Messines to CARRICK HILL

WRITING HOME FROM THE GREAT WAR

TOM BURKE

D1343019

MERCIER PRESS

04495755

MERCIER PRESS

Cork

www.mercierpress.ie

© Thomas Burke, 2017

ISBN: 978 1 78117 484 5

10 9 8 7 6 5 4 3 2 1

A CIP record for this title is available from the British Library

Printed and bound in the EU.

Contents

Abbreviations & Acronyms

BEF	British Expeditionary Force
CBS	Christian Brothers School
CF	Chaplain to the Forces
CWGC	Commonwealth War Graves Commission
DCM	Distinguished Conduct Medal
DSO	Distinguished Service Order
GHQ	General Headquarters
GOC	General Officer Commanding
GPO	General Post Office
HMT	His/Her Majesty's Transport
IWM	Imperial War Museum
LHCMA	Liddell Hart Centre for Military Archives
NAK	National Archives, Kew
NCO	Non-commissioned Officer
OR	Other Rank
OTC	Officers' Training Corps
RAMC	Royal Army Medical Corps
RASC	Royal Army Service Corps
RDF	Royal Dublin Fusiliers
RDFA	Royal Dublin Fusiliers Association
RFA	Royal Field Artillery
RFC	Royal Flying Corps
RHMS	Royal Hibernian Military School
SJ	Society of Jesus
SP	Strong Point
UCD	University College Dublin
UVF	Ulster Volunteer Force
VC	Victoria Cross
VD	Venereal Disease

Preface

On 28 January 1999 Mrs Rosemary Kavanagh of Warner's Lane, Dublin, wrote me a letter addressed to the Dublin Civic Museum in South William Street.[1] She informed me in the letter that she had recently come into possession of a bundle of documents containing letters, telegrams and some photographs that had once belonged to Michael Wall, a young relative of her husband. She explained that Michael was an Irish officer who served in the Royal Irish Regiment during the First World War. The majority of the letters by Michael were written from the trenches in Flanders to his mother in Carrick Hill near Malahide in north County Dublin. The documents had come into Rosemary's possession following the death of Michael's younger brother Bernard, or Barney as he was known to family and friends. Barney never married and safely kept Michael's papers for many years in his home in Blackrock, County Dublin. He died in August 1998 at the age of ninety. Rosemary graciously offered the documents as a donation to the archive of The Royal Dublin Fusiliers Association (RDFA).

It wasn't until the middle of March 1999 that I got round to visiting Rosemary, her husband, Andy, and their daughter, Jane. I spent an entire afternoon and evening reading these simple but heart-rending letters. So emotionally moved was I by these letters that I made a promise to myself, to Rosemary and her family, and most of all to Michael that someday I would use his letters to write an account of his time in Flanders.

No matter how Michael's story was going to be told, it had to be set within the larger story of the First World War and in particular the Battle of Wijtschate and Messines, which took place in early June 1917.[2] After I received Michael's letters, I spent several years researching the Irish participation in this battle in great detail. The end product of the research was an unpublished 500-page treatise that essentially told the story of how the 16th (Irish) and 36th (Ulster) Divisions took the village of Wijtschate from the Germans on 7 June 1917.[3] Having completed the work, I realised that Michael's story was lost in this vast script, in which the emphasis was on the battle itself and not on Michael Wall.[4] Consequently, I decided the best way to tell this young man's story was to let him tell it himself, by reducing emphasis on the battle and paying greater attention to the content of his letters. To add a sense of place and reality, the letters – all of which are dated – are set against his battalion's locations and activities in Flanders.[5] Moreover, to explain the background of the sentiments Michael expressed and the topics to which he referred, the narrative is expanded and contextualised.

I would like to thank some of the people who helped me produce Michael's story. There are few regrets I have in life, but, sad to say, one I do have is the fact that Rosemary never got to see the fruits of my work. She died peacefully at St Vincent's University Hospital in Dublin on 23 June 2016. So to Rosemary, Andy, Jane and all the Kavanagh family, I simply say thank you for giving me his letters and the privilege of writing his story. To my dear friends and comrades in the RDFA – Sean Connolly, Brian Moroney, Captain (retired) Seamus Greene, Philip Lecane, Nick Broughall and the late Pat Hogarty – thank you for your friendship, kindness and generosity.

I have always believed that if one is going to write about a battle, one must walk the battlefield – or in my case cycle it. For many years I have cycled round the laneways and roads that once passed through the battlefield on the eastern and western sides of

Wijtschate and Messines to see where a camp called the Curragh Camp and hutment lines called Tralee Lines and Shankill Lines once stood full of Irish men. I simply could not have survived in the Heuvelland region of Flanders without the help of Mrs Trees Vanneste, her husband, Marc, and also Mr Johan Vandelanotte, who, sadly, passed away too young on 26 October 2016. I thank them for their kindness and hospitality on my many trips to the region.

I thank, too, my dear friends Erwin and Mia Ureel. Erwin is a Flemish man who for many years, unknown to most people in Ireland, has worked tirelessly to keep alive the memory of the Irish soldiers who fought and died in his country. To mark the 100th anniversary of the Christmas Truce of December 1914, Erwin, Sean Connolly and I camped out on the old front line near Prowse Point Cemetery on Christmas Eve 2014. It was a magical experience.

There were many people who read parts of my script and offered their opinions, which I valued. For their contribution I would like to thank Sean Connolly, Philip Lecane, Dr Tim Bowman of the University of Kent and Dr David Murphy of the National University of Ireland, Maynooth. There are also many people to whom I am very grateful for their advice on the location and sourcing of primary source material: Ellen Murphy and Dr Mary Clarke of the Dublin City Library and Archive; Billy Ervine of The Somme Heritage Centre in Newtownards; Fr Fergus O'Donoghue SJ of the Jesuit Archive in Leeson Street, Dublin; Cliff Walter of the Royal Signals Museum in Dorset; Alan Wakefield of The Photographic Archive in the Imperial War Museum, London; Aoife Lyons, librarian, National Gallery of Ireland; and Brother Tom Connolly, Edmund Rice House, Dublin. Thanks, too, to Martin Steffen for his help on German regiments. Thanks also to Mr George (RIP) and Mrs Mabel Pearson, Hillsborough, County

Down, for allowing me access to the papers of Sergeant Andrew Lockhart; the editorial staff of Mercier Press, Wendy Logue, Noel O'Regan and Trish Myers Smith; my brother-in-law Trevor Wayman for his artistic skills; and my friend at Ulster Television, Paul Clark, who was so encouraging to me along the way.

To my mother, Annie, and my father, Ned, long since passed away, thank you for giving me the gift of an education. To my wife, Michele, and children, Carl, Jamie and Rachel, thank you for your support and encouragement during difficult times.

And so, after many a twist and turn to complete it, here is the story of one of Ireland's lost generation of unfulfilled potential. This is my anthem for their doomed youth.

Tom Burke

June 2017

1

Innocence

Michael Thomas Wall, or 'Al' as he was known to family and friends, was born on 21 March 1898 in the fishing village of Howth, north County Dublin.[1] His father, also named Michael, had been born on a farm near the village of Coolrain, County Laois; he worked as a bookkeeper in Howth.[2] Michael's mother, Theresa Carr, was born on 24 February 1872 and came from Dunbo Cottages, near Dunbo Terrace, behind the police station in Howth.[3] Theresa and Michael Wall senior (who was a widower) met in Howth and were married in the old Catholic church in the village on 21 May 1897.[4] Within a year of their marriage, Michael junior was born at Glentora, an elegant house situated on the fashionable Balkill Road in Howth. Over the next ten years, Michael senior and Theresa brought three more children into the world: Patrick Joseph, or 'Joe', in 1899; Agatha Mary in 1901; and Bernard, or 'Barney', on 20 August 1908.

In May 1906, at a little over eight years of age, young Michael enrolled in St Joseph's Christian Brothers School (CBS) in the north Dublin suburb of Fairview.[5] Each morning he travelled to school by tram from Howth along the coast road. The full fourteen-and-a-half kilometre journey to Nelson's Pillar in central Dublin took about forty-five minutes; the fare was five pennies.[6] Within a month of his being at St Joseph's, Michael had made an impression on his teacher, Brother M. S. O'Farrell, who wrote to Mrs Wall telling her that 'Michael is a fine, talented child. He's bound, if God spares him, to become a fine man.'[7]

The year 1908 was a good one for Michael. In August his mother gave birth to a baby boy she named Barney, and Michael passed his Standard III exam and advanced to Standard IV. Written on Michael's Standard III certificate was a quotation by the writer John Ruskin (1819–1900), which the brothers used as a kind of motto: 'Education is the leading of human souls to what is best.' Brother Reid signed Michael's certificate.

The following year St Joseph's – or 'Joey's' as it became known to generations of Dubliners – reached its twenty-first year and metaphorically had come of age (the school had been in operation since 1888). It had three Christian Brothers and three lay teachers teaching under the supervision of Brother Patrick Berchmans Reid (1880–1956), Master of Method in the Christian Brothers' training school. The school hours were 9 a.m. to 3 p.m. In that year, Joey's had a state inspection. The inspectors were pleased with the layout of the school, its cleanliness and the provision of blackboards and maps. They noted the presence of a library containing some 600 volumes, mostly books of adventure. They also noted that discipline was very good and that punishment was by means of a strap on the palm of the hand.[8]

Sometime after Barney was born, the Wall family had moved from Howth to 7 Hollybrook Road, Clontarf, a well-established parish about five kilometres north-east of Dublin city and near Fairview.[9] A terrible tragedy struck this young family in December 1910 when Michael's father died, aged forty-five, from cancer of the colon. He was buried in St Fintan's Cemetery, Sutton, County Dublin. Michael was just twelve. The death of her husband left Theresa with a very young family and no regular source of income; the future looked bleak indeed.

Theresa's sister Margaret, or 'Margo' for short, was one year older than her and had married a wealthy landowner, Sir Percy

Willan. Their family residence was at Carrick Hill House, a grand country house with thirty-two rooms, near Portmarnock, also in north County Dublin. In an act of kindness, Margo offered Theresa and her young family part of her home in which to stay. Margo had suffered her own share of tragedy. She had married in 1899 and in 1903 gave birth to a boy named Cyril. Four years later, however, her husband ran off with Cyril's nanny. He also left Margo near-penniless at the time by selling most of the farm's livestock.[10] Before he had died, Theresa's husband, Michael, with his farming experience, had helped to restock the farm at Carrick Hill. The exact date on which Michael junior and the rest of his family moved to Carrick Hill is not known, but it may well have been soon after he left Joey's in January 1911.

The estate around Carrick Hill House consisted of about 263 acres of excellent farming land. It was a very active farm, with the main business coming from cattle, sheep and the growing of Russet eating apples for export.[11] The house itself was surrounded by beautiful gardens. It was customary with such large country houses to have live-in maids. Two lived at Carrick Hill: Bridget Marshall, aged thirty-one, who was single and from County Westmeath, and Elizabeth Clynn, seventeen and also single, from County Longford.[12]

Portmarnock was the nearest village to Michael's new home.[13] In the early twentieth century, it was a typical small Irish country village with an economy that was based mainly on agriculture. Like many such villages at the time, Portmarnock had its share of local landlords and gentry. The bulk of the land around the village was in the hands of four families, namely the Jamesons (Protestant and associated with the distilling of Irish whiskey), the Plunketts (Roman Catholic), the Trumbulls (Protestant) and the Willans (Protestant). Probably the earliest landowners in the area were the

Plunkett family, who were in Portmarnock as far back as 1733. They were also related to St Oliver Plunkett, who had been primate of Ireland in the seventeenth century. The Plunketts ran a brick factory in the village for nearly 200 years and, along with farming, provided the main source of employment in the parish. Out of the twenty-three families who lived in Portmarnock, sixteen lived on lands owned by the Plunkett family.[14]

Front (*top*) and rear views of Carrick Hill House, Carrick Hill, Portmarnock, County Dublin. *Courtesy of the Kavanagh family.*

Living and working on the Willan estate were six families.[15] Tommy Cunningham, the Land Steward who worked on the estate, lived there all his life. When Sir Percy departed, Margo had known nothing about farming and had relied on Tommy, who, through hard work, brought the farm back from near-bankruptcy. Cunningham was a decent, honest man, respected by those who worked under him. He died, aged eighty-eight, in 1956 and is buried in the Old Cemetery in Portmarnock.[16] Harry Kealy, the local coalman's brother, was the Willans' shepherd.[17] John Donnelly was the blacksmith; his forge and thatched family home were on the road leading up to the big house.

Mrs Connie Fowler, née Donnelly, was one of the blacksmith's daughters. She could recall her father working in his forge when she was a little girl: the only light was 'daylight which came in through the double door at the front ... Among Dad's regular customers was Cyril Willan, James Kealy, the local coalman, the Jamesons and the locals who had ponies for Sunday mass.' She had fond memories of life in Portmarnock during the years of the First World War, especially on market day, which began with the collection of cabbages from the Willan estate. In the summer months, when the beach and golf course at Portmarnock attracted visitors, Connie's mother opened a tea garden in the front garden of the house, with tables set with white linen tablecloths and decorated with flowers from the garden.[18]

Martha Reilly was born in Portmarnock in 1894. Her recollections of lazy, peaceful summer evenings present a further image of life around the Willan estate in the early twentieth century:

The Jamesons used to rent the Martello field from Willan for grassing and the cows used to walk from that field across the road and down onto the strand near the rocks at the Martello Tower. They used to paddle in the water and lie on the beach. It was lovely to watch them. At evening they would then move down the strand and across the sandy banks on their way to Jameson's stables for milking.[19]

The Dublin artist Walter Osborne (1859–1903) was a regular summer visitor to Portmarnock. His paintings *Cattle in the Sea*, *Milking Time in St Marnock's Byre* and *On the Beach* depict the scene Martha talked about.[20]

There was no Catholic church in the village of Portmarnock for centuries until the first one was dedicated on Sunday 22 July 1934. Consequently, folks had to travel, mainly by horse and cart, on the coast road from Portmarnock and Carrick Hill to the Church of St Peter and Paul in Baldoyle. The parish priest who looked after the spiritual needs of the Roman Catholics of Portmarnock, Carrick Hill and Baldoyle was Fr Robert Carrick (1833–1932). The children of the village went to the Jameson School, so named after the family who were the school's early patrons from 1868. When the Jamesons visited the school, the children all had to stand up and sing 'God Save the King'. The school was a national school for the village children between four and twelve years of age, and was in use until 1965.[21]

Apart from Michael, all of Theresa's children were sent to Mount Sackville boarding school at Chapelizod in Dublin. Their fees were paid for by Margo. The common practice for boys who had completed their junior education at St Joseph's was to transfer to the senior CBS – O'Connell Boys' School in North Richmond Street, Dublin, named after Daniel O'Connell – and Michael, like many before him, followed this path. The compliments his teacher at St Joseph's wrote about him being a 'fine, talented child' were quite genuine.[22] Michael brought these talents with him into his early adolescence. In 1915 the Scholarship Committee of Dublin

County Council offered Michael, who was by then seventeen, a county scholarship to study at University College Dublin (UCD).[23] During the summer of 1915 he completed his matriculation exams for entry into the National University of Ireland. His late application, however, denied him a place in college that year. Judging by the science subjects he studied over his four years at O'Connell CBS, such as elementary physics and magnetism, he no doubt would have pursued a degree in engineering or science.[24]

Life for Theresa's young family seemed idyllic. Fresh air and all the pursuits of country living helped to ease the loss of a husband and father. Michael soon took on the mantle of being the man of the family. He settled into his new home and assumed the role of a young country squire. His destiny seemed to lie in a university education and a career in science or engineering. It is incredible to think that effects of the shock wave created by the assassination of an Austrian aristocrat and his wife by a Serbian nationalist on the streets of Sarajevo on 28 June 1914 trickled their way to a little coastal village in north County Dublin, and brought with them disaster and misery for some of its inhabitants.

2

Smitten by War

Michael Wall was only sixteen when the First World War broke out. At such a young and impressionable age, war and boyhood adventure went hand in hand. In early March 1915 he wrote to an acquaintance of the family, Francis Gleeson, who by then was a padre with the Royal Munster Fusiliers serving in France.[1] On 14 March Fr Gleeson replied to Michael's letter; he thanked Michael for the shamrock he had sent. He found life at the front, 'desolate and cheerless … a very hard one, but the loneliness is the worst'.[2]

Like so many young men of his generation, Michael may have been seduced by a vision of war presented to him in what he read in his youth. In the years leading up to the First World War, young boys who could read and afford them bought magazines such as *The Boy's Own*, *Pluck* and *The Boy's Friend*, which mythologised war with romantic and chivalric stories. Not only were these fictions a source of exciting escapist adventure, but they also promoted 'patriotism, manliness and a simplistic imperial world view that emphasised duty and the need for sacrifice if the British Empire was to endure'.[3] According to Michael Paris, 'adventure fictions, generally written for boys and young men aged between 10 and 18 years, were intended to inculcate patriotism, manliness, and a sense of duty to Crown and Empire among readers'.[4] The library in St Joseph's CBS in Fairview may not have had many books relating to the glory of the British Empire, but boyhood adventure was a central theme of many of the books.

Young German boys had their choice of pre-war patriotic, martial juvenile literature to read too. According to Sonja Muller:

> Historic juvenile literature was the main genre and related to battles and wars of the past. Also popular were books on contemporary history. Titles like *Um Freiheit und Vaterland* (For Freedom and Fatherland), *Die Helden des Burenkrieges* (Heroes of the Boer War) or *Der Weltkrieg, Deutsche Träume* (World War, German Dreams) offered various ranges of militaristic literature.[5]

To add to the martial influences acting on Michael's juvenile mind, the boys from the Royal Hibernian Military School (RHMS) in Phoenix Park, Dublin, spent their summer camp in the fields round Carrick Hill, where they practised drill and lived the outdoor life under canvas. The RHMS boys were at Carrick Hill in August 1915.[6] With recruitment posters on display throughout the land, the war had come to Ireland, and recruitment was in full swing by late 1914. By the beginning of February 1915 approximately 50,107 Irishmen had enlisted in the army.[7]

Michael was too young to enlist legally. Recruits for the army at that time had to be between eighteen and thirty-eight years of age. However, despite his age, this war was not going to pass him by. Having an interest in science and engineering, on the advice of his friend R. W. Smyth at the RHMS, Michael applied for work in the engineering department at the Ministry of Munitions, which had an office at 32 Nassau Street in Dublin. On 25 September 1915 Staff Captain R. B. Kelly, who represented the Ministry of Munitions in Ireland, wrote to Michael declining his application but suggested that he should 'communicate with Messrs Watt Ltd of Bridgefoot Street in Dublin'.[8] Michael didn't seem to have much luck in obtaining work with Watt Ltd either, so, keen as ever, he reapplied to the Ministry of Munitions for work.

On 16 November he received another letter, from a Captain Browne, superintendent engineer for Dublin and South of Ireland, who informed Michael, 'I have forwarded your application to W. H. Morton Esq. Loco Engineer, Midland Great Western Railway, Broadstone, Dublin, who will no doubt write to you in the course of a few posts.'[9] But Michael's ambitions to work in munitions never materialised. A week later, Smyth wrote to Michael suggesting he should try to enlist in the army.[10] Two days later, on 25 November 1915, Michael filled out Army Form W.3075, which was to be completed by a 'Candidate for a Commission in the Regular Army, Special Reserve or Territorial'.

The language used in Smyth's letter to Michael is interesting to note. By using the words 'they will all think the more of you for doing so', Smyth tapped into the Edwardian sense of honour and manly pride, suggesting to Michael that 'they' – that is, those who knew him and perhaps his mother – would be proud of him for enlisting. In truth, his mother may have been proud of her son, but as Smyth also suggested, Michael's enlistment did nothing for her peace of mind. No doubt some difficult words were exchanged between Michael and his mother when he told her that he had applied to join the army.

Michael had applied for a cadetship as an officer and not as an ordinary private soldier. His young country squire self-image and his coming from the 'big house' at Carrick Hill, with all the social standing and imagery associated with the big-house class, conditioned his ambition to take part in this war as an officer. It was adventure that drove Michael to enlist. He certainly did not do so out of economic necessity; after all, he came from comfortable surroundings and had a good academic career ahead of him in UCD. He was going to wear the uniform of an officer, a leader, an imagined heroic character from an adventure book and a representative of his assumed class.

Michael's ambition to join the officer ranks was in contrast to a neighbour of his who also enlisted. Patrick (Pat) Redmond was the son of Plunkett's chauffeur, James Redmond. Pat was twenty years of age when the war broke out, and he enlisted as a private in the 9th Royal Dublin Fusiliers (RDF).[11] He was a general labourer and lived with his father, two sisters and two brothers in their three-room tenant-cottage on the Plunkett estate. His mother was dead.[12] Pat's and Michael's different levels of entry into the army were dictated by their social class and were a reflection of the society from which they came. Their motivation for enlisting may also have been different. While Michael's was adventure, Patrick's may well have been economic.

Michael was not the only ex-Joey's CBS boy who enlisted in the British Army. Tom O'Mara from the Howth Road in Clontarf was commissioned a lieutenant. Thomas Saurin from 3 Seafield Road, also in Clontarf, who had passed the Middle Grade exam at St Joseph's in 1910, served with the Royal Army Medical Corps (RAMC) on the Western Front. In contrast, his brother Charles James Saurin would fight with the Irish Volunteers in the Dublin Metropole Hotel during the Easter Rising of 1916. Twenty-four past pupils, some possibly classmates of Michael Wall, would fight with the Irish Volunteers and others in the Easter Rising.[13]

Like all recruits, Michael underwent a medical examination. He was examined by Lieutenant Colonel Dr M. O'Connell of the RAMC. Michael's medical report noted that he was a healthy young man but had suffered from typhoid and diphtheria in the past. The report also noted that he was eighteen years of age. This was wrong, of course; he was in fact seventeen years, nine months and four days old, and so underage for military service.[14] His application for a commission in the regular army was turned down, and he was told to reapply for a commission in the Reserve of Officers. Three days before Christmas 1915, Michael completed Army Form B.201, an application to the Special Reserve of Officers. His choice of unit was the Royal Irish Regiment. Because he was under twenty-one years of age, his mother had to sign the form as his guardian. Attached to the application was a Certificate of Moral Character signed by Fr Robert Carrick. His school principal at O'Connell CBS also signed a statement saying Michael had obtained a 'good standard of education'.[15]

Christmas 1915 at Carrick Hill passed happily for Michael and his family. On 8 January 1916 Michael received a letter from Captain Cecil Stafford, writing on behalf of the assistant military secretary, Irish Command, at 32 Nassau Street, Dublin. The letter invited Michael to attend an interview at the headquarters of the 25th Reserve Infantry Brigade. The interview took place at the Royal Hospital Kilmainham, some time between 10.30 a.m. and 3.30 p.m. on 13 January 1916. The invitation noted that 'owing to the large number of candidates registered, no undertaking as to your appointment to a Commission can be given or implied … No claim for travelling or other expenses in attending the Board can be sanctioned.'[16]

There was, indeed, a large number of applications from young, enthusiastic Irishmen just like Michael, who wanted to be officers. In fact, by 14 December 1914 Lieutenant Colonel W. B. Rennie, a senior staff officer with the 16th (Irish) Division, informed Sir Maurice Moore that 'in junior officers, the division is already over establishment'.[17]

Before February 1916 one method of appointing officers was through self-appointment from amongst the ranks of men in their battalion, simply on the grounds of their standing in society. This created tension in some battalions, particularly the 7th RDF. Bryan Cooper notes that men found it difficult to work under their peers: 'The preservation of rigid military discipline among men who were the equals of their officers in social position was not easy.'[18] The main danger of this self-appointing system was that men with no military training or experience were given positions of command. Take Ernest Julian for example, a barrister educated at Trinity College, Dublin. He enlisted and was 'Elected to Commission' by his comrades in September 1914. He was commissioned a lieutenant one month later.[19] Another example is Robert Douglas, who was educated at the grammar school in Kingstown and The Abbey in Tipperary. Like Julian, he was elected for a commission by his comrades in 'D' Company of the 7th RDF simply because 'he had been known to most of them in sport'.[20] Poole Hickman was another Trinity graduate and a barrister on the Munster circuit before the war. On 22 September 1914 he was gazetted a second lieutenant in the 7th RDF, was made captain on 7 January 1915 and from that date was officer commanding 'D' Company 7th RDF. In fewer than six months, this man transferred from being a civilian barrister on the Munster circuit to commanding a company of soldiers on their way to war.[21]

This internal appointment of officers proved disastrous in combat, and lessons were learned at the War Office in London as to the consequences of self-appointed temporary commissions. According to Ian Beckett and Keith Simpson, 'as a result of increasing subaltern casualties and the continuing expansion of the army, the War Office decided in February 1916 to establish a new system for selecting and training junior officers'.[22] The new system resulted in the formation of the Officer Cadet battalions set up throughout the United Kingdom.

However, in Ireland, Cadet Company No. 7 was established at Moore Park in Cork as early as November 1914.[23] Up to 5 December 1915 the general officer commanding (GOC) of the 16th (Irish) Division was Lieutenant General Sir Lawrence W. Parsons.[24] A disciplinarian, Parsons also knew of the tragic consequences of internally appointing officers. To become an officer in the 16th (Irish) Division would demand dedication. In November 1914 Parsons left no young man in any doubt as to what was required of him:

> If he (the applicant) has not had any previous military training, I tell him that he must enlist as a Private soldier in the 7th Battalion Leinster Regiment in which 'C' Company is kept as the Candidates Company ... I tell him plainly that if I do not consider him fit for Officer's or NCO's [non-commissioned officer's] rank he will have to go on service and, possibly die in a trench, as a Private.[25]

According to Lieutenant Colonel Frederick E. Whitton, 'several hundreds of young officers were gazetted from time to time to various regiments' from the 7th Leinster's Cadet Company No. 7.[26] Between November 1914 and December 1915, some 161 young men were commissioned from this company at Blackdown Camp near Aldershot.[27]

To be accepted into a cadetship, applicants first had to sit an interview with a senior officer. Michael Wall received his cadetship through this method when he met Captain Cecil Stafford at the Royal Hospital Kilmainham. His interview went well; on 15 January he received a letter from Captain Stafford stating, 'I have the honour to inform you that your application for a Special Reserve Commission has been forwarded to the War Office.'[28] Ten days later Michael received his letter of appointment (opposite)

Any further communication on this subject should be addressed to—

The Secretary,
War Office,
London, S.W.,

and the following number quoted.

WAR OFFICE,

LONDON, S.W.,

25th January 1916.

91/Gen. No./2208 M. S. 2.
Special Reserve.

SIR,

I am directed to inform you that you have been appointed to a commission as Second Lieutenant (on probation) in the Special Reserve of Officers. You have been posted to the 3rd Battalion Royal Irish Regiment stationed at Richmond Barracks, Dublin but, prior to joining that Unit, you have been selected to attend a class of instruction at the Dublin Univ. School of Instruction, and should report yourself without fail to The Officer Commanding at the following address Dublin Univ.O.T.C.,Trinity College,Dublin. on 2nd February 1916. MXX, between 2 and 4 p.m.

You should provide yourself with bedding and kit as per enclosed lists, and should join in uniform, but if your uniform is not ready, in plain clothes.

To enable you to draw your outfit allowance (as per enclosed Form M. T. 394), you should, after reporting yourself in person, apply to the Commandant of the School of Instruction to which you have been ordered to attend, for a "Joining Certificate," and forward the same, duly completed, to your Army Agents.

Expenses incurred in travelling to join on first appointment must be paid by yourself. This letter need not be acknowledged.

I am,

SIR,

Your obedient Servant,

TECK, Lieutenant-Colonel,

Assistant Military Secretary.

Michael.T.Wall Esq,
Carrick Hill,
Malahide,
Co.Dublin.

Letter from the War Office offering Michael a commission as a second lieutenant (on probation) to the 3rd Royal Irish Regiment, 25 January 1916.

DUBLIN UNIVERSITY OFFICERS SCHOOL OF INSTRUCTION
CLASS 1?.
SIX WEEKS COMMENCING FEBRUARY 2nd 1916
STANDING ORDERS

ORDERS...Orders will be published daily or as required and will be posted up in the Mess Room and School Armoury with the weekly programme. All Officers should make a point of reading Orders etc. carefully.

DUTIES For the purpose of maintaining discipline in the Hotel and generally, a Senior Officer will be appointed who will act as Officer of the Week, also an Officer who will act as Officer of the day or Orderly Officer. The Officer of the Week will be responsible to the Commandant for the good order and discipline of the Class in the Hotel and generally. In this duty he will be assisted by the Orderly Officer of the day. The Officer of the Week will act as President of the Table at Meals, and the Orderly Officer will act as Vice-President. The Orderly Officer of the day will wear his sword-belt all day, and will not leave the Hotel during his tour of duty. He will assist the Senior Officer in seeing that no unnecessary noise takes place in the Hotel, and that Lights are out in the Mess and ante rooms at 12.p.m. He will also furnish the usual Orderly Officer's report to the Acting Adjutant before first parade each morning.

)DISCIPLINE
Officers of the Class are reminded while they are billeted in the Hotel they must act as if they were in their Regimental Mess, and in the absence of the Commandant or other Officers of the Staff, they must conform to the Orders given by the Officer of the Week or the Orderly Officer. Any complaints that Officers may wish to make about their quarters etc. must be made to the Officer of the Week and the latter will bring them under the notice of the Quartermaster each morning at 8.45.a.m. On no account is any Officer to make PERSONAL COMPLAINTS TO ANY OF THE HOTEL STAFF. Officers must be in their quarters before or at 12.p.m. each night. If they desire to be out after that hour they must give their names and reasons to the Orderly Officer before lunch time. The latter will bring the list to the Adjutant for approval and will report to him the names of Officers out after 12.p.m. without leave. The Hotel Staff are instructed to take the names of Officers out after 12.p.m. and serious notice will be taken of any Officer out after that hour without leave. Strict regard must be paid to punctuality and Officers must be in their places on parade 10 minutes before the time appointed.

)MESSING
For Officers living in the Hotel the charge of Messing will be 6/- per day to include breakfast, lunch and dinner. Afternoon tea may be had by arrangement at a nominal charge. Officers who are to live outside must lunch in the Hotel except on Saturdays and Sundays, and will be charged 1/6 per day. Breakfast will be at 8.a.m. (9.a.m. Sundays) Lunch 1.p.m. and Dinner 6.30.

:)GUEST NIGHT
Every Wednesday evening will be MESS GUEST NIGHT, and Officers desiring to bring Guests may do so. Charge for Guests 3/-

:)DRESS....Officers must always wear Sam Browne Belts and carry sticks and Gloves outside quarters.

James H Kellip

LIEUTENANT & ACTING COMMANDANT
DUBLIN UNIVERSITY OFFICERS SCHOOL OF
INSTRUCTION

Dublin University OTC Standing Orders for Class 1.

from the War Office informing him that he had been offered a commission as a second lieutenant in the Special Reserve of Officers and was posted to the 3rd Battalion, Royal Irish Regiment, at Richmond Barracks in Dublin.[29]

On 2 February 1916 Michael became a member of Class 12 and began a six-week course at the Dublin University Officers' School of Instruction. Before he presented himself at the school, he was informed in a letter from the commandant that:

> Officers will be billeted during the course and need not bring bedding, special billeting allowances is [*sic*] granted. Officers must report in uniform, swords are not necessary. Officers should bring with them the following books. *Musketry Regulations, Infantry Training, Field Service Regulations Part 1* and *The Manual of Map Reading*.[30]

While with the Dublin University Officers' Training Corps (OTC), the trainee officers were billeted in local hotels and had to obey a set of standing orders (opposite) on topics such as the maintenance of discipline in their hotel, eating and dress.[31]

The seduction of a uniform, status and future adventure had won the battle between Michael's heart and his head.

Michael in uniform.
Courtesy of the Kavanagh family.

3

'Fancy the Royal Irish captured Moore Street'

Towards the end of March 1916 Michael finished his six-week training course at the Dublin University OTC and was sent for further training to Ballykinlar, County Down. For Michael and his fellow trainees, the wooden billets at Ballykinlar were a far cry from the comforts of a plush hotel in the centre of Dublin. On 18 April Michael began a process of regular letter writing to family and friends. He wrote to his younger brother Bernard, who

Group of officer cadets at Ballykinlar Camp, County Down in April 1916. Michael is standing third from the left.
Courtesy of the Kavanagh family.

had just made his First Confession. Michael was pleased to hear the news that young Bernard was going to become a soldier. Not a British soldier, but, as all first confessors are told, a soldier of Christ. Michael promised to bring home his rifle and bayonet to show to Bernard.[1]

Michael spent Holy Week 1916 at home in Carrick Hill. On a rainy Easter Sunday morning, he left to return to Ballykinlar. He caught the Great Northern train from Amiens Street Station in Dublin and arrived back in camp in the early hours of Easter Monday morning. He missed the beginning of the Easter Rising in Dublin by one day. Had he been in Dublin, he would have been called up. He wrote to his mother on Tuesday:

> Officers Company
> Ballykinlar Camp
> Co. Down
>
> April 25th 1916.
>
> Dear Mother,
>
> I arrived here quite safe about 1 oc[lock] on Monday morning. We stopped in Newry and had supper with a fellow called Frank, his father is a Veterinary Surgeon there. Do you know who has just got a commission in the R.A.M.C. – Willie O'Neill … I hear there was a great racket in Dublin with the Sinn Feiners and that there was some damage done to the post office. I have not seen any papers yet so I cannot say that it is true. It poured rain all the way back on Sunday from Drogheda and it is still raining … When are you going to the opera? Write and tell me if it was any good. I am sending a few cigarette pictures, I suppose Bernard will be pleased to have them. Do you know what you might do – send me on every Saturday night's Herald as they publish the

Officers Company
Ballykinlar Camp
Co Down

April 25th 1916.

Dear Mother

I arrived here quite safe about 1. o.
on Monday morning. We stopped in Newry and
had supper with a fellow called Maxie,
his father is a veterinary Surgeon there. Do you
know who has just got a commision in the
R. A. M. C. - Willie O'Neill the factors son. He
travelled down on the train with us and I
think he went to Belfast. I hear there was a
a great racket in Dublin with the Sinn Feiners
and that there was some damage done to the
post office. I have not seen any papers yet
so I cannot say that it is true. It poured
rain all the way back on Sunday from
Drogheda and it is still raining. I never saw
such rain and this place is in a queer state
of mud & water. Cyril and Bernard I am
sure must be very downhearted. When the

Roll of Honour of the different schools. Must close now. Give my love to Auntie and all at C. H.

I remain, your fond son,
Michael.

Please excuse scribble as I have a bad pen.[2]

The letter shows that the Rising came as a surprise to Michael, as it did to many of the people of Dublin. It is interesting to note that it is only the third item he refers to in his letter, after the supper with Frank and news about Willie O'Neill obtaining a commission in the RAMC.

However, reflecting the general change in the public attitude when the full impact of the Rising was realised, it became the first item in his next letter home. Indeed the excitement of the unfolding events may explain why Michael incorrectly dated this letter to 6 April (he probably meant 6 May). His ambivalent attitude had also changed:

Officers Company,
Ballykinlar Camp,
Co. Down.

April 6th [sic] 1916.

Dear Mother,

I hope this letter finds you all well and safe at Carrick Hill. Wasn't it a terrible week. I hope Auntie has not sustained any damage as I saw in the paper that there was an outbreak at Swords but whether it is true or not I cannot say. I got back to camp too soon. I wish I had been in Dublin. It would have been great. Fancy the Royal Irish captured Moore St under Col. Owens. One of our officers was killed – Lt. Ramsey [*sic*] – I am sure Mrs Clifford must have been in a terrible state. About six hundred of the Rifles left here on the Tuesday after Easter and they held the Railway embankment at Fairview. Have you been to see poor old Dublin yet. There are a good many of our fellows gone up to Dublin for the weekend armed to the teeth with revolvers. Of course they had to motor up. The bugle sounded the alarm Saturday morning at one o'clock and we had to turn out as quickly as possible. I managed to get out in five minutes with my clothes on anyway and a rifle and bayonet. Some fellows ran out in their pyjamas. Then we were served out with fifty rounds of ammunition each and we were told that a party of Sinn Feiners had left Newry and were coming on to Newcastle with the intention of attacking the Camp. Then we started off and posted pickets and sentry groups and barricaded all the roads. That brought us up to 6:30 a.m. Then we had breakfast after which we were to fall in at eight o'clock. This gave us an hour's rest and we all set to sharpening our bayonets on the door step. I have got an edge on mine like a razor. At eight o'clock, a portion of our platoon went off to dig a trench overlooking Dundrum and my party were sent out with wire cutters and gloves and we put up barbed wire entanglements and then occupied the trenches. We were relieved at 8 o'c[lock] p.m. but had to stand by so I was up for two nights and days. But we were sorely disappointed as the beggars never came out at all. Of course we were confined to camp up to Wednesday last and now we can go about freely enough. As soon as the train service is restored I will try and go up. I would like to see Dublin. I suppose Joe barricaded the house and had his air gun ready. What about Cyril and Bernard? Have they gone back to school yet. I saw Mrs Fogarty of Artane House in Newcastle on Wednesday and there are a couple of fellows here very keen on Miss Fogarty. I hope this letter will reach you all right, I'm sure it will as I see the Rotunda Rink is made into a post office. I must close now but I hope to hear from you soon. Give my love to all at Carrick Hill and kindest regards to Auntie.

I remain, your fond son,
Michael.[3]

Officers Company
Ballykinlar Camp
Co. Down.

April 6th 1916.

Dear Mother,

I hope this letter finds you all well and safe at Carrick Hill. Wasn't it a terrible week. I hope Auntie has not sustained any damage as I saw in the paper that there was an outbreak at Swords but whether it is true or not I cannot say. I got back to camp too soon. I wish I had been in Dublin. It would have been great. Fancy the Royal Irish captured Moore St under Col. Owens. One of our officers was killed — Lt. Ramsay. — I am sure Mrs. Clifford must have been in a terrible state. About six hundred of the Rifles left here on the Tuesday after Easter and they held the Railway embankment at Fairview. Have you been to see poor old Dublin yet. There are a good many of our fellows gone up to Dublin for the week end armed to the teeth with revolvers. Of course they had to motor up. The bugle sounded the

News about the Rising in Dublin was slow to reach the front lines in Flanders, France and beyond. The authorities did their best to contain the news.[4] The Irish serving overseas heard about the Rising in various ways. Private George Soper, a signaller serving with the 2nd RDF in France, read about the Rising in an Irish newspaper.[5] Like Michael, Private Soper may well have read *The Irish Times*, which printed three editions during the week of the Rising. While serving with the Royal Artillery in Mesopotamia, Tom Barry found out about the Rising from a bulletin posted in his unit's orderly room. He found the news 'a rude awakening'.[6] Soon after the Rising, Irish papers reported that Irish troops felt betrayed and angered. Some of the nationalist newspapers gave their support to the Irish regiments that put down the Rising. On 5 May 1916 *The Freeman's Journal* sang their praises:

> Not regiments of professional soldiery of the old stamp, but reserves of the Irish Brigade who had rallied to the last call of the Irish leader, true Irish Volunteers … defending their city against the blind self-devoted victims of the Hun.[7]

German newspapers were aware of the Dublin rebellion and this news travelled to their troops at the front. They raised placards opposite the Irish lines informing them of the rebellion. One read: 'Irishmen! Heavy uproar in Ireland: english guns are firing at your wifes and children! 1st May 1916.'[8] The placards asked the Irish to desert, but little heed was paid to the German enticements. The war diarist of the 9th Royal Munster Fusiliers recorded a revenge taunt on 21 May, when his battalion hung up an effigy of Roger Casement in full view of the German trenches. The battalion's war diary recorded that the effigy 'appeared to annoy the enemy and was found riddled with bullets'.[9]

The Easter Rising could be argued to be the beginning of the Irish Civil War. *The Freeman's Journal* thought so. Captain Stephen Gwynn, a nationalist MP serving with the 6th Connaught Rangers, noted that the 10th RDF, who fought the Irish Volunteers at the Mendicity Institution building during the Rising, included men who 'had been active leaders in the Howth gun-running. It was not merely a case of Irishmen firing on their fellow countrymen: it was one section of the original [Irish] Volunteers firing on another.'[10]

Feelings about and reactions to the Rising varied among the thousands of Irishmen serving at the time in the British Army at home and at the front. There were feelings of surprise. Private Soper wrote to Miss Monica Roberts in Stillorgan in Dublin on 20 May 1916: 'I was more than surprised when I heard of the Rebellion in Ireland and I could scarcely believe it until I read it in the papers …'.[11] Michael Wall, as his letter revealed, was also surprised, and delighted to learn that his regiment had taken Moore Street from the rebels.[12]

Others felt angry and wanted revenge. On hearing news of the Rising, Lieutenant Patrick Hemphill speculated on 29 April: 'I suppose they'll hang the ringleaders. It's what traitors deserve. It appears to have been got up by Roger Casement.'[13] Michael told his mother that he was 'sharpening' his bayonet ready for any encounter with 'the beggars' in Sinn Féin. This young, middle-class Catholic Irishman, educated by the Christian Brothers in St Joseph's and O'Connell School in Dublin, was totally against the Rising.[14]

Michael's anger would later turn to a desire for retribution. Almost a year after the Rising, he reckoned that 'those Sinn Feiners should be sent out here [to the front] to do a few nights on the fire step, I will guarantee it will cool their air down.'[15] Private Christy Fox of the 2nd RDF, from North King Street in Dublin, felt the same way as Michael. He remembered the poverty in Dublin following the strikes in 1913 during the Lockout. Writing to Monica Roberts in Dublin, Fox noted:

> I am glad to hear all the trouble is over in Dublin. I would like to have a few of those rebels out here, I can tell you I would give them 2 oz of lead. But in ways the poor fools, that's what I would call them, were dragged into it by Connolly and a few more of his colleagues. Deed [*sic*] I know them very well, the lot of robbers. I remember the strike in Dublin, look at the way Dublin was left poverty stricken that time. It is the same click [*sic*] that has brought on all that destruction on our dear old country. However they are put down now and I only have one hope and that is I hope they are down forever.[16]

Such sentiments were common amongst the ranks of the 2nd RDF in France. Writing to Monica Roberts on 11 May 1916, Private Joseph Clarke told her what he and many of his comrades felt about the Rising:

> I was sorry to hear of the rebel rising in Ireland, but I hope by the time this letter reaches you, the condition will have changed and things [are] normal again. There is no one more sorry to hear of the Rising than the Irish troops out here, it worries them more than I can explain. Their whole cry is, if they could only get amongst them for a few days, the country would not be annoyed with them anymore. Some of the men in this battalion is [*sic*] very uneasy about the safety of their people and one or two poor fellows have lost relatives in this scandalous affair. We just have had some men returned off leave and they tell us that Dublin is in ruins. It is awfully hard to lose one's life out here without being shot at home.
>
> The Sherwood's [*sic*] lost heavily but I expect the Rebels got the worst of the encounter. We of the 2nd Battalion, the Dublins, would

ask for nothing better that [*sic*] the rebels should be sent out here and have an encounter with some of their 'so called Allies', the Germans. I do not think anything they have done will cause any anxiety to England or her noble cause. We will win just the same. These men are pro-German pure and simple, and no Irish men will be sorry when they get justice meted out to them, which, in my opinion, should be death by being *shot*.[17]

Men feared for the safety of their families back in Ireland. Private Andrew Lockhart of the 11th Royal Inniskilling Fusiliers, a battalion in the 36th (Ulster) Division, was worried that the Irish Volunteers would cause trouble around his home farm near Bruckless in County Donegal. Writing to his sister Mina in Donegal he noted: 'I was glad to hear that things are getting quiet in Ireland, had you any trouble with them at home …'.[18]

Private Christy Fox was initially very worried because he had not received any letters from home following the Rising. Since he lived near the Linenhall Barracks in Dublin, he was worried that his family had been caught up in the fighting. However, by the end of May 1916 he had received word that all was well. Writing to Monica Roberts, he noted:

I'm glad to be able to tell you I have got news from home, all my people are quite safe. There was [*sic*] a few people killed where I live. Those two men that were dug up in the cellar in 177 North King Street, I live in the house facing it at the corner of Linenhall Street. There were four men killed in a house only three doors from me at 27 North King Street, I live in 24 when I'm at home and I knew one of them well.[19]

One thing soldiers in any army must feel is that they have support from the home front. Loss of that support creates uncertainty in the ranks. According to Captain Stephen Gwynn, the Rising left Irish soldiers 'in great measure cut off from that moral support which a country gives its citizens in arms'.[20] Nationalist officers in particular believed the Rising was a betrayal and that it damaged the prospects of Irish Home Rule. Gwynn told his fellow nationalist MP Major William (Willie) Hoey Kearney Redmond (who, incidentally, was Michael Wall's commanding officer in the 6th Royal Irish Regiment): 'I shall never forget the men's indignation. They felt they had been stabbed in the back.'[21] According to Jane Leonard, 'Captain Stephen Gwynn's subsequent speeches to the House of Commons and his letters to the press were bitter about the damage done to Home Rule.'[22]

Willie Redmond, who had been on leave in England at the time of the Rising, in turn, wrote to Gwynn: 'Don't imagine that what you and I have done is going to make us popular with our people. On the contrary, we shall both be sent to the right about at the first general election.' Redmond, who was also devastated by the fighting in Dublin, clearly feared he would lose his seat in the next election. It was Patrick Pearse's appeal to the 'Gallant German allies' that particularly shocked him.[23] The Rising had undermined his political life's work. His wife wrote that 'often since the rebellion he said he thought he could best serve Ireland by dying'.[24]

Irish Nationalist MP and officer in the 9th RDF Tom Kettle was also aghast at the Rising. He denounced the venture as madness, seeing it as destructive of what he had striven for throughout his adult life.[25]

Following the execution of leaders of the Rising between 3 and 12 May, attitudes of some of the civilian population began to change in favour of Sinn Féin. Robert Barton, a Wicklow landowner, was gazetted from the Inns of Court OTC to the RDF just as the rebellion began. As a soldier he experienced that change in civilian sentiment. By June 1916 he noted that 'everyone is a Sinn Feiner now ... Ireland will never again be as friendly disposed to England as she was at the outbreak of the war'.[26]

Some of the soldiers also started to question whether they had made the right choice in joining the British Army. They may well have felt disillusioned. Men like Second Lieutenant O'Connor Dunbar of the Royal Army Service Corps (RASC), a friend and colleague of writer and poet Monk Gibbon, who wrote about Dunbar's participation in the gun-running at Howth and was a Redmondite National Volunteer. Gibbon, who was also an officer in the RASC, stated that 'it had taken the Easter executions to make Dunbar begin to doubt the wisdom of the step he had taken'.[27]

Like Michael Wall, Charles Duff had just missed the Rising, going to England for officer training on Easter Monday from Fermanagh. He noted in his memoirs that he 'had joined the British Army as a volunteer in Dublin – to fight Germans', but presumably not to fight his fellow countrymen.[28] Tom Kettle was also distressed by the executions; he was friendly with several of those who were shot. Moreover, the murder of his brother-in-law, Francis Sheehy Skeffington, during the Rising deeply affected Kettle. Kettle's wife, Mary, and Francis's wife, Hannah, were sisters. Sheehy Skeffington's murderer, Captain Bowen-Colthurst, and Kettle wore the same uniform. Kettle, too, began to doubt his vocation.[29]

Writing in 1970 about 'that affair in April 1916', William Mount, an ex-officer with the RDF and friend of Seán Heuston (who had commanded the Volunteer garrison in the Mendicity Institution), stated, 'there were times when I wondered if we were on the right side'. Referring to the executions he said, 'That was a cowardly, unforgivable thing to do.'[30] John Lucy of the 2nd Royal Irish Rifles was anguished by the news of the executions. He noted that 'my fellow soldiers had no great sympathy with the rebels but they got fed up when they heard of the execution of the leaders'.[31] The poet Francis Ledwidge was also deeply troubled by the executions in Dublin: 'Yes, poor Ireland is always in trouble,' he wrote to an Ulster Protestant friend on the day the first leaders were executed. 'Though I am not a Sinn Feiner and you are a Carsonite, do your sympathies not go to Cathleen ni Houlihan? Poor MacDonagh and Pearse were two of my best friends and now they are dead, shot by England.'[32]

Some nationalist-minded men felt powerless, realising that they could do little more than get on with the task in hand at the front. Lieutenant Michael Fitzgerald, serving in the Irish Guards, noted: 'We were too preoccupied with what was in front of us and what we had to do … whatever might happen in Ireland after we'd gone we could do nothing about it. That was our attitude.'[33] Others found the whole affair uninteresting. Anthony Brennan of the 2nd Royal Irish Regiment wrote in 1937: 'Although we were mildly interested, nobody took the thing very seriously.'[34] The commanding officer of the 1st Battalion Irish Guards was summoned to the War Office in June 1916 to discuss the political situation in Ireland. The officer summoned noted that the Rising made 'no impact on the men of the battalion'.[35]

For unionist officers and men of other ranks, particularly from Ulster, feelings and reaction to the Rising fell along predictable lines. The Rising had disrupted the war effort and was a useful reminder of nationalist treachery. At the time of the Rising, Basil Brooke, later Viscount Brookeborough, was a regular officer in Dublin. He was on special leave, as his wife was having a baby. He felt ashamed 'for his country, for his regiment and for those who had died in the war'.[36] Major Frank Crozier, serving with the Royal Irish Rifles in France – a regiment that recruited its service battalions mainly in loyalist areas of Belfast – found very little talk of the Rising amongst his men.[37] And yet there was concern amongst some of the Rifles. The trench journal of the 14th Royal Irish Rifles, which was created from the pre-war Young Citizen Volunteer battalion of the Ulster Volunteer Force (UVF), noted: 'Speaking for ourselves, we'd rather have seen a little less mercy to some of the rebels … what kind of death do those insurgent dogs deserve … Ugh! Doesn't it make your blood boil lads.'[38]

One man, who later became a unionist MP for North Down, Lieutenant Walter Smiles, serving with the Royal Naval Armoured Train, hoped that Sir Edward Carson would be appointed chief secretary for Ireland.[39]

There was a certain amount of solidarity expressed towards the Irish Volunteers by Irishmen in the British Army at the time of the Rising. Commandant W. J. Brennan-Whitmore, director of Field Intelligence for the Volunteers and officer commanding the North Earl Street area of the city, who was captured by the 3rd Royal Irish Regiment, noted:

> Many of the NCOs and men of the 18th Regiment were very dis-satisfied that we had not given them a chance to join us. Practically all those whom I knew personally, and some I didn't know, came and unhesitatingly voiced that sentiment to me.[40]

Nationalist officers in particular were keen to emphasise the sensitivity with which Irish regiments handled themselves during and after the Rising when contrasted with the heavy-handed methods used by non-Irish units. Captain Eugene Sheehy stressed the restraint with which his battalion, the 4th RDF, had conducted itself.[41] The 4th RDF was based in Templemore, County Tipperary and, much like the 3rd Royal Irish, was a training battalion.[42] One officer of the Leinster Regiment declined to command the firing party at the execution of Joseph Plunkett. He cited their childhood friendship and was excused this duty.[43] Robert Barton spent the week in Richmond Barracks and was in charge of gathering prisoners' effects after their surrender. The prisoners found him sympathetic and helpful.[44] Brennan-Whitmore noted that he and his fellow prisoners at Richmond Barracks 'were received and treated with the greatest kindness by the NCOs and men of the 18th Royal Irish'.[45]

However, despite Sheehy and Brennan-Whitmore's positive accounts of the handling of Irish rebels by the 4th RDF and the 18th Royal Irish, there was undoubtedly an amount of hostility shown to the Irish rebels. Indeed, Lieutenant Arthur Killingley, also of 4th RDF, presents a contradictory account to Sheehy's. When he and his men arrived at Kingsbridge (now Heuston) Railway Station from Templemore, they came across a batch of Irish rebels who had been taken prisoner. Killingley's concerns and doubts about his men's attitude towards their fellow countrymen were soon removed. His men, he noted, 'booted the prisoners with great gusto'.[46] Moreover, on the afternoon of Thursday 27 April, the commanding officer of the 4th RDF, Colonel Meldon, issued special orders from battalion headquarters at Dublin's Broadstone Station to 'E' Company headquarters near the Richmond Hospital for an officer and machine-gun crew to proceed to high ground on the North Circular Road, and, according to Major T. C. H. Dickson, from there to 'spray with machine gun fire Aughrim Street and Grangegorman districts. No reason was given but possibly rebel escapists were thought to be collecting.'[47] It wasn't the only time the Dublin Fusiliers fired a machine gun into civilian houses in their own city. On the same day, Lieutenant Killingley claimed that, further down their cordon line at the end of the North Circular Road at Dorset Street, in order to flush out snipers, 'a machine-gun of ours at the five cross-roads peppered a few suspected houses'.[48]

The variation of feelings expressed by Irish soldiers during the Rising led to an atmosphere of uncertainty about the loyalty of some Irish troops at British political and army command levels. At the political level, Colonel Maurice Moore, senior training officer in the National Volunteers, noted in June 1916 that 'all nationalists are Sinn Feiners in War Office eyes'.[49]

At command level, concerns seemed to vary. High-ranking British officers in Dublin did not express any such fears. General Maxwell, in his army order of 1 May 1916, commented favourably on the 'Irish regiments that have so largely helped to crush this rising'.[50] General William Robertson, chief of the Imperial General Staff, agreed with Sir John French, the former commander-in-chief of the British Expeditionary Force (BEF) who had become commander-in-chief of Home Forces, that there was no evidence to doubt the dependability of the Irish troops. David Satterthwaite has suggested that there appeared 'little to suggest that there was a widespread belief that following the Rising there was a concerted effort on behalf of the British military authorities to suppress or undermine the national identity of Irish units'. The higher level military command still had confidence that the Irish units at the front would fight.[51]

And yet, at a lower level of command – perhaps at battalion or brigade level – there were concerns amongst the officer corps of the Irish regiments as to whether or not their Irish troops could be depended upon, both in Dublin during the Rising and at the front in France after it. Noel Drury, a unionist officer in the 6th RDF, experienced the doubt which had filtered down through the ranks as far away from Ireland as Ismalia in Egypt, where he was stationed. He and his men liked to look at the aeroplanes, but he found the pilots a bit stand-offish in their conversations: 'They were very chary [*sic*] of letting us see much of the machines.

Suppose they thought the Irish couldn't be trusted.'[52] Anthony Brennan's unit in the 2nd Royal Irish Regiment was held out in the countryside in France for a few extra weeks 'to guard against any possible sympathetic reactions to affairs in Dublin'.[53]

Even a year after the Rising there was concern at battalion level about the loyalty of Irish troops. In April 1917 the Roman Catholic chaplain to the 2nd Royal Irish Rifles, Fr Henry Gill SJ, was asked by his commanding officer if he 'thought it likely that any of the Irish would think of deserting and if it would be advisable to talk to the men'. Fr Gill responded by saying he thought 'that nothing could do greater harm than to suggest that any of the men were thought capable of treachery ... We were free from anything of this kind.'[54]

Michael Wall's mother would have disapproved of the Rising and those who caused it. She, too, would have felt betrayed. In fact she had an awful scare when she saw a notice in the *Irish Independent* referring to Michael being wounded during the Rising. Michael was very upset about this notice, which apparently was a joke set up by a fellow officer.[55]

It is well-known that the rebels were treated with contempt by a section of Dublin's citizenry, some of whom were women, as they marched through Dublin on their way to detention camps in England. Commandant Brennan-Whitmore noted:

> On the 30th of April, no less than 200 prisoners were evacuated from Richmond Barracks for internment in Knutsford Jail, England ... As we tramped and hobbled down the quays, under heavy escort, we were pelted by garbage and filthy epithets by the scum of the City.[56]

Brennan-Whitmore's reference to the scum of the city may be a bit unfair. It is true that the rebels were treated with contempt by a section of women from the back streets of inner-city Dublin. J. C. Carrothers found it 'pitiable to see some of the Sinns [*sic*] that have been captured by women in the back streets. They are all scratched and stabbed with hat pins.'[57] Lieutenant John Wilson-Lynch sent a vivid account of escort duty to his family in Galway. He stated that the Sinn Féin prisoners 'were a sad sight'.[58]

There is perhaps one possible reason why some women from the back streets of Dublin pelted these men with rotten vegetables and other less savoury projectiles and stabbed others with their hair pins. On 27 April 1916 the Germans launched a gas attack over the Irish lines facing Hulluch, north of Loos in the front line, occupied at the time by Irish battalions of the 16th (Irish) Division. There were 2,128 casualties as a result of the attack, approximately 538 of whom were killed. The remainder were to suffer chronic lung and breathing conditions for the rest of their lives.[59] Almost to the day one year previously, on 25 April 1915, the 1st RDF in Gallipoli and the 2nd RDF at St Julien, suffered appalling casualties and losses. Later, on 25 May, the 2nd RDF was almost wiped out following a gas attack at Mouse Trap Farm, north-east of Ypres. Some 2,166 men of the 1st and 2nd RDF battalions were killed, wounded or missing following the landing at Gallipoli in April and the gas attacks on St Julien and Mouse Trap Farm in April and May.[60] April 1916 was the first anniversary of these losses and one can reasonably assume that this, coupled with the tragic news of Hulluch, filled the women of Dublin's inner streets with grief. It was perhaps out of a sense of solidarity with their loved ones suffering at the front and of grief, rather than out of political disapproval of or disrespect to the Rising or the rebels, that the women took their anger out on the Volunteers. It should also be noted that the women's reaction of anger followed by retribution is similar to the feelings and reactions shown by the soldiers themselves at the front.

Service certificate for
Private Joseph Pender,
9th RDF, from Blackrock,
County Dublin. Private
Pender was killed in action
at Hulluch on 27 April
1916. He was seventeen.
*Courtesy of the RDFA
Archive.*

To date, there is no evidence of any mass defection or mutiny amongst the Irish regiments in Dublin or at the front as a result of the Rising. However, there was a drop in morale among some Irish soldiers.[61] More than a year after the event, resentment of the Irish rebels had not gone away. Sergeant Edward Heafey wrote to Monica Roberts in August 1917. Feeling somewhat depressed, he seemed to link his depression with the state that Ireland was in following the Rising:

> We are having awful weather just now, raining day and night and what a pity too just as we were making so much success. No one knows how we are going through it all, we are having a most awful time of it just now and I have lost nearly all of my platoon. Poor boys, it has upset

me very much. I went to see them after our last battle and there are only nine of them left. So you see Ireland is doing her share in the great struggle. I had a very narrow escape last week myself. A piece of a shell just missed me (thank God). I have great faith and I believe I shall pull through this war all right, but still, we have much to go through yet and by the time you get this we will be in the thick of the fray once more ... I am sorry to hear the old country is so much upset. If I had my way with the Sinn Feiners, I would put them where I am just at the present, up to our eyes in muck and wet and then they would know what war really was like. Anyway, they will get what they are looking for when we Boys see this over.[62]

Despite fears of a breakdown in discipline and a mass fall off in morale in the ranks of the Irish regiments on account of the Rising, neither happened on a large scale. Evidence to support this may be taken from the fact that courts martial held in Irish regiments serving on the Western Front in the months from the Rising to September 1916 were not above average. Moreover, there was no significant increase in the courts-martial records of the home battalions of the Irish regiments in Dublin after the Rising.[63]

On the same theme of the effect of the Rising on morale and the fighting effectiveness of Irish battalions, according to Terry Denman, 'from the magnificent achievements of the 16th (Irish) Division on the Somme a few months after the Rising, it is clear that whatever disquiet the events in Ireland produced, they did not damage its fighting performance'.[64] As can be seen from the 9th Munsters and their treatment of Casement's effigy, although the Rising dismayed and embittered men in the trenches, it did not seem to weaken the morale of that regiment. Private Soper, who had read about the Rising in the Irish newspapers, wrote to Monica Roberts on 20 May 1916. Rather than damage his morale, the Rising had made him more determined than ever to fight on:

It took no effect on us chaps out here except to make us more determined to stick. I suppose their idea was that the Irishmen out here would be for them but they were greatly mistaken and we wished we had a chance to get even with them. I don't know where their bravery was if they call killing wounded soldiers a brave deed.[65]

Using the incidence of reporting sick for duty as a means of measuring morale in an infantry battalion, Lynn Lemisko noted that the incidence of reporting sick amongst Irish troops in the 16th (Irish) Division after the Rising was not above the average. She further noted:

While Irish Catholic soldiers of the 16th (Irish) Division were not completely divorced from the politics of their homeland, political incidents did not have pronounced or long-term ramifications on the morale of the Irish division. Although their English comrades occasionally labelled Irish soldiers as Sinn Feiners, most Irish troops were clear on their position in the spectrum of Irish political opinion. When asked his views about the relative aims of the nationalists and the Sinn Feiners, an Irish corporal told Rowland Fielding, 'the nationalists aim at getting independence by constitutional, the Sinn Feiners by unconstitutional, means.'[66]

By mid-May 1916 things had quietened down in Dublin and indeed for Michael Wall at Ballykinlar. 'This is such a dull place,' he wrote. He and two other trainee officers spent many a long summer's evening playing golf at the nearby town of Newcastle. 'It is for all the world like the pictures one sees of the Dargle.' On 16 May he wrote to his mother and asked her to get Joe to send some 'golf balls that is [sic] without any cracks and some golf ball paint that is in that room where you had the jam stored'. He also enquired about the condition Dublin was in after the Rising and whether well-known Dublin retailers Arnotts had survived the rebellion: 'I hear they have restarted to rebuild Sackville Street. Did Arnotts shop escape.'[67]

Orders circulated round the camp for savings to be made in every way possible. For example, paper became a bit scarce, with the result that Michael had to write on both the back and front of his letters. The summer months drifted away at Ballykinlar.

By the end of August 1916 Michael had moved down south to Richmond Barracks at Templemore, County Tipperary, where living conditions were very basic. One of his friends who later trained there noted in a letter to Michael that the barracks was dirty and had no sanitary arrangements. The walls in his room were covered with pink distemper. The men had their meals in Hickie's Hotel and did very little other than walk in and out of the town.[68] In contrast, for Michael the pace of training quickened at Templemore. His days were busy and in the evening he was so tired that he was not in much humour for writing to anyone. Nor did he have much time for golf in Thurles. When it rained, Michael passed the time in the evening by sleeping and sitting in front of the fire in his billet. In one letter he wrote:

> Richmond Barracks,
> Templemore,
> Co. Tipperary.
> Thursday.
>
> Dear Mother,
>
> Many thanks for parcel. You must forgive me for not writing since Saturday as I am very busy all day and I don't feel in the humour of writing when the day is done. I must try and get up home when the visitors are there. What is all this nonsense about

travel in Dublin? I hope there is nothing wrong. … The weather is shocking here – always raining, but I have a good fire every night so I manage to pass the time. We went for a fine long route march yesterday and I quite enjoyed it. …

Your fond son,
Michael.[69]

Soon enough, however, the quiet nights by the fire at Templemore would end.

4

Dear Mother, You Are Not to Worry

In early September 1916, for further training, Michael moved from Templemore to the main British Army training camp at Aldershot in Hampshire. Before leaving Ireland he spent a short time training at Portobello Barracks in Dublin. When he arrived in a bustling London, the sights and sounds dazzled him. Having arrived at his hotel in Charing Cross, he wrote home to his mother telling her of his rough crossing to Holyhead and of a couple of men he had met who were on their way back to the front, one of whom was from his regiment. He spent a day in London looking around the famous sights. In a follow-up letter to his mother and younger brother Joseph, he told them he had seen the Strand, Piccadilly, St Paul's Cathedral and the Houses of Parliament, but there was no street like Dublin's Sackville Street.

Michael arrived in Aldershot on Tuesday 5 September and was temporarily attached to the 27th Middlesex Regiment. The camp resembled the Phoenix Park in Dublin and there was nothing to be seen but men in khaki. The Royal Flying Corps (RFC) impressed him, doing their aerial loops above the camp. He heard rumours of men being offered cushy staff jobs at Aldershot. No doubt he also heard stories from men who had served at the front; these may have given him second thoughts about getting involved in this war, as the reality of what lay ahead of him may have hit him at Aldershot.[1]

Physical training at Aldershot was given by Australian and Canadian NCOs. The tough training didn't seem to go down too well with Michael. He told Joseph that he 'wished this course was over, the work is too hard to continue daily for five hours'.[2]

Drill training class at Aldershot, September 1916. Michael is seated third from the left. *Courtesy of the Kavanagh family.*

His training as an officer lasted seven months, from 2 February 1916 at Dublin University to 2 September 1916. On Friday 29 September his physical training course finished at Aldershot. He returned to Dublin and when he got home a letter was waiting for him from his friend Smyth of the RHMS. He told Michael that 'Fritz was getting more than he bargained for just now!' The letter was dated 28 September 1916 and no doubt Smyth was referring to the fighting at the Battle of the Somme, which had begun back in July and was still going on. Fritz may well have been getting more than he bargained for, but as the newspapers of the day failed to mention, so too was 'Tommy Atkins'.[3]

The night before he left for France, Michael and some of the Trinity OTC lads he had trained with stayed at the Grosvenor Hotel on Westland Row in Dublin. No doubt their last night in Dublin went well into the early hours. He wrote a brief note to his mother asking her not to worry and reassuring her he would be fine:

21.X [October].16.

Dearest Mother,

I am going to ask you not to worry about me as I shall be as safe as houses. I know you will find it very hard but do cheer up and look forward to happy days that are to come when this strafe [*sic*] is over. There are some of the old Trinity lot going out tomorrow and they are staying here. Give my love to Auntie and all the young 'uns and tell Joe to buck up & pass his exam.

Always your fond son,
Michael.[4]

Postcard from Michael to his mother, sent from the Grosvenor Hotel in
Westland Row, Dublin, 21 October 1916.

Two days later, on 23 October 1916, Michael arrived at a base depot
in Boulogne. He was destined for Flanders and, more precisely, the
Flemish village of Loker on the southern edge of the Ypres salient.

5

The Road to Wijtschate

In order to understand how Michael Wall and his comrades ended up fighting the Germans who occupied the Flemish village of Wijtschate, just east of Loker, in June 1917, it is important to set his story in the context of the bigger picture of why – and indeed how – British Commander-in-Chief General Douglas Haig and his staff would take the war to the Germans in June 1917.

By the end of 1914, following the First Battle of Ypres, stalemate had resulted along the Western Front. For the Central Powers – that is Germany, Austria-Hungary, the Ottoman Empire and Bulgaria – 1915 was a somewhat successful year of the war. No Allied breakout initiative, such as that in Gallipoli or Salonika, had delivered much, and the Russians and Serbs had been routed.[1] Rather optimistically, General Joseph Joffre, the French commander-in-chief, believed the autumn breakout offensives in Champagne and Artois (including Loos) had brought tactical results, and he ascribed their overall failure to bad weather and a shortage of ammunition. He took the lead in seeking a concerted response to the Allied breakout failures of 1915.

On 6 December 1915, at a conference in Chantilly – the great horse-racing town north of Paris – at Joffre's headquarters, representatives of the Allied high command from Britain, France, Russia, Serbia and Italy agreed to aim for a synchronised offensive on the Western, Eastern and Italian Fronts on some date after March 1916. The ever-increasing size of the Allied armies would allow these offensives to be carried out. The philosophy behind this synchronised offensive was to prevent the Germans from using their central static position to switch their reserves in turn from front to front. The representatives also agreed that if the Central Powers attacked one ally, the others would assist.[2]

The Italians would attack the Austro-Hungarians along the central Isonzo river; the Russians' Brusilov Offensive would attack along the southern sector of the Eastern Front; and the British and French would attack the Germans astride the river Somme, but would then switch their main effort to break the German hold on Flanders via the British-held Ypres salient and attempt to take the Belgian ports of Ostend, Blankenberge and Zeebrugge, which had been in German hands since the end of 1914.

These occupied Belgian ports presented a particular strategic threat to the cross-channel BEF supply routes. They had been used as bases from which German destroyers, submarines and submarine minelayers struck at the British supply routes from the ports of Dover and Folkestone to Dunkirk, Calais and Boulogne in France. This threat was identified very early in the war. On 7 December 1914 First Lord of the Admiralty Winston Churchill proposed to Field Marshal Sir John French, the then commander-in-chief of the BEF, a scheme for recovering the stretch of Belgian coast that contained these occupied ports by means of a combined naval and military operation. However, at the time, General Joffre opposed the plan as he was more concerned with his plans to remove the German threat to Paris. In November 1915 the Admiralty stated that the use of the Belgian ports by the German navy was 'a growing danger to the transport of troops and supplies to France' and, in the light of this danger, again pressed for a combined naval and military action to free them.[3]

At the request of the British Admiralty, the General Staff at the War Office, in consultation with the Admiralty war staff and others, produced a memorandum dated 12 November 1915, which essentially outlined the project to remove the Germans from Ostend. The recommendation was either to make a surprise landing at Ostend with a British force embarking from Dover, Calais and Dunkirk, or to advance along the Belgian coast that was in Allied hands far enough to enable heavy artillery to make Ostend at least non-functional as a harbour.

Unfortunately that particular plan foundered after Admiralty warnings that its light ships could not stand up to the German coastal artillery and that its battleships could not be risked in such confined waters.[4] The project was shelved, but the naval threat and dangers emanating from these occupied ports remained and grew, although in November 1915 the Admiralty could not have envisaged just how much the loss of shipping would increase. By 1917 the German U-boats that operated out of Ostend and Zeebrugge would contribute to the sinking of one-third of the total British and Allied shipping sunk. The remaining two-thirds were attributed to the fleets at Kiel and Wilhelmshaven.[5] Regardless of this, the British Admiralty wanted the Germans out of Zeebrugge and Ostend. In 1917, according to A. J. P. Taylor, 'the number of ships sunk by U-Boats rose catastrophically'.[6] British Merchant Navy shipping loses in January 1917 totalled forty-nine ships, comprising 153,666 tons. In February tonnage loses had more than doubled. Ship losses amounted to 105 and tonnage loss to 313,486 tons. By April 1917 the total British Merchant Navy shipping losses amounted to 450 ships, comprising 1,365,912 tons. The losses were so severe that the then First Sea-Lord Admiral Sir John Jellicoe informed Haig that 'if the army cannot get the Belgian ports, the Navy cannot hold the Channel and the War is lost'.[7]

On 14 February 1916 Haig met Joffre at Chantilly; in accordance with the combined-offensive policy agreed at the Allied conference of 6 December 1915, both commanders-in-chief agreed to a joint offensive astride the Somme river, where both armies stood beside each other. At the age of fifty-four, General Haig had been given command of the BEF on 19 December 1915. He replaced Field Marshal Sir John French, who had resigned.[8]

Haig and Joffre set a target date for their joint offensive for the end of June 1916. Haig then instructed General Sir Henry Rawlinson to prepare a plan for the Somme offensive. However, to keep his Flanders project alive, which included the capture of the Belgian ports, he also instructed General Sir Herbert Plumer to prepare plans for offensive operations there.[9] General Plumer was the commander of the 2nd Army in Flanders; since the Second Battle of Ypres in April and May 1915, the Flanders sector of the Western Front had been relatively quiet.

Joffre considered the Somme offensive a predominantly French operation. This may well have suited General Haig, who believed that once the German's reserves had been drawn off at the Somme, he could then launch his Flanders breakout project.[10] Haig viewed the joint Somme offensive as a preliminary attack that would take place before his breakout from Ypres. Given the choice of offensives in 1916, the Flanders project was always going to be Haig's preferred option.[11] Haig's plan of assisting the French first on the Somme and then turning his efforts on Flanders had Joffre's approval.[12] He also had the approval of the War Committee of British Prime Minister Herbert Asquith's cabinet, which indicated that there was no operation of war it regarded of greater importance than the expulsion of the Germans from the Belgian coast.[13]

Coupled with the original project to take the German-occupied ports at Ostend, Blankenberge and Zeebrugge, there were further sound strategic reasons why Haig believed in the Flanders project. In January 1915 French operations staff at Chantilly had begun to analyse how to break the German defences and their lines of supply to their armies along the Western Front. They identified the rail-communication lines that supported the German armies in the field. Three rail systems led from the Western Front back across the Rhine into Germany. If any of these lines were cut and supplies curtailed, perhaps the Germans might fall back. This would create conditions for open warfare, which was believed to offer the best chance of a decisive Allied victory in Europe. Of the three railway links, two supplied the German armies in Flanders and Verdun. The former was of specific interest to the BEF stuck in Flanders. The German railway line to their Flanders front came along the Roulers–Thourout line. Breaking out from Ypres in a north-east swoop from the city and taking Roulers (now Roeselare), which lay eight kilometres beyond the Passchendaele Ridge, would be a strategic success. In contrast, a break through the German lines astride the Somme would be of no strategic value to the British. There were no major strategic communication lines or industrial complexes beyond the German lines facing the British sector of their Somme offensive. All the British would face along the Somme front would be an uphill battle against fortified villages and some of the strongest German positions on the Western Front.

Planning for the Flanders breakout went through several ideas and personalities. Rather than the surprise landing from the sea at Ostend, which he believed would be too difficult to effect and support, Haig proposed to operate from the Ypres front with two armies and not attempt a coastal advance and landings until the main offensive north-east out of the Ypres salient had made progress. The 2nd Army that protected the Ypres salient was already on the ground in Flanders under General Plumer.

As warden of the salient, Plumer held a heavy responsibility with little chance of glory, for there was hardly a point within the loop of ground around Ypres that German guns could not enfilade. It was a state of affairs hardly calculated to improve his nerves or those of his troops. Nonetheless, he had made the salient a hard nut to crack, and the Germans had not tried to do so since he had taken over in 1915.[14]

Following a meeting with his army commanders on 7 January 1916, Haig proposed that the new British 4th Army should take over the southern sector of the Ypres salient, thus completing his two-army attack formation. He asked General Rawlinson to work out a plan for an offensive north-eastward from the Ypres salient that would use General Plumer's 2nd Army as support. Moreover, he discussed the proposed naval assault with Lieutenant General Sir Aylmer Hunter-Weston, who had gained experience of combined operations during the Gallipoli campaign, together with Vice Admiral Sir Reginald Bacon, who had already planned the framework of the naval arrangements. Both were to work out details for the coastal attack and landings. French and Belgian divisions were also to make plans, since they were holding the Allied side of the coastal sector south of Nieuport.[15]

When Haig took command of the BEF, his intention was to hold meetings every week at the headquarters of the armies under his command. 'The object of these meetings,' he noted, was 'to develop mutual understanding and closer touch not only between the Army Commanders and myself but also between our Staff.'[16] At one of those weekly meetings, at 2nd Army headquarters on 13 January 1916, special emphasis was placed on the need to capture the Gheluvelt Plateau, which ran around the east of Ypres, before the 4th Army could launch its breakout from the Ypres salient. German artillery concealed behind the ridge in its woods and on its slopes dominated the ground below in the Ypres salient, where the British had been since the end of 1914. General Plumer pointed out that before any attempt to capture the plateau was attempted, the Wijtschate–Messines Ridge – which formed the southern part of the arc of the Ypres salient and which the Germans called the Wytschaete–Bogen – would have to be taken. He added that plans for such an event were well advanced, with the digging of mines under the German strong points along the Wijtschate–Messines Ridge.

The mines were dug by Tunnelling Companies made up of men drawn from the ranks, mixed with drafts of men experienced in mining in coal pits and the London Underground. The inspiration behind the establishment of these companies was an engineer named Major John Norton-Griffiths, who was known as 'Empire Jack'. He was a professional civil engineer, an entrepreneur, a member of parliament and an officer with the 2nd King Edward's Horse Regiment. His nickname was a fitting one, as he had literally helped build parts of the pre-war British Empire.[17]

The Messines Ridge, won by the Germans in 1914, had been one of their principal ramparts on the Western Front. A captured German order showed the importance they attached to it: 'The unconditional retention of the independent strong points, Wijtschate and Messines, is of the increased importance for the domination of the whole Wijtschate salient. These strong points must therefore not fall even temporarily into the enemy's hands …'.[18]

Haig saw the logic in Plumer's proposal and agreed to this extension of his plans. He asked that the capture of the Messines Ridge should now be incorporated into the larger project of clearing the Belgian coast and the breakout from Ypres.[19]

On 27 February 1916 General Rawlinson presented the outline of his breakout proposal. A week or so later, on 5 March, with some revisions, the staff at General Headquarters (GHQ) had put the Rawlinson plan together in terms of strategy, manpower and equipment needed to implement his proposal. Initially set up in St Omer in October 1914, the GHQ of the British Army was subsequently transferred to Montreuil-sur-Mer in March 1916. Rawlinson's and GHQ's plans consisted of a phased operation over six stages. The general concept was to oust the German 4th Army first from the Wijtschate–Messines Ridge south of Ypres, secure the Gheluvelt Plateau and then, by stages, extend over the high ground north-eastwards of the Ypres salient, through Passchendaele and beyond to the Roulers–Thourout railway junction.

On 10 April 1916 GHQ issued a memorandum to General Plumer that informed him of the plan under consideration, and also asked Plumer to submit his plan for the capture of the Wijtschate–Messines and Pilckem Ridges. The target date set for the opening of the Flanders offensive with the attack on Wijtschate would be 15 July 1916, that is after the Somme offensive had begun.[20]

There is a wise and true saying, 'God disposes what man proposes.' In the spring of 1916 it was German General Erich Ludendorff, the metaphorical figure of God in the above saying, who disposed of what Haig and the Allies at Chantilly had proposed for their 1916 offensive. Ludendorff's offensive at Verdun, which began on 21 February 1916, had developed into a long, drawn-out attritional battle that wore the French and, indeed, the German armies down, and upset the Allied plans for the 1916 Flanders breakout. On 27 March 1916 General Joffre informed Sir Douglas Haig that the British might have to deploy the whole of their available resources alongside the French in a combined operation astride the Somme, in order to relieve and prevent the total destruction of the French at Verdun. However, even as late as 27 May 1916, as preparations for the Somme offensive were in full swing, the Flanders project was still on the table and GHQ ordered that preparations be pressed ahead with at full speed.[21]

By 4 June 1916, however, it was evident that whatever shape the Flanders part of the British and French summer offensive might take, General Rawlinson – who by that time had been appointed commander of the 4th Army in the area north of the Somme river – would now be too far committed on the Somme to participate in it. Consequently, Haig ordered Plumer to be prepared to direct the Flanders operation with restricted resources.[22]

General Plumer continued to work on his original plan with considerably reduced resources. By June 1916, as part of that plan, twenty-four mines beneath the Wijtschate–Messines Ridge had been dug to depths of 20–30 metres and packed with almost 396,530 kilograms (874,200 pounds) of ammonal – explosive powder made up of ammonium nitrate and aluminium powder. The end points of the tunnels in which the explosives were placed were located under German strong points along their line, such as machine-gun positions and redoubts.[23] Removing these strong points would be vital to give Plumer's attacking infantry a clear run into the German lines.

Even after the attack by the 4th Army at the Somme on 1 July 1916, the attack on the Wijtschate–Messines Ridge was still being considered and proposed as a subsidiary attack to the Somme battles. As per the original plan, 15 July was provisionally set for the attack on Messines. In the end, however, this operation could not be undertaken. The duration of the Somme offensive, and the enormous loss of men and material, prevented the Messines Ridge stage of the Flanders project from going ahead.[24] Haig's plans for a Flanders breakout fell apart in early July 1916, due to the losses on the Somme. Plumer's men, the mineshafts and tunnels dug under the Wijtschate–Messines Ridge would have to wait and withstand the winter of 1916. The explosives would sit in their galleries for almost a year following their completion, where they were regularly maintained by members of the Royal Engineers. Meanwhile, the battle along the Somme raged on throughout the summer and autumn of 1916.

On 15 November 1916, with the Somme petering out, Haig's breakout at Flanders was back on the agenda when he attended an Allied conference held at Chantilly, which considered the Allied plans for 1917. The Flanders project was discussed and the French put their own offensive ideas to General Haig. Joffre urged that no rest should be given to the German army, which had suffered terrible and irreplaceable losses at Verdun and the Somme.[25] The slaughter of the previous two-and-a-half years on the Western Front also played heavily on the French army, whose losses, too, had been horrendous.

However, plans for the 1917 offensives were interrupted by political and military developments on both sides of the English Channel. First, General Joffre – who had been the French commander-in-chief since the outbreak of the war – was dismissed; on 12 December 1916 the French government chose their hero of Verdun, General Robert Nivelle, as their new commander-in-chief. He brought his own ideas for breaking the stalemate and keeping up the pressure on the Germans along the Western Front. Second, in the same month, in Britain Asquith's government fell; his position as prime minister was taken by David Lloyd George, who, much to the displeasure of Haig, agreed with the placing of Nivelle in supreme command of the BEF in France.[26]

Instead of being nursed back to strength after the previous two years of fighting, particularly at the Somme, the French, under their new commander, planned another offensive in the Soissons-Reims area. Nivelle believed that if he was successful in this major offensive, the Germans would probably abandon the Belgian coastline and that Haig's proposed operation in Flanders would be unnecessary.[27] If, however, Nivelle's offensive failed, the British would, as quickly as possible, turn their attentions to the Flanders breakout.[28] Haig's project was yet again to be put on hold for another French-led offensive.

Haig reluctantly agreed to co-operate with Nivelle in this offensive, with the latter being in charge. It is important to note that up to the end of May 1917 many of the main battles in which the British took part along the Western Front were in conjunction with the French army. The British objective in most of these battles was to draw away German reserves from the French, who led the main attack. In Nivelle's new offensive, the British and Commonwealth forces would again play a subsidiary part, by attacking a few days before the French. The British and Canadians would attack the Arras to Vimy sector in April 1917, in yet another attempt to draw German reserves away from the French main attack.

As a result of the decisions taken at the Chantilly conference of November 1916, two days after the end of the conference, on 17 November, General Haig asked General Plumer to suggest any changes needed for his earlier plan, or else to come up with a new plan keeping in mind the post-Somme reduction in resources. Plumer's proposals were sent to GHQ on 12 December 1916. The naturally cautious Plumer had restricted his horizons to the capture of the Messines Ridge and the low-lying Pilckem Ridge immediately to the east of Ypres. His proposals followed the same lines as those he had first submitted earlier in the year, which were that before any major advance either eastward or north-eastward from the Ypres salient could be made, the offensive for the main breakout should begin with two armies simultaneously attempting to capture the Wijtschate–Messines Ridge in the south, and Hill 60 and Hill 29 (Pilckem Ridge) in the north. Preparations for the

Messines attack were to be advanced so that it could be carried out at a month's notice in the spring or summer of 1917.

The plan that Plumer submitted to GHQ on 12 December fell short of Haig's more ambitious plans to rout the Germans out of Belgium entirely. Plumer suggested a bite-and-hold project, whereas Haig wanted something more rapid. Consequently, on 6 January 1917 Haig asked Plumer to recast his scheme. He also sought a second opinion from Rawlinson, who had borne the brunt of the Somme offensive, with the intention of giving Rawlinson responsibility for the northern sector of the attack. Moreover, perhaps by way of an alternative, Haig put together a special subsection of the Operations Branch of his own GHQ staff under Lieutenant Colonel C. N. MacMullen, assisted by Major Viscount Gort, which produced another proposal for the main breakout project.[29] Both groups received a letter from GHQ that set out the revised objectives.

On 30 January 1917 Plumer presented his revised second plan.[30] It was a little more ambitious than his first. He proposed an initial operation intended to capture Pilckem in the north and Messines in the south, with a small advance across the plateau, followed by the capture of the village of Passchendaele, north-east of Ypres. Ultimately, he proposed a push towards the Belgian coast. The attack was to be staggered and made by two armies, one to attack the north of the salient (that is Pilckem), and the other the south (that is Messines) – he had initially proposed the attack be carried out by both armies at the same time.[31] He concluded, however, that an attack north of the Ypres salient on Pilckem would not succeed unless the ridge – that is the Wijtschate–Messines Ridge to the south – was taken first.

However, once again Plumer's plan fell short of Haig's expectations. Haig asked Rawlinson for a second opinion on Plumer's revised plan, but Rawlinson disappointed him by basically agreeing with Plumer's assessment. Rawlinson felt that the attacks on Pilckem and Messines should not occur simultaneously and should instead be staggered. The first target should be Messines. If that fell, then the operation should be moved against the Gheluvelt Plateau and Pilckem Ridge.

In his analysis of Plumer's plan, Rawlinson believed that maximum advantage could be taken with the fall of the Messines Ridge, and that no great interval should follow before the launch of the attack on Pilckem. He recommended a gap of between forty-eight and seventy-two hours, which was the minimum time, he believed, needed to reorient the artillery.[32]

Still dissatisfied, Haig turned to the other option being prepared by Lieutenant Colonel MacMullen's team. MacMullen's plan, submitted on 14 February, involved the massive use of tanks. This plan impressed Haig, who had great hope for the tank. However, tank experts at GHQ shot down MacMullen's plan, because they deemed the land over which the attack would take place – the swamps and dense cluster of shattered woods of the Gheluvelt Plateau – unsuitable for tanks.[33] This plan was shelved; in the end, Haig had no option but to go with Plumer.

On Easter Monday 9 April 1917 – in accordance with Haig's agreement with Nivelle – under the command of General Edmund 'Bull' Allenby and General Sir Julian Byng, the British attacked Arras and made one of the most outstanding advances in the war to that date. Canadian and Moroccan troops captured the strong German defences at Vimy Ridge. However, despite the gains, the overall state of the British attack ended in stalemate.

On 16 April 1917, in icy rain, Nivelle went ahead with his attempt to break through the German lines along the Chemin des Dames Ridge. Converting a breakout into a breakthrough on the Western Front was always the great challenge that confronted commanders in major infantry offensives. Nivelle's attempt failed catastrophically, petering out in early May; the Germans, it turned out, had captured a document that revealed Nivelle's plan of attack. Units of the French army had had enough and began to mutiny. Some 30,000 French soldiers left their trenches along the Chemin des Dames. Nivelle was subsequently sacked and replaced by another hero of Verdun, General Henri Phillippe Pétain.

With the failure of the Nivelle offensive, General Haig turned his attention to his plans for the Flanders breakout. His time had come at last, and this time he would be in charge. On Monday 7 May 1917, following an Inter-Allied Conference in Paris, Haig brought his army commanders together for a conference at Doullens. He announced that the Nivelle offensive had achieved only a limited advance and that the attack had been halted. The Arras campaign would continue in the hope of wearing the Germans down and misleading them as to British intentions. However, the troops and material involved in Arras would be gradually reduced and moved north to Flanders for the attack on the Wijtschate–Messines Ridge. To bridge the gap between the end of the attack on the Wijtschate–Messines Ridge and the beginning of the offensive on the Gheluvelt Ridge/Pilckem Ridge, the French, Italians and Russians had agreed to undertake operations to hold the attention of the Germans elsewhere.[34]

Haig's ambition of more than two years had come at last. He asked Plumer when he would be ready to carry out the attack. Plumer replied, 'In one month from now.'[35]

If what would become known as the Third Battle of Ypres, or, as some simply called it, Passchendaele, were to be considered a stage drama, then the Battle of Wijtschate and Messines would be considered act one, scene one. Thus would come – after all the planning, proposals and counter-proposals that had gone into this grand breakout plan to capture the German-occupied Belgian ports and the railhead at Roulers – Irishmen from the four corners of the island of Ireland, along with thousands of soldiers from Britain, Australia, New Zealand and the West Indies. Among those thousands of Irishmen, whose first objective would be to kick the Germans off the Wijtschate Ridge on 7 June 1917, was Michael Wall from Carrick Hill in north County Dublin.

6

Michael's New Home in Flanders

After their part in the Battle of the Somme in the summer of 1916, both Irish infantry divisions moved north towards the quieter Ypres salient. The first to move was the 36th (Ulster) Division. Following their tragic loss of approximately 5,500 men at Thiepval on 1 July during the Battle of the Somme, the Ulster Division was placed in reserve and temporarily came under the administration of 2nd Army headquarters for a period of recovery.[1] On 13 July they headed north to the well-known training area around the city of St Omer. When they eventually arrived in Flanders, they set up their headquarters at Saint-Jans-Cappel near Bailleul.[2] To make up for their dreadful losses at the Somme, the Ulster Division was reinforced with 193 officers and 2,182 other ranks.[3]

On 12 September 1916 units of the Welsh Guards and Grenadier Guards relieved the 16th (Irish) Division at Ginchy. The division had suffered a loss of some 240 officers and 4,090 other ranks; a total of 4,330 men were killed, wounded or declared missing during their Somme campaign between 1 and 11 September 1916.[4] Over the next three days, the three infantry brigades of the Irish Division also moved north towards Flanders, to the village of Loker, some eight kilometres west of the then German-occupied village of Wijtschate. They relieved Canadian troops on their arrival at the village.[5]

At 9 a.m. on 24 September 1916 GOC 16th (Irish) Division

General Sir William Hickie assumed command of the Vierstraat–Wijtschate sector.[6] This sector lay between the crossroads hamlet of Vierstraat in the north and Maedelstede Farm in the south, the latter being the southernmost end of the division's sector. The 16th (Irish) Division's front line in this sector was a little over two kilometres long. The 36th (Ulster) Division's sector was named the Spanbroek sector after a windmill that once stood on the Spanbroekmolen hill facing the Ulstermen. The British front line covering this sector ran from Maedelstede Farm southwards to a townland named Kruisstraat on the Wulverghem to Wijtschate road. The Ulster Division's front line was a little under two kilometres long.[7] Both divisions' sectors were subdivided into small sub-sectors. The line separating the two Irish divisions was the road from Kemmel to Wijtschate, known to the men of both divisions as 'the Suicide Road'.[8] For the next nine months or so, the 16th (Irish) and the 36th (Ulster) Divisions served with 9th Corps in General Plumer's 2nd Army.

Upon their arrival in this southern sector of the Ypres salient, soldiers of the 16th (Irish) moved into billets and tents around the villages of Loker and Kemmel. The landscape was mainly hilly; the region in Flemish is known as Heuveland ('hilly land') with Kemmelberg ('Mount Kemmel') being the highest point, at approximately 150 metres high. Before the war the area had been covered with woods consisting of oak, beech and holly trees. By the autumn and winter of 1916 it resembled a lunar landscape. The 16th (Irish) front line lay roughly halfway between the foot of Mount Kemmel and the village of Wijtschate to the east.

The 16th (Irish) Divisional artillery had arrived in the sector not long before the infantry and set up their wagon lines in the village of Westoutre. They set up their gun positions in front of De Klijte (La Clytte), covering the ridge that led up to Wijtschate.

The 16th (Irish) Division's sector within which Michael's 6th Royal Irish Regiment operated up to 7 June 1917 ran from Vierstraat crossroads (north) to Maedelstede Farm (south). The 36th (Ulster) Division's sector ran further south, from Maedelstede Farm, through Spanbroekmolen to Kruisstraat crossroads.

Source: 'Supplement to 1:10000 (British) Series I. Trenches corrected
to: 1.4.17. Sheet name and no. 28SW 2. Edition no. 5A. Lines: A/G
Production: OS GSGS no. 3062', National Archives Kew, WO297/6580.

For a while, Sergeant R. H. Newman of the 177th Brigade Royal Field Artillery (RFA) and his comrades in 'C' Battery had a quiet time when they arrived at their new front. According to Newman, they were even welcomed by the Bavarians on the other side of the wire. He claimed things were so quiet that they met some of the Bavarians and exchanged treats with each other, such as white bread for German cigars. He noted in his diary:

> When we took over, our infantry were not with us, but the Bavarians were in the opposite trenches with a notice put up. WELCOME 16TH IRISH. This was supposed to demoralise us. However, we knew that the Bavarians were never aggressive troops and it was not long before both sides were sitting on the top, swapping bully beef for cigars, as they had not time for the black sausage or black bread, the Bavarians would give anything for a piece of white bread and would not believe that it was still a standard issue. The authorities soon put a stop to all that by bringing the artillery into action. Then they took the Bavarians out and brought the Prussians in and that was the end of our quiet interlude.[9]

Placed along the British front line in the Irish sector were positions designated on trench maps as Strong Points (SPs). For example, SP7 was in the Ulster Division's sector. These positions were used as front-line or advanced battalion headquarter dugouts, some of which could accommodate a company of men in each. They were well wired and protected, because they were also the entrance to some of the mine shafts that led to the gallery in which the mine explosives were placed, ready to blow on Zero Day, 7 June.[10] The average distance between these points was about 275 metres.[11]

Running through both the 16th and the 36th Divisions' sectors was a huge wall of sandbags, known as the Chinese Wall, named after the Chinese Labour Corps who had originally helped to construct it. It straddled the Haringhebeek stream, which in winter swelled to create a swampy valley held by the Irish facing the Germans in Wijtschate. It had dugouts along its length and was constructed behind the front line to serve as a support trench and protected assembly place for gathering before a raid or attack on the German line.[12] Beginning from the dugout known as Irish House and going straight north along the line, sections of the wall were named Canton Trench, Hong Kong Trench, Peking Trench, Spantung Trench and finally Yum Trench, which joined up with the Vierstraat–Wijtschate Road.[13]

The Chinese men who worked in the Chinese Labour Corps were treated disgracefully. Due to the labour shortage created by the war, the French government allowed private firms to employ Chinese labourers throughout France. Their contract, signed before they left China, obliged them to work ten hours a day, seven days a week, with 'due consideration' made for Chinese festivals. Such considerations were not always given. Before the end of the war some 100,000 Chinese people were employed on menial tasks throughout the war zones of the Allied armies. *The Times* in London thought they all looked alike and were not to be trusted:

> He has his own little tricks and dodges. As one Chinaman is, to the Western eye, indistinguishable from another, there is always the danger that 'Ah Lung' may try to draw the pay of 'Weng Chow' who is on the sick list or has gone home. Consequently every coolie has his fingerprints taken and registered under the supervision of Scotland Yard.[14]

Chinese labourers were disgusted with their treatment. Letters home reflected their bitterness: 'though well-clothed and fed, we are treated like animals. Nobody takes any notice of us ... we get no credit for the work we do.'[15] The bodies of approximately 1,612 of these untrustworthy 'coolies' lie in scattered graves around northern France and Flanders.[16]

Part of the trench system facing Wijtschate that the Irish troops occupied was made by Canadian troops; it was not very protective, being mainly parapets built above ground level on account of the high water table in the region.[17] Lieutenant Frank Laird described the trenches in his sector of the line, which was at the end of York Road and on the left of the sector where Michael Wall was stationed:

> The front line trenches were not what we had been taught to expect in the text books and lectures of the Cadet Battalion … They had traverses and fire bays all right, but, in place of being six or seven good feet underground, they were mainly a breastwork towards the enemy of sandbags with a parados of a rather so so kind marked by gaps here and there. There were spots where the breastwork itself was on the low side, and it was necessary to proceed in a humble and undignified stoop to avoid the attention of snipers.[18]

When the Canadians were in this sector, they named some of the trenches after places in Canada, such as Fort Saskatchewan and Fort Halifax.[19] They also set up a cemetery along the York Road, later named La Laiterie Cemetery. Men from the Canadian New Brunswick Regiment were buried there before the Irish arrived.[20]

Soon after their arrival, both Irish divisions began to rename some of their trenches after places back in Ireland. In the 16th (Irish) Division's sector there was Watling Street Trench, named after a street near the Guinness brewery in Dublin. It was a communication trench that ran in a north-west to south-east direction behind Vandenberghe Farm. Mayo Trench and Fermoy Trench ran just north-west of Vandenberghe Farm. The Ulster Division's trench names included Ulster Road Trench, which ran north to south in front of the Spanbroekmolen salient facing Wijtschate.[21]

The Irish troops also named their huts and billets after towns in Ireland. For example, a camp on the road linking Loker with the village of De Klijte was named Fermoy Camp. Names such as Derry Huts, Tralee Lines, Birr Barracks and Curragh Camp appeared on official trench maps. Just outside Loker, on the road going south-east towards Dranouter, was Birr Barracks, which on and off was occupied by the 7th Leinsters and 9th RDF.[22] The huts at Birr Barracks were partially finished when the men occupied them in January 1917; they were draughty and very cold.[23] The Curragh Camp lay halfway along the road that linked Loker with Westoutre.[24] When in reserve, the 8th and 9th Dublin Fusiliers camped at the convent in Loker.[25]

Initially Michael was not sure which unit he would be attached to following his arrival in France. But, true to form, on the very day he arrived in France he wrote a letter home: '23rd October 1916. B.E.F. France. Just arrived here after a horrible crossing. I am moving off now somewhere else but have no permanent address yet. Hope to have it soon. Must clear out now. Love to all, Michael.'[26]

Indeed, over the next seven days, Michael would write a further five letters, including the following letter the very next day to his mother:

B.E.F.

France

24.X.16

Dear Mater,

Did you get my previous letter? ... It is raining like the very dickens and everywhere is very wet. We are billeted in tents for the present. I have not been definitely told who I am to be attached to yet and until I know I can't give you any address ... I feel very fit except for a little nauseous [?] after the journey over. The English daily papers come over here every day, so one knows all the news from "blighty". We landed at Boulogne and it is a fine looking place & of course busy. ... By the way, I left my pipe behind me and had to get another ... Remember me to everyone at home.

Your fond son
Michael[27]

On 25 October 1916 Michael found out he was being assigned to the 6th Battalion of the Royal Irish Regiment, which at that time was in a reserve camp at the north-western end of Kemmel Hill on the Kemmel–Reningelst Road near De Klijte. The 6th Royal Irish Regiment had been raised at Fermoy, County Cork in October 1914 and became part of the 47th Infantry Brigade under the command of Brigadier General George E. Pereira, a Catholic officer educated at the Oratory School in Birmingham.[28]

The weather for much of October 1916 was cold and wet. During the month, forty-eight men of the 8th Dublins were sent to hospital, the majority suffering from trench fever. The part of the front line the Dublins occupied was quiet during the day, but at night it was strafed by rifle and machine-gun fire mainly from the German positions at Maedelstede Farm and Petit Bois. Occasionally at night the Germans used Minenwerfers – trench mortars the British nicknamed 'Rum Jars' or 'Moaning Minnies'.[29] One of these mortar weapons was located near the corner of Grand Bois and was regularly used to shell the Irish lines at Watling Street Trench.[30]

The communication trenches were a particular target for the German machine gunners during the late evening. They were aware that some battalions changed over in the line at this time and were thus exposed and vulnerable in the half light. This happened on the day Michael arrived at his battalion. On his first evening the battalion moved from their reserve camp into the front line, with battalion headquarters at York House, situated roughly halfway along the Kemmel–Vierstraat road. There they relieved the 7th Leinsters.[31] Prior to the changeover, Michael wrote a brief note home to his mother telling her that he hadn't met anyone he knew yet and that he was heading up to the line for the first time the following morning.[32] During the changeover one man, Private John Stringer from Belfast, was killed. Another, Private Patrick Doherty from Templemore, County Derry, was wounded; he died the next day.[33]

The average routine for trench tours of duty that Michael experienced was eight days and nights in the front or support line. During that period, companies in the front line rotated with companies in Brigade Support. Following this tour of front- and support-line duty, the battalion went into Brigade Reserve, which was further back from the front and support lines, and out of the way of short-range shell fire. Here the men could wash, clean up and take some rest. Following this time out, they returned to the front line and began the sequence of changeovers again.

One of the first activities Michael's battalion carried out in their first tour of front-line duty was to send out a patrol to inspect the German defences facing them at York House. They found the German wire was 'very thick and in good condition generally'.[34] From his front-line dugout, Michael wrote to tell his mother of his first trench experience:

Att[ached to the] 6th Royal Irish Regt.
B.E.F.
France
28.X.1916.

Dear Mater

This constitutes my second day in the trenches and funny to relate it does not seem to have any effect on me. I don't know how it is. This part of the line is not too bad except at night. The Huns sent over a few whizz bangs just now while we were having lunch but what they give us is nothing to what we repay them with. There is plenty of mud all the same, fine thick stuff that sticks to everything. I know all the officers that are in the company with me and we are all quite happy. Some of them have musical instruments in the way of mouth organs and tin whistles and we have some music every day though sometimes we can't hear it with the row that is going on all round. One can hear the shells flying overhead and bursting in the Bosche line. All night, lights are soaring all round and machine guns and snipers keep up a continual fire while the bullets zip–zip over the parapet. There are rats of all sizes running about all night. I saw one fellow as big as a cat last night, they are beastly things. It is now starting to rain, as it usually does towards evening. Trees and houses alike have suffered from the effects of shell fire. I expect we shall all soon go back to billets … You might send out my pipe, I forgot it coming away. Please write soon and let me have all the news. Love to everybody.

Your fond son,
Michael[35]

The next day Michael's battalion was relieved in the line by the 6th Connaught Rangers. It had been an uneventful time in the line.

att 6th Royal Irish Regt.
B.E.F.
France

28. X. 16.

Dear Mater
            This constitutes my second
day in the trenches and funny to
relate it does not seem to have any
effect on me. I don't know how it is.
This part of the line is not too bad
except at night. The Huns sent
over a few whizz bangs just now
while we were having lunch but
what they give us is nothing to
what we repay them with. There is
plenty of mud all the same, fine
thick stuff that sticks to everything.
I know all the Officers that are in the
company with me and we are all quite
happy. Some of them have musical
instruments in the way of mouth organs
and tin whistles and we have some

However, the 49th Brigade on their right had carried out a raid during which they took six German prisoners.[36] When he got back to his billet, in a reassuring letter, Michael wrote home to tell his mother he was safe and that she should not worry. He had survived his first period of front-line duty, was in good form and wanted *The Irish Times* and the December edition of *Nash's Magazine*:

> Att. 6th Royal Irish Regt.
> B.E.F.
> France.
>
> Monday. 30th.x.16.
>
> Dear Mater,
>
> I am just back from the trenches for a rest, a few days I expect. We are all under canvass at present and it is raining very hard. I was quite happy & comfortable in my dug out up the line and the weather was good. Indeed it seemed too fine to be fighting. I have not seen any bosches so far as they keep very low. It is great fun trying to talk to some of the people about though some of them can speak English very well. I saw Mrs Hughe's [*sic*] son of Hazlebrook, he was with the regiment that relieved us … You need have no fear of me at all as I am as safe as houses and quite happy. The bosches got a nasty dig in the eye last night. I wish we could only give them a few more and finish the beggars. … Could you send me out some papers now and then. The "Irish Times" especially and get me the December "Nashes Magazine". Joseph will know it. … Well, give my love to everybody & same to [your]self.
>
> Ever your fond son,
> Michael.[37]

Att. 6th Royal Irish Regt.
B. E. F.
France.
Monday. 30th. v. 16.

Dear Mate,

I am just back from the trenches for a rest, a few days I expect. We are all under canvass at present and it is raining very hard. I was quite happy & comfortable in my dug out up the line and the weather was good. Indeed it seemed too fine to be fighting. I have not seen any bosches so far as they keep very low. It is great fun trying to talk to some of the people about though some of them can speak English very well. I saw Mrs. Hughes son of Hazelbrook he was with the regiment that relieved us. I have no idea how long he has been out here. You need have no fear of me at all as I am as safe as houses and quite happy. The

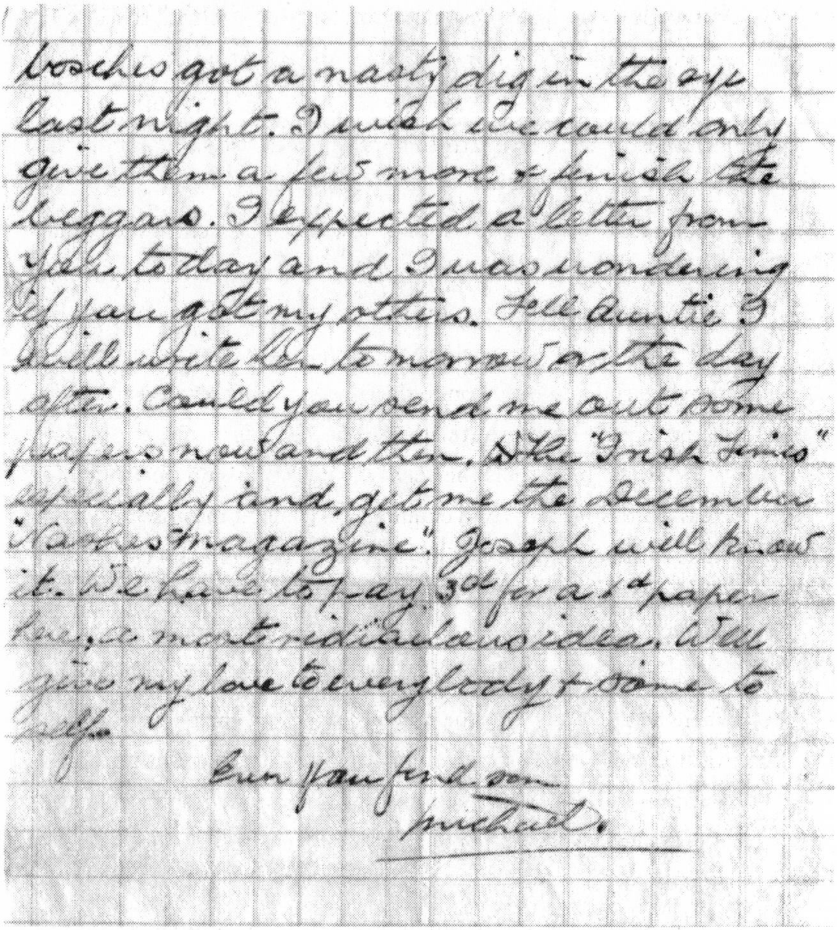

[Handwritten letter, partially legible:]

> boches got a nasty dig in the eye
> last night. I wish we could only
> give them a few more & finish the
> beggars. I expected a letter from
> you today and I was wondering
> if you got my others. Tell Auntie I
> will write to her tomorrow or the day
> after. Could you send me out some
> papers now and then. The "Irish Times"
> especially and get me the December
> "Nashes magazine" Joseph will know
> it. We have to pay 3d for a 1d paper
> here, a most ridiculous idea. Will
> give my love to everybody & some to
> yourself.
>
>   Ever your fond son
>   Michael.

By the end of October 1916 Michael seemed to have settled in well to the routine of trench life. With music from mouth organs and tin whistles echoing around camps at night, to the Irishmen who were there it must have seemed as though a little bit of Ireland was planted in Flanders. He had met a few officers whom he knew, such as Mrs Hughes's son Tommy from Hazlebrook, mentioned in the letter above, who was a second lieutenant with the 6th Connaught Rangers.[38]

For a young and inexperienced officer like Michael, the duties for a typical day and night in the front line at that time would have been comparable to those experienced by a similar young officer, Frank Laird, who served with the 8th RDF in the same sector:

I found that night was the strenuous time in the trenches, and that my particular job consisted in taking my turn as officer in charge in the front line, two hours on and two hours off. The two hours on were spent in stumbling along the inequalities of our duck-boards from one end of our section to the other, with my revolver handy in the pouch and my servant with his rifle behind.

Visiting in turn all the sentries and Lewis gun posts to pass them the time of night and enquire as to whether they saw anything outside. There was about time to do this twice in the two hours, progress being slow even though the Bosch kindly lit up the way with his frequent Verey lights ... When my two hours were over I pulled aside the blanket of the signaller's dugout in the parapet, where he sat all night by the light of a candle at the field telephone, crawled over the sleeping Tommies who carpeted the floor and rolled myself up in a blanket in the corner where, despite the rattle of machine-guns and the pop of bullets against the parapet, I slept the sleep of the just.

It seemed only ten minutes when I was roused again for another tour in the dark and cold, and the last sleep was generally abridged by 'Stand To', when the whole Company stood to arms in the trench from an hour before sunrise till it was quite light. Then the pleasantest function of the day – the distribution of rum ration – took place. Attended by the Company Sergeant-Major, the officer proceeded along the trench with the rum jar, filling out a small dose in the measure and handing it to each man in turn, occasionally putting in an extra drop for the older hands, whose well-seasoned throats required an extra warming ... To men who had stood the biting frost, or, worse still, the rain and the mud of a winter's night in the trenches, it was a godsend ...

The men's breakfast came up ... hot bacon and hot tea carried in a tank strapped to the orderly's back, with hot coals in the bottom to keep up the heat. Having finished breakfast and a cigarette and performed the meagre toilet possible, the officer whose first turn it was went along the line to inspect the rifles and equipment and to see that all was O.K. in case the Colonel should come to pay one of his frequent visits ...

The morning inspection over there was little else to do in the daytime during quiet hours. One officer had to be in charge of the Company front, but had little to do but smoke. The others had leisure on their hands, except the Captain, whose pen was generally busy ... Indents, strength reports, wind reports etc. seemed to be cropping up all day. As dusk fell the watch became once again more alert, working parties were mustered for wiring in no man's land or trench repairing and two hours on duty and four hours off for the 2nd Lieutenant dragged through another night, till the blessed sun rose again.[39]

On 1 November Michael's battalion moved into the new billets at the Curragh Camp. They provided good accommodation for one full battalion and would act in the future as a 16th (Irish) Divisional Reserve Camp.[40]

Att. 6th Royal Irish Regt.

B.E.F.

France

1st.11.16

Dear Joseph,

... So far France is alright. I would rather have it than Temple-more. ... I am back in billets for a rest after having been in the trenches. ... I feel very fit out here and am always ready for every meal. Yes I want my pipe badly and I hate a new pipe and I think I mentioned in one of my letters that I wanted it. ... Tell mother to write soon & let me have all the news, gossip, scandal or any-thing else you can. Letters are the only thing I look forward [to] and I am writing to every damn girl I know just for the sake of getting an answer & something to pass the time. ...

Your frère,
Michael.[41]

For some reason Michael wrote about being in France, though he was in fact in Belgium. He may have been obliged simply to write France on all his letters home as a censorial precaution. All the men's letters were censored for security purposes. So far as is known, Michael did not have a girlfriend back in Carrick Hill or the village of Malahide nearby, so, perhaps to keep in step with the lads around him in the billet who received letters from their girlfriends, Michael wrote to every girl he knew to try to create such a friendship.

For long periods trench life was extremely boring. To move along the humdrum time, Michael wrote letters to almost anybody he knew, hoping they would write back. Nothing much happened in Michael's section of the line going into November 1916. In fact, he began to get very bored and lonely. The days were short, the evenings long, dark and cold. They passed with the same old drudgery. Sundays were distinguished from other weekdays by virtue of the fact that 'the peasants', as he referred to the locals, dressed up in all sorts of colours.[42] The main enemies at this time were the cold, boredom, mud and rats, although the men did

Att. 6th Royal Irish Regt.
B.E.F.
France
1. 11. 16

Dear Joseph.

Your letter arrived O.K.
yesterday and I am glad to hear
all mine reached their destination
Yes I did feel a bit tired after my
journey and French trains are
none too fast I assure you. So far
France is alright. I would rather
have it than Templemore. The weather
here is not too bad at all. At present
I am back in billets for a rest
after having been in the trenches. The
boches sent over a bit of shrapnel
as we were coming out but no harm
was done. I feel very fit out here
and am always ready for every
meal. Yes I want my pipe badly
and I hate a new pipe and I

think I mentioned in one of my letters that I wanted it. I took three photos before I came away. Glad to hear you can print them alright. How are those I printed? Tell mother that I am writing to everyone as fast as I can. Thanks so much for forwarding the other letter. Tell mother to write soon & let me have all the news, gossip, scandal or anything else you can. Letters are the only thing to look forward and I am writing to every damn girl I know just for the sake of getting an answer & something to pass the time. I wrote to Gyrts yesterday. Well don't forget to send out an odd "Irish Times" you know. Give my love to master and auntie & all the rest & ask Bernard when he is coming out. Well here's the best of luck in your exams. Cheers

your frind
Michael

apparently become accustomed to the rodents. Colonel Fielding of the 6th Connaughts noted that the rats 'have come to be accepted so much as part and parcel of the war that their presence is generally ignored'. When a huge rat ran along the parapet beside him, Fielding wrote: 'instead of trying to kill it, the men in the trench started calling "puss, puss"'.[43]

It would appear the only way home, or to 'Blighty' as Michael called it, was to be wounded. Amongst the able men there seemed to be a certain amount of envy towards those who fell foul of a German sniper or other source of wounding. Michael called them 'lucky sods'.[44] The language he used exposed the fact that after less than a couple of weeks in Flanders, disillusionment had set in.

On 4 November 1916 a member of the British royalty, Prince Arthur, visited the sector in which Michael's battalion was based, and for his highness's entertainment, the 16th (Irish) Division's artillery let fly at the Germans in the Petit Bois woods near Wijtschate, as recorded in its war diary: '4 November 1916. Billets. Curragh Camp. Visit to this area by the Duke of Connaught. Divisional Artillery bombardment carried out for his benefit in the afternoon. 2nd Lt M. Wolf joined this day for duty with the battalion.'[45] The Germans didn't find this bit of royal entertainment amusing and later in the afternoon returned the compliment with trench mortars, resulting in the blowing in of a 9th Dublins' trench known as Ketchen Avenue. Luckily there were no casualties.[46]

Amongst the visiting party was General Plumer, as well as corps, divisional and brigade commanders. It was a grand display of top brass. The GOC of the 2nd Anzac Corps was Lieutenant General Sir Alexander Godley, an ex-Dublin Fusilier who had served as a brevet major with the 2nd RDF (The Old Toughs) in the Anglo-Boer War (1899–1901).[47] On his walkabout, Godley talked about old times with some of the older Dublins in the billets at Loker.[48]

Lieutenant Frank Simon, a former officer in the 9th Dublins, who was transferred to the 1st Otago Regiment, had his own opinion of Godley: 'He looks like a machine, cold and insuperable and inhuman.' However, he thought Godley was 'probably a good soldier'. Simon didn't have much time for what he called 'Imperial Officers', and he believed that Godley fell into that category of men.[49]

Michael's next letter home reassured his mother that he was tending to his spiritual duties as well as his military ones. He told her that he went to Benediction and wrote to Fr Gleeson, and thanked her for sending him the Catholic magazine *The Messenger*. However, in the same letter, he jokingly boasted about cracking a German's nut with a piece of lead.[50]

A few days before Michael's battalion went back into the line to relieve the 7th Leinsters, the battalion's war diary noted that Second Lieutenant Wall had been sent 'to hospital; with influenza'.[51] Michael wrote home from hospital:

6th Royal Irish Regt.
B.E.F.
France.

13.11.16.

Dear Mater,

Just a line to let you know that your parcel has come and everything is in good condition. However I can't touch any of them for the present as I am in hospital and am on a milk diet. I don't know what is the matter with me except a slight touch of influenza ... I don't like being here I may tell you, I would much rather be up the line. You need not be very much alarmed as I am quite alright and a few days will see me out. ... It is just a month ago today that I got orders to come out. The time was not long slipping by. ...

Your fond son
Michael.[52]

6th Royal Irish Regt.
B.E.F.
France.

13. 11. 16.

Dear Mater.
                Just a line to let you know
that your parcel has come and
everything is in good condition. However
I can't touch any of them for the present
as I am in hospital and am on a
milk diet. I don't know what is the
matter with me except a slight touch
of influenza. However I will be out
again in a few days I hope. I don't
like being here I may tell you, I would
much rather be up the line. You need
not be very much alarmed as I am
quite alright and a few days will
see me out. Is there any news about
Charlie Ward since? I should like
to know his address. It is just a
month ago today that I got orders
to come out. The time was not long
slipping by. Please excuse me for I have
no more to say. Love to everyone + many
thanks.
                Your fond son
                        Michael.

On the day Michael wrote this letter from hospital, his battalion was on a section of the front line known as Vankeep. Their signallers suffered casualties from a German mortar attack, as their war diary recorded:

> 13 November 1916. Trenches. York House. Hostile activity by their trench mortars, especially on VANKEEP blowing signals dug out and signal to add that Captain Phillips and one other rank were killed and two other ranks wounded. The battalion relieved this day by the 6th Connaught Rangers and moved into Brigade support at Butterfly Farm. Captain Phillips buried this day at Kemmel Cemetery. Cpl Richer buried at the Military Cemetery near York House.[53]

Captain Edward George Phillips was twenty-two and came from Clonmel in County Tipperary. He was in the battalion signals dugout when it was hit by a trench mortar. Corporal John Henry Richer, aged twenty-five, was a Channel Islander who came from St Peter Port, Guernsey. He may have been with Captain Phillips in the dugout. He was buried by his comrades at a military cemetery near York House, but his body was later exhumed and reinterred at La Laiterie Military Cemetery.[54]

By November 1916 the ground in many of the front-line trenches was so soaked that the sandbag parapets began to slide in and collapse. 'Signs of winter, all exposed water pipes to be covered against frost' and 'all lights in Corps area must be screened by 5:00 p.m.' wrote the diarist of the 8th Dublins.[55] The onset of cold and wet weather had a detrimental effect on the men's health. Trench foot, a terribly ugly and painful condition, was, in such conditions, an ever-occurring threat. To try to avoid this terrible affliction, the RDF in particular had a system of issuing each man every night with a dry pair of socks and a tot of whale oil to rub into his feet. In October the 8th Dublins had lost the forty-eight men mentioned earlier to trench fever, and in November they lost the same number. As a precaution against further depletions of the line through illness, each member of the battalion was inoculated against typhoid.[56]

Michael was no different to any other man who had to stand for long hours in cold and damp trenches. His illness, which he thought was influenza, was more likely trench fever, and he was admitted to the field hospital on 7 November. He was still there more than a week later when he wrote the letter quoted above. His mother had sent him a comforts parcel that contained his beloved pipe, along with some OXO cubes, cakes, biscuits and *The Irish Times*. The parcel seemed to cheer him up and restore him to his old self.

Much-needed comforts for the troops in the form of food parcels – containing cakes, fruit, flour, sugar and tobacco – were sent by mothers, wives, family and friends to soldiers in the front line. These parcels were a lifeline to home and gave a boost to the men's morale. Receiving one told a soldier that someone back home was thinking of him; he was not forgotten. Michael received regular parcels of food and other comforts from his mother.

However, many men had nobody at home to send them parcels. Consequently, some of the Irish regiments had regimental comfort committees back in Ireland, who arranged for food and clothing parcels to be sent out regularly to the front. The RDF, for example, had a very active home-front committee. In August 1914 the Committee of the Dublin Women's Unionist Club held a meeting at the offices of the club at 10 Leinster Street in Dublin. Following this meeting, the women decided to work for the men serving with the Dublins through 'the collection and dispatch of a large quantity of newspapers, magazines and books to the battalions of the regiment serving with the Expeditionary Force in France and Flanders'.[57] A Dublin Fusiliers Warm Clothing and Prisoners Aid Fund was established, and anybody who wanted to contribute to it could send their donations to 'The Countess of Mayo' at Palmerstown, Straffan, County Kildare, or to Mrs Loveband, c/o The Barracks, Naas, County Kildare.[58] As the war progressed, demands on these regimental voluntary organisations increased. This led to the establishment of a Dublin Fusiliers Central Advisory Committee for the Regimental Area of the City and County of Dublin and the Counties of Wicklow, Carlow and Kildare.[59]

The women of the Dublin Women's Unionist Club were not the only ones who worked for the Irishmen in the trenches. Throughout the war, at their north County Dublin convent in Baldoyle, not far from where Michael lived, nuns from the Irish Sisters of Charity took to making shirts for the British Army. However, unlike the unionist ladies, there was nothing charitable about this work. It was strictly business. At the end of the war, when there was no further need for army shirts, the nuns turned their skills to crochet work, making knitwear, and the manufacture of silk garments.[60]

Individual women performed magnificent voluntary work at the outbreak of the war. One such woman was the previously mentioned Monica Roberts, who, with a friend, set up the Band of Helpers for the Soldiers. Both young ladies were musically talented and went round parish halls on Dublin's south side, performing on the piano and singing recitals. The money they collected from these events went towards the funding of comfort parcels they made up and sent to the troops in France and Flanders. The main recipients of these were men serving in the RDF or RFC. Men wrote to

Monica expressing their thanks and, in some cases, their inner thoughts on the war. Many of them looked upon Monica as their distant sweetheart and pen pal. Some of the soldiers who wrote to Monica asked her for a photograph of herself; some even sent photographs of themselves. Typical of these letters is one written by Private J. Kirwin of the 2nd Dublin Fusiliers to Monica when his battalion was in reserve near Kemmel on 22 February 1917:

> The boys of my platoon gave me your card and told me to write a letter to you to thank you for your cigarettes that they received and enjoyed very much … they were glad to get the cigarettes from someone Irish as they are all Irish and I am Irish myself, they said they never enjoyed a better smoke in their lives as they were in the trenches when they got them … No more to say at present, wishing you the best of luck from all the boys of my platoon of the Dubs.
>
> Pte. J. Kirwin.
> 2nd RDF.[61]

Sadly, one or two men were killed not long after they had written to Monica. One was Private Patrick Byrne of the 2nd RDF, who came from St John's Street West in Dublin. He wrote to Monica on 5 April 1916, when the 2nd Dublins were in the trenches facing Bienvillers in the Somme sector:

> I just received your most kind letter which I always long to get from Ireland, it reminds me of the happy time I spent there. I came out to France with the 1st Expeditionary Force and I have been twice down the line. Once gassed at Ypres on the 9th of May. Wounded the 23rd January this year and could not get home, but I am still in the land of the living, so I have a chance yet of seeing dear old Dublin. We had very bad weather all the winter, what with snow, rain, frost and all

the worst kind of times you could expect in winter. I did not spend a very good St Patrick's Day [scribbled out by censor] outside, but not inside. But still, you would never hear of us chaps grumble. We just [scribbled out by censor] got our own back by way of throwing bombs, rifle grenades and sniping at the Huns, so I had amusement after all. Of course I'm well used to the game by now, as well as my comrades so you can expect we give the Germans a lively time. I would like you to send me a parcel of eatables as we are rather short of grub sometimes.

I would be very thankful to you for it. I expect to get my leave in a few months' time and then I will relate to you some of my experiences if it pleases you.

Yours truly,
P. Byrne.[62]

He never did get home to tell Monica about his experiences. Patrick Byrne was killed on a miserable wet day, 20 April 1916, a little over two weeks after he wrote this letter. The battalion diary of the day noted: 'Enemy bombarded 'B' Company with 4.2 and 9.5 Inch shells doing much damage to dugouts and trenches: Trenches becoming very bad owing to very heavy rain.'[63] There was no mention of the loss of Private Byrne, or of the man who died with him. For the record, he was Private William Carroll, aged twenty-four, from 66 Corporation Place in Dublin. William left a wife and a four-year-old daughter behind. Both men were buried in Bienvillers Military Cemetery, France.[64]

By the end of November 1916 the Somme campaign had ended, with unprecedented loss of life and very little strategically to show on either side of the wire. Michael Wall had recovered from his illness and was back in the support line near Kemmel, in the cold, wet, boring and rat-infested trenches facing Wijtschate.

7

Back to School

Before they went back to the front line on 26 November 2016, the 6th Royal Irish had a rest while in reserve. During this time the battalion took stock of their supplies and tidied themselves up for their next tour in the support and front line trenches. It was time to open the comfort parcels sent from home, write letters and wash off the mud from the previous tour of duty. The whole battalion was allocated baths at the village of Westoutre near Loker. The officers played a rugby match against the officers of the 7th Leinsters and were trashed twenty-four points to nil. The match was played in a field near their billets at a place called Butterfly Farm about two kilometres north-east of Loker. Also during this time the battalion received a draft of eighty-six other ranks, mainly composed of Englishmen from the surplus of recruits to the RFA. The battalion diarist noted that some of them were 'old soldiers' who were 'very badly needed'.[1]

The time out gave Michael a chance to write home to his mother and aunt and tell them he had recovered. He was 'perfectly content' so long as he could get his *Irish Times* now and then.

> 6th Royal Irish Regt.
>
> B.E.F.
>
> France
>
> 18th Nov. 1916
>
> Dear Mater,

Just a line to let you know that I am quite alright again … I am my old self once again. Your letter, parcel and papers have just arrived this moment. Thanks ever so much, the cake was top hole. Those OXO cubes you sent me are awfully good, also the biscuits. But please don't send all these things out so often, it is not fair to you. So long as you send me the papers I don't mind. … We can get all papers and magazines now except the Irish papers. … I have plenty of warm clothes and any I want I can get here. Most of the leading London tailors have agents out here. My socks are all right thanks, I have got another muffler and mittens, they are on issue. I have got all your letters so far but please don't be uneasy if I don't write regularly as it is very hard to find anything to say … Please don't dream of sending out candles, we got plenty of them [sic] and when we are in the trenches we have electric light in our dug-out, so what do you say to that! …

Your fond son
Michael.[2]

Towards the end of November the 6th Royal Irish Regiment went back into the line at Vankeep. They had a tough time, as their war diarist noted:

26th November 1916. Front line trenches. York Street. The battalion relieved the 7th Leinsters in the front line at VANKEEP and Mayo Street, bombarded with aerial darts. Two other ranks killed, four wounded.

27th November. Mayo Street again bombarded with aerial darts, they have the range of this trench to a nicety. Two other ranks killed.

29th November. A strong patrol went out under Capt. Day

and Lt Wolf to get a prisoner, no patrols discovered and wire much too thick to get through. Gun cotton was placed under the enemy's wire and a dummy raid was carried out with the help of the artillery. The patrol returned safely at 1:00 a.m. when the dummy raid was started.

30th November. Evidently did some damage to the Germans as all day long we were bombarded by trench mortars and aerial darts without causing any material damage. The battalion was relieved this day by the 1st Royal Munster Fusiliers and went into Divisional Reserve at the Curragh Camp.[3]

Under this German trench-mortar barrage, Michael sent home a quick-fire Field Service postcard from his dugout in the front line to say all was well: 'I am quite well. Letter follows at first opportunity.'[4]

In parts of the sector for which the 16th (Irish) Division was responsible, the German and British front lines were very close to each other. So much so that on one occasion Michael claimed he could see some Germans shaving.[5]

NOTHING is to be written on this side except the date and signature of the sender. Sentences not required may be erased. If anything else is added the post card will be destroyed.

I am quite well.

I have been admitted into hospital

{ sick } and am going on well.
{ wounded } and hope to be discharged soon.

I am being sent down to the base.

I have received your { letter dated
{ telegram,,
{ parcel ,,

Letter follows at first opportunity.

I have received no letter from you { lately.
{ for a long time.

Signature only } M. J. Wolf

Date: 28/11/16

[Postage must be prepaid on any letter or post card addressed to the sender of this card.]

The closeness of the lines was ideal for sniping, yet strangely enough there were few or no reports of sniping in November and December

1916. However, the Irish front and support lines were intermittently hit by German shelling, which increased during December, more than likely as a response to British tri-weekly trench and Stokes mortar bombardments.[6] The commanding officers of the 9th RDF commented on these mortar duels, noting: 'The enemy Trench Mortars appeared to out-class ours, but whereas their artillery fire was pliable, ours was very acute.'[7]

The Germans, or more precisely the Prussians, who faced the Irish troops in late November 1916 had no fear of their shells falling short near their front line and hitting their own men. This was mainly due to the fact that they did not occupy their front line on a regular basis. This was discovered by night raids into the German front line by parties from the 6th Royal Irish and other battalions.[8]

On the Irish side of the wire it was pot luck where a German shell landed. On 23 November three Dublin Fusiliers were buried alive when a Rum Jar shell hit their trench at Rossignol Wood on the Vierstraat–Kemmel Road. Luckily they were in the dugout, but suffered shell shock as a result of their experience.[9] Three days later, two men belonging to Michael's battalion were killed in a similar attack: Private Henry Brown from Rockfort Avenue, Dalkey, County Dublin and Private Edmond Taylor from Leverington in Cambridgeshire. Brown enlisted at Kingstown (Dún Laoghaire) at the outbreak of the war and was thirty-four when he died. Taylor was one of the English drafts who had joined the battalion two days previously. Before the war he had lived at Wisbech in Cambridgeshire and was formerly a member of the RFC.

The next day two more men were killed. They were Private William Sweeney and Private George Edward Bullock. Sweeney was from the Parish of St Peter and Paul, Clonmel, County

Tipperary. He enlisted at the depot of the Royal Irish in Clonmel. Bullock was a Channel Islander, from St Peter Port, Guernsey. He surely would have known Corporal John Richer from 2 Collings Road, St Peter Port, Guernsey, who had been killed on 13 November. They may even have been neighbours.[10]

For both sides, the bad weather in November 1916 was a common enemy. The winter of 1916/1917 was the coldest for nearly thirty years.[11] Men found it impossible to use picks and shovels even to maintain the trench in which they stood. According to Rowland Fielding:

> The weather has been and is Arctic, with a biting east wind and the strain in the front line is considerable … The breastworks are in a horrible state, frozen hard as stone, the ground is white with snow, and the garrison stands for days and nights in the paralysing cold, without exercise, numbed.[12]

Colonel Bellingham of the 8th RDF also commented on the detrimental effect the cold weather had on his trenches: 'It is difficult to keep the front line trenches in a proper state of repair. They are constantly falling in owing to weather effects.'[13]

The increasing cold and dampness exacerbated the problem of the dreaded trench fever. During December the number of men within the ranks of the RDF suffering from fever increased from the previous months. Of the men sent to hospital in November and December, more were suffering from fever than were suffering from shattered limbs as a result of German artillery fire.

On 1 December the 6th Royal Irish came out of the line and went into billets at the Curragh Camp. Michael wrote home as usual the following day. Whatever heroic and chivalrous image Michael had of the war before enlistment, it was now gone:

6th Royal Irish Regt.

B.E.F.

France.

December 2nd 1916.

Dear Mater,

Many thanks for your letter. I got it while I was in the front line. We are now out for eight days rest and I am going on a course tomorrow. I think it lasts four weeks. Well you say you heard the front lines is not so dangerous. But they all are. One never knows when something will come over. I got a pretty hot five minutes while I was crossing a bit of open ground. The enemy turned a machine gun and started to sweep the ground. The bullets were hopping just a few feet in front of us. ... Well we all wish the war was over. ... my fingers are very cold and writing is rather difficult. I am well and as fit as a fiddle. You will say I am rather blood-thirsty when I tell you that I sniped two bosches this time in the line. It is quite good sport after stand-to. The enemies' [sic] line is none too good and they are always showing themselves. One of the men in a letter to his mother said that he killed fourteen but he added "they were on my shirt." I thought it was rather good. ... I don't know what my new address will be but I shall let you know as soon as possible. ...

Your fond son,

Michael.[14]

While his battalion was out of the line, Michael was sent on a training course. Given past and often bitter experiences in all aspects of trench warfare, as the war progressed a desire had grown in the BEF to learn from these experiences. These lessons and improvements were passed on to soldiers through a variety of training

6th Royal Irish Regt.
B.E.F.
France.

December 2nd 1916.

Dear mater.

Many thanks for your letter. I
got it while I was in the front line. We
are now out for eight days rest and I
am going on a course tomorrow. I think
it lasts four weeks. Well you say you
heard the front line is not so dangerous.
But they all are. One never knows when
something will come over. I got a pretty
hot five minutes while I was crossing
a bit of open ground. The enemy turned
a machine gun and started to sweep the
ground. The bullets were hopping just a
few feet in front of us. The cake was quite
alright thanks. I got the papers along with
your letter but I have not had time to
read them yet. I shall be on the look-out
for the plum pudding. Well we all wish the
war was over. The weather here is very
cold but dry and it is not unpleasant.
All the same my fingers are very cold and
writing is rather difficult. I am well and
fit as a fiddle. You will say I am rather

blood-thirsty when I tell you that I sniped
two bosches this time in the line. It is quite
good sport after stand to. The enemies' line
is none too good and they are always showing
themselves. One of the men in a letter to his
mother said that he killed fourteen but he
added "they were on my shirt." I thought
it was rather good. How is Joseph getting
on by the way? Has he got a move on yet?
I don't know what my new address will
be but I shall let you know as soon as
possible. Remember me to Mrs Crawford
when you see her next. I did not hear
from Mrs. Perkins or Mrs. Jones yet. I must
close now but will let you have
another letter soon. Give my love to
everybody at home.
        Your fond son
            Michael.

schools set up behind the lines in France. Army and Corps schools had developed rapidly in 1915.[15] For example, in early February 1915 the 4th Division (10th Brigade, 2nd RDF) began trench-mortar classes under Captain Smithson in an effort to increase the proficiency of their trench-mortar gunners.[16] To improve communications skills, the Royal Engineers Signal Service set up training schools for division and brigade signallers.[17] Learning and improvement became important and, from September 1915 on, each school in the 4th Division was improved 'to provide training for signals, machine guns, gas warfare, and for practicing methods of attack'.[18]

Michael's army commander, General Plumer, placed a huge emphasis on training. Consequently, training schools were set up all across his 2nd Army's Ypres-salient sector, stretching from Bailleul to St Omer.[19] The 16th (Irish) Division set up a school near Saint-Jans-Cappel, a small French village about three kilometres north of Bailleul. They also set up a divisional gas school at Canada Corner, about one kilometre north of Loker.[20] The Ulster Division set up their divisional school in Dranouter.

By December 1916 training schools offered courses on a wide range of subjects.[21] Gas instructors were sent round brigades and battalions to train the officers and men in gas protection methods, such as the use of sprayers and the new box respirators, which had been introduced to the 2nd Army in October 1916.[22] This step also gave the men 'confidence, and to show them with proper care there is little to fear from the enemy's use of this new weapon'.[23] There were even pigeon-flying and sanitation courses offered in Bailleul.[24]

Frank Laird joined the ranks of the 7th Dublin Fusiliers at the outbreak of the war and had fought in Gallipoli in 1915. He was commissioned into the 8th Dublins at Loker and attended the divisional school at Saint-Jans-Cappel. He described some of the courses he attended:

> The month's instruction was pretty much a replica of the Officer's Cadet Battalion at home. Any amount of squad and arms drill was provided for us the officers being put through it in a squad by themselves. Revolver practice, Lewis gun firing, gas instruction, marching at night by compass ... The lectures were attended by officers, N.C.O.s and men ...[25]

Michael's course was 'a sort of refresher course for some things, others are entirely new'.[26] Although the day was long, going back to this sort of school was a welcome break from the front line for Michael and his brother officers. According to Frank Laird:

> On Fridays we had a gala dinner in the mess, followed by a concert, one of which was given by the staff and other given by Pierrot troupes. Saturday was a day for visiting Bailleul and dining and doing a show there. Sunday we had to ourselves and usually spent it in the same pleasant burg.[27]

Michael's time at the 16th (Irish) Divisional School coincided with the change of prime minister from Asquith to David Lloyd George. Winston Churchill claimed that Lloyd George was the one person in the government who possessed 'any aptitude for war or knowledge of it'.[28] News of Asquith's resignation travelled to the front quickly. Michael saw it in the papers and wrote home to his mother. He wondered what would happen next.[29] The change in prime minister seemed to please him and may even have boosted his morale a bit. He noted, 'I see at last we have got a decent Cabinet with people in it who know their job.'[30]

Also while he was in school, Michael's battalion moved from their billets at the Curragh Camp into a new line named Cooker Farm, where it came under shell fire on 16 and 17 December 1916. The war diary of the 6th Royal Irish for 16 December 1916 read:

New lines. Cooker Farm. At 11:00 a.m. the enemy shelled our Dressing Station also near battalion headquarters. Three direct hits were obtained on the dressing station which killed one man and wounded eight. Our trench mortars were very active during the afternoon.[31]

Eight of Michael's comrades were killed over those two days. The men came from towns and villages such as Castlecomer in County Kilkenny, as well as County Tipperary towns such as Clonmel, Killenaule, Cashel and Thurles.[32] The killing of Michael's comrades just before Christmas 1916 made him think the German offer of peace made on 12 December was a bit cheeky.[33]

On 18 December 1916 the 16th (Irish) Division had been one year in France. To mark the occasion General Hickie wrote to his men:

To-day is the anniversary of the landing of the 16th Division in France. The Divisional Commander wishes to express his appreciation of the spirit which has been shown by all ranks during the past year. He feels that the division has earned the right to adopt the motto which was granted by the King to the Irish Brigade which served in this country for a hundred years. 'Everywhere and always faithful.'[34]

Perhaps as a morale booster for the Irish troops coming up to Christmas, a lot of 'Red Hats' (slang name for senior army officers) were seen around the villages of Kemmel, Loker and Dranouter between 18 and 20 December. On 19 December General Plumer visited the 153rd Brigade RFA attached to the Ulster Division. Ernest Kingdon, an observation officer with the 153rd Brigade attached to the Ulster Division, noted in his diary about Plumer's visit:

> Motors and red hats by the score. Never saw such fuss. What amused me most of all was that he never wore a tin hat. I had to conduct him round the battery position. I showed him everything, even my bedroom. He was a nice amiable fatherly old thing.
>
> The Colonel told me afterwards that our Brigadier said I wasn't obsequious enough and that I talked to the old man as if he had been a friend, but then our Brigadier doesn't know that we were both Old Etonians.[35]

On the following day General Haig visited the Irish troops at Loker. He inspected some battalions who were out of the line at the time, such as the 2nd Dublins. Haig's visit didn't seem to cheer Michael up much; the visit merited just one line in a letter home to his mother. Michael was more concerned with the delay in the post:

> 6th Royal Irish Regt.
> 16th (Irish) Divisional School
> B.E.F.
> France.
>
> December 20th 1916.
>
> Dear Mater,
>
> I am still wondering if you got my last three letters. I have not heard from anybody for over a fortnight, I can't understand it at

all. Everybody else's letters seem to have gone through alright …
We have just had Sir Douglas Haig round to inspect us. … hope
to hear some news soon. Love to everybody and Auntie.

Your fond son
Michael[36]

The Christmas Truce of 1914 was a thing of the past. No such fraternisation was allowed by Christmas 1916. However, the spirit of Christmas was not entirely lost among the men who faced each other across no man's land. Morale among some of the Irish troops in the week leading up to Christmas seemed fine. Fr Wrafter SJ, a chaplain with the 7th Leinsters, noted in a letter home to the Provincial in Dublin: 'The men are quite wonderful. They know it will take time but they never grumble and never think it impossible that they should be beaten.'[37]

To add a bit of *esprit de corps*, Christmas cards were printed for the 16th (Irish) Division on white cards, with the division's new motto and a harp with no crown over it drawn in green. On the inside was a sketch of two men carrying on their shoulders a steaming pot with the inscription 'XMAS DINNER 1916'. The words 'Wishing you a Happy Christmas From [Soldier's name]' and 'And my heart goes back to Erin's Isle and the [Recipient's name] I left behind me' were also written on the inside. Michael signed this simply, 'Your fond brother Michael'.[38]

XMAS DINNER 1916

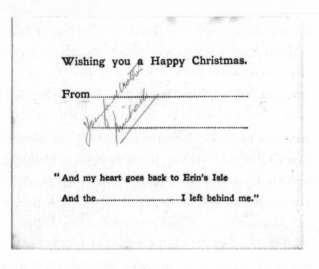

The 16th (Irish) Division Christmas card that Michael sent to his brother Joseph in 1916.

Many of the men used these cards for their sweethearts. However, despite Michael's writing to every girl he knew, and although it seemed a certain nurse back in Dublin may have had his fancy, as he sent this to his brother it seems as if Michael didn't have a Christmas sweetheart in 1916.

The war diary of the 6th Royal Irish Regiment leading up to Christmas read: '20 December 1916: Trenches. Cooker Farm. Relieved by the 6th Connaught Rangers. Capt. Day left on leave. 25th December Christmas Day. Billets. Derry Huts. X.M.A.S. Dinner.'[39]

There was no shelling from either side of the wire at Wijt-schate on Christmas Day 1916. It was a quiet day. However, on St Stephen's (Boxing) Day the Germans fired some trench mortars over the 16th (Irish) Division's front line, to which British artillery and Stokes guns retaliated on the same day.[40] The 2nd and 9th Dublins along with the 6th Connaught Rangers were rather unfortunate in having to be the ones who held the 16th (Irish) Division's section of the front line on Christmas Day 1916.[41]

Monsignor Ryan from Tipperary, who was in Loker on a visit at the time, gave some men of the 2nd Dublins midnight mass at Siege Farm.[42] On Christmas night, one or two of the Connaught Rangers' officers made an effort to bring Christmas to their candle-lit dugout. They ate tinned turkey and tinned plum pudding, and washed it down with a drop of whiskey.[43] Those men who were not on duty at the fire step on Christmas Day received mass in the open at Shamus Farm, a pile of rubble about 270 metres behind the front line. Second Lieutenant C. A. Brett, who was in command of a company of Rangers at the tender age of twenty, described the event in his diary:

> It was the most impressive service I ever attended. There were perhaps 500 men there, all on their knees in the mud and it was something not to be forgotten. During the Service there was no gunfire, but occasional shots could be heard during the day.[44]

The 8th Dublin Fusiliers were out of the line on Christmas Day

1916. Having set up a big marquee in the grounds of the convent at Loker, the nuns laid on a Christmas dinner for the officers of the battalion, after which they were visited by General Hickie and General Ramsay, their 48th Brigade commander.[45] However, it wasn't until early in the new year that the 2nd Dublins sat down to their Christmas dinner at Birr Barracks in Loker. The night before, more than forty sergeants attended the Annual Sergeants' Dinner that was hosted by the battalion. The 2nd Dublins applied to the local *estaminet* (café) in Loker for an extension of the opening hours, but were refused.[46] There seemed to be a right Irish hooley in Loker that night. Considering what the Dublins had come through, and what lay ahead of them, the argument can be made that they deserved every minute of it. Private Christy Fox certainly thought it was a good night:

> We only had our Christmas Dinner four days ago, we had a grand night of it, and we couldn't enjoy ourselves better. We had plenty of singing and dancing. I think I eat [*sic*] too much pudding; I blame it for me being sick.[47]

Back from his course at the divisional school, who else would Michael write to on Christmas Day, but his mother?

> 6th Royal Irish Regt.
>
> B.E.F.
>
> France
>
> 25th Dec. 1916
>
> Dear Mater,
>
> … I have changed the address at the top as we go back next Sunday so your letters will all come to the right place without

any delay. I had a very nice card from Capt. Smyth. It was a view of the Camp at Carrick Hill ... Tomorrow night we are going to have a bit of a spree. Four of us have clubbed together and pooled our parcels so we shan't do too badly. By the way I had a very nice sweet cake sent to me by the nurse I met in Dublin, so you see I have not done too badly. Out here French people don't put too much pass on Xmas. New Year's Day is their great feast. Whom do you think I met yesterday but my old chum O'Sullivan. Lord I never saw him look better. He is what we call a "tip-it-and-run-man" that is to say he is in the T.M. (Trench Mortar) Battery. He is going on leave today ... The snow has worn off for the present and we are having a very high cold wind. I'm afraid I must close now. Please give my love to everybody at home.

Your fond son,
Michael.[48]

The lace Christmas card Michael sent home to his mother in 1916.

Three men of the 2nd Dublins were injured on St Stephen's Day 1916 as a result of defective trench-mortar ammunition. The name 'tip-it-and-run-men' for trench-mortar men was perfect, as firing one of these weapons was a hazardous operation. Apparently, some of the trench-mortar ammunition was defective and unreliable, so a trench-mortar man could never be certain if it would fire at the Germans or explode in his face.[49]

A few days after Christmas Michael received a brief note from one of his friends back in Dublin, where, despite the destruction caused by the Rising, Christmas pantos were presented at the Empire Theatre.[50] As well as the pantos, a film made by the French company Le Film d'Art and called *The Spirit of France* was shown at the Masterpiece Picture Theatre in Talbot Street, Dublin. Starring Jane Hading and Raphaël Duflos, it presented a 'powerful story of love and war'. The film had been released in Britain and Ireland in November 1916.[51]

The war diary of the 6th Royal Irish recorded on 30 December 1916: 'Trenches. Cooker Farm. Enemy's Artillery more active than usual.'[52] Michael's battalion saw out the traumatic year of 1916 in the front line at Cooker Farm. Feeling bored, he wrote a brief note home to his mother from a damp and cold front-line dugout:

6th Royal Irish Regt.

B.E.F.

France

Dec. 30th 1916

Dear Mater,

Just a few lines to let you know how things are. I am at present in a dugout in the front line. Things are pretty quiet on the whole tonight. It simply spilled rain last night and everywhere is in a devil of a mess. You have only to look round and you are covered with mud. Well so long as it is only mud, what matter. How is everything going in the old country … No more time at present. Love to all.

Your fond son,
Michael[53]

On 31 December 1916 the battalion diarist of the 6th Royal Irish noted: 'Lieutenant Rennison reported missing believed killed.'[54] Walter Rennison was twenty-three years of age and the son of the Rev. Chancellor Henry Rennison of The Rectory, Wexford. The lieutenant's body was never found. He may have fallen victim to the active artillery reported in the battalion's war diary, a single line in which noted the end of this young Irishman's existence.

Also on New Year's Eve the diarist of the 8th Dublins wrote, 'our guns fired for several minutes rapid, probably saluting the New Year'.[55] Over in the Derry Huts at Dranouter, just as midnight struck, the Connaught Rangers sang 'Auld Lang Syne'.[56] Over the previous twelve months, hundreds of thousands of human beings had died at Hulluch and Verdun, and during the Somme campaign. In Ireland, a rebellion had taken place that would forever change the course of Irish history. For the thousands of men in the trenches along the Western Front, however, 1916 ended as it had begun: lonely, cold, hopeless and miserable.

8

'Shamrock grows
nowhere else but Ireland'

The new year in Flanders began as the old year had ended, with freezing cold weather and trenches in a terrible state. The new huts at Birr Barracks were not yet completed. The cold weather had held up work on the chimney in some of the billets, resulting in bitterly cold bunks at night.[1] Private Christy Fox wrote home to Monica Roberts and told her how things were at that time:

> I am wearing two pairs of socks at present and still can't keep my feet warm. The weather is something awful out here. I am nearly choked with a cough, in fact every second one of us out here is the same and I could tell you more that in fact some men have died with the cold. This [sic] few days it is so severe no matter what clothes we have on, we cannot keep ourselves warm. I never put in a harder winter since I was born.[2]

Up in the front line, night patrols and wiring, which involved repairing damaged wire entanglements and installing new wire, carried on as usual. With the ground frozen hard, revetting damaged trenches proved almost impossible. Given the freezing conditions, the quartermaster of the 8th Dublins ensured that the men coming in from the front line off a night patrol or from a bit of trench-maintenance work were given a hot cup of tea with sugar or an Oxo soup in which to dip some bread.[3] Those men who did go out on night patrols had the luxury of wearing gumboots, waterproof boots similar to modern wellington boots. However, these boots were in short supply, and men had to hand their boots back to the same quartermaster when they returned from the patrol for the next man to wear going out.[4]

On New Year's Day 1917 the 6th Royal Irish were still in the front line at Cooker Farm. The battalion diarist noted: 'Our artillery active all day.'[5] The new year was greeted with a couple of salvos. Michael Wall was hoping that by this time the next year he would be home.[6] When he came back from the front line to his billet at the Curragh Camp, Michael sent yet another reassuring note home to his mother to tell her he was fine so far:

6th Royal Irish Regt.
B.E.F.
France

January 6th 1917.

Dear Mater,

I am out of the trenches once again for eight days' rest. We did look nice sights coming back all covered with mud and sleepy as could be. It was rather exciting this time. A piece of shell about the size of a piece of lump sugar just missed my eye by inches … A great many letters went astray at Xmas. I am just wishing for the time to roll by and bring my turn for leave … I am sending a cheque which I hope will reach you alright. I would have sent it before but I was afraid it would get lost in going from the line …

Remember me to everyone,
Michael.[7]

6th Royal Irish Regt.
B.E.F.
France
January 6th 1917.

Dear Mater.

I am out of the trenches once again for eight days' rest. We did look nice sights coming back all covered with mud and sleepy as could be. It was rather exciting this time. A piece of shell about the size of a piece of lump sugar just missed my eye by inches and I missed a blighty. Well as I don't particularily wish to get one it does not matter. I had a letter from Mrs. Jones yesterday and she said it was the third she had written. She also sent a xmas box but I never saw either. A great many letters went astray at Xmas. I am just wishing for the time to roll by and bring my turn for leave round. Mother Cecilia I think it was, told me how Bernard carries the news up to Auntie piece by piece when my letters

On the morning of 5 January 1917 General Hickie held a battalion commanders' conference at York House.[8] Plans for the coming weeks were discussed and prepared. For the month of January, the three RDF battalions of the 48th Brigade, along with the other battalion of the brigade, settled into a routine of rotational duties in the front and support lines facing Wijtschate. From now on, when in reserve, battalions had to be ready to move to any part of the divisional front at four hours' notice.[9]

The war diary of the 6th Royal Irish for 7 January 1917 reads: 'Billets. Curragh Camp. 2nd Lt Wall and 25 OR [Other Ranks] left for railway construction duty.'[10] Behind the routine trench duties carried out at local level, as laid out by General Hickie, the development of infrastructure for General Plumer's breakout plan also began to move forward. On 7 January Michael was removed from front-line duties and given the task of being a quartermaster to a party of twenty-five other soldiers assigned to work on railway construction duty.

At last Michael was getting to work on something challenging and away from the boredom of trench life. The task was also important. After all, the improvement and development of light railways and roads around the Ypres salient and, in particular, around Kemmel, were a vital strategic part of General Plumer's breakout plans. A network of standard-gauge double and single rail lines was installed from Hazebrouck (France) to provide rail transport to supply the ammunition dumps along the Wijtschate–Messines front. Bailleul was the railhead town that linked Hazebrouck with St Omer and Boulogne. There was an end-of-rail line or railhead on the southern side of Kemmel Hill and another at La Clytte, which acted as a supply point to the Irish and other troops stationed around Kemmel and Loker.[11] Work on the railway line was safe and out of reach of German artillery.

Michael now had time to read his *Irish Times* and relax a bit. With no sign of a break in the war, alone at night with his thoughts, his mind drifted back to the safety of Carrick Hill. He had been nearly a year in the army and at the front for three months. His mother still worried about him. Her latest parcel contained food for body and soul. She sent him *The Evening Herald* and *The Messenger*. She also sent him a parcel containing Oxo cubes, apples and sweets. While making up this little parcel for her son, placing the goodies in the box, one can imagine her saying to herself: 'Well now, he might need those,' placing a pair of socks in the parcel. 'A cup of hot Oxo will keep him warm. I'll give him an apple and a few sweets, he'd like that … Dear God, please look after him, won't you.'

It was difficult for a soldier, particularly an officer, to write home about his feelings towards the war. The battalion censor made sure such sentiments were prevented from leaving the front. However, despite all the attempts by the censor to hide valuable information from the eyes of the opposition, it seems the censorship rules didn't apply to all. Ernest Kingdon wrote in his diary about the issue of censorship in letters from the front. He had his own opinions as to who was breaking the rules:

> I have been most religious and given no hint in any of my letters about anything taking place, and yet you write to me about things you hear and what the papers say. Censorship seems useless. It isn't the soldiers who write things. I am afraid the Staff babble more than ordinary beings – I suppose they get more opportunity as they get more leave.[12]

Like the comfort parcels, mail from home was vital; it provided that link with home. It provided relief to Michael and the other men from the madness that surrounded them. Any breakdown in the supply of mail affected the men's morale deeply, and letters played an important role in sustaining it. In the weeks before the 6th Connaught Rangers had attacked Guillemont back in September 1916, Second Lieutenant J. F. B. O'Sullivan had written of how a letter from home gave him a lift. Having been told he would act as liaison officer between the 47th and 59th Brigades in the attack, he wrote:

> As a gloomy postscript to the exciting news, a few remnants of the day's ration party came straggling in and told us that nearly all of their party (and rations) had been destroyed in the attempt to get through the barrage. However, what did get through when the food and rum were lost was some home mail for me. Letters from Nora, Tom and Blanche. It would probably sound ridiculous to describe what those letters did for my morale; better than food or rum. For an exquisite spell, fear and fatigue, dirt, stench and death were forgotten.[13]

Battalion censors were normally officers of middle rank such as lieutenants or captains. Reading letters written by their men offered these officers an insight into their men's state of mind. For example, Andrew Lockhart was happy when he went to France. However, within weeks of his arrival, he wished he was out of it. Not long after he and his 11th Royal Inniskilling Fusiliers arrived in France, Andrew wrote several letters home. He wrote on 5 November 1915, 'I must say that I am keeping in the best of form.' However, by 4 December he had a different view: 'I only wish this war was over, for there isn't much pleasure in being out here.'[14] Within the space of a month, his feelings towards the war had changed. The reality of war had hit him.

As an officer, Michael would have been very concerned about his men's morale. The war was bad enough without adding to men's misery by the loss of their letters from home. The problems with the army postal service annoyed Michael so much that he wrote about them in a letter to his mother, knowing well that the censor would read it, and that maybe something would be done to solve the problems of mail going astray:

6th Royal Irish Regt.

8th [*sic*] Corps Troops Supply Column

B.E.F.

France

January 16th 1917.

Dear Mater,

This is to answer your letter of Jan 10th or as you say (No. 1) ... I am with a party of men working on a railway. I am glad you received my letter with cheque alright. I wish you would not worry, I am safe as houses. My beads are quite alright. I don't mind whether I have to go back or not provided I get my leave. Three of my letters have gone astray and it is the fault of the Battn as they sent them to the wrong address. Auntie L. wrote and said she had sent out a parcel but I have never seen it. It is a shame the way some mail is treated. A little more care on the part of those who deliver them would make a great difference. I am not grousing because my own have gone astray but because some of my men have been disappointed ...

I suppose the casual mill labourers want as much money as ever and no risks. What about the Tommy on the fire step with a shilling a day and can't call his life his own. I get fed up with these strikes and discontentments [*sic*] that are always going on at home. I wish they were out here ... I got The Evening Herald and Messenger with your letter. What a funny marriage, fancy old Vinny O'Brien popping the question, well I never. All these old nuts will get the girls and when we go home there will be none left ... What do they say at Mount Sackville? I feel I should like to write volumes if I had some news to tell you but you know I can't so I must say goodbye for now.

Love to all.

Your fond son,

Michael.

Chiero [*sic*], You may expect to see me pop into the yard any morning in a taxi. You never can tell.[15]

6th Royal Irish Regt.
8th Corps Troops Supply Column
B.E.F.
France
January 16th 1917.

Dear Mater

This is to answer your letter of Jan 10th or as you say (No. 1). I suppose you know my new address by now. I have no idea how long I will be here. I am with a party of men working on a railway. I am glad you received my letter with cheque alright. I wish you would not worry I am safe as houses. My beads are quite alright. I don't mind whether I have to go back or not provided I get my leave. Three of my letters have gone astray and it is the fault of the Batt. as they sent them to the wrong address. Auntie L. wrote and said she had sent out a parcel but I have never seen it. It is a shame the way some mail is treated. A little more

As well as problems with the post, news of men back home going on strike also seemed to annoy Michael and affect his morale. In his opinion, those striking men undermined the efforts he and his comrades were making at the front. He wished they were with him to see what deprivation was really like. He wasn't the only soldier who felt let down and expressed such sentiments on hearing of strikes back home.[16] Rowland Fielding wrote to his wife and complained about the striking workers too:

> It makes one feel ashamed for those Irishmen, and also of those fellow countrymen of our own [Fielding was English] earning huge wages, yet forever clamouring for more; striking, or threatening to strike; while the country is engaged upon this murderous struggle. Why, we ask here, has not the whole nation, civil as well as military, been conscripted? ... It makes me feel sick. It makes me think I never want to see the British Isles again so long as the war lasts.[17]

The origin of these men's discontent was the labour shortages created in most combatant economies by the war. According to Niall Ferguson:

> Workers were in a position to bid up wages and or to lower their productivity by going slow, or, if management sought to resist wage demands, by striking ... In all countries labour shortages in strategically vital sectors gave bargaining power to groups who were traditionally at the lower end of the income scale.[18]

One sector of the Irish economy that was crucial to the war effort was agriculture. Striking mill labourers at Boland's Mills in Dublin, who were traditionally at the lower end of the income scale, fit exactly into Ferguson's category of potential strikers. *The Irish Times* of 3 and 15 November 1917, under headlines of 'Labour Unrest', carried announcements of arbitration talks between a number of Dublin companies in industrial disputes with their workers. Examples were The Alliance and Dublin Consumers'

Gas Company and Boland's Mills Ltd, whose labourers wanted an increase in pay.[19] Unlike the workers at the Dublin Gas Company or Boland's Mills, Michael and his team working on the rail line couldn't go on strike. But there was no use in complaining. Nobody was listening.[20]

During the period Michael was away from the battalion, Second Lieutenant Toohey was killed during the battalion's tour of duty in the front line at Cooker Farm. He was shot by a sniper on 18 January 1917. Toohey was a married man of thirty-five who had served in the Boer War. Another man was killed the next day. He was Sergeant Patrick Smyth, 'B' Company, from St John's Green in Kilkenny, who was forty-six and also married.[21] The day-by-day killing went on, and the men almost became accustomed to it. Death was a part of everyday life at the front.

Michael could never mention the deaths of Second Lieutenant Toohey and Sergeant Smyth in his letters home; the censor would prevent such news getting out. However, it was unlikely that he would have mentioned them anyway. He avoided referencing such things in his letters, as he wanted to isolate his mother from the reality of war and not give her any more reasons to worry. The truth of war had to be kept from home. Ultimately, though, his concerns did not matter as all he was allowed to write home about were family matters, such as how novel 'Vinny O'Brien popping the question' was, or Joseph not being successful in an exam.[22] He drifted between two worlds, one of homely peace and another of war and death from which there was no escape.

On a quiet day off from his duties on the rail line, Michael came across some shamrock growing. He wrote and told his mother of his discovery. At the same time he could hear the muffled noise of British artillery up near the front line firing on the German lines, using a heavy trench mortar they had nicknamed 'The Duchess'.[23]

6th Royal Irish Regt.

8th [*sic*] Corps Troops Supply Column

B.E.F.

France

January 28th 1917.

Dear Mater,

Just a few lines to let you all know that I am quite well in spite of the intense cold that prevails here. The ponds are in great form for skating and the ice is in some cases eight inches thick. A bitter east wind has been blowing for the last week and makes one stick indoors whenever possible. ... I had a very nice letter from Mrs Nolan, quite a long letter in fact. They live in Kingstown and are at present living in Earlsfort Terrace, Dublin. Woodmere is the name of the house. I suppose you know yesterday (27th) was the Kaiser's birthday. This Sunday evening reminded me very much of home and I was thinking of you all and what you would probably be doing. I do wish the wind would shift as it is bitter at present. It gives one all sorts of aches and pains. I was looking out for a letter from home today but none turned up. I found a piece of genuine Shamrock growing here the other day so whoever says that Shamrock grows nowhere else but Ireland is a gentleman [*sic*] ... Write soon.

Your fond son,

Michael.[24]

Michael's battalion was relieved from the front line on 29 January 1917 by the 7th Leinsters. The men proceeded back to Derry Huts for their rest and recuperation. The freezing winter was beginning to cut into the battalion's strength. In early February ninety-five men from the 8th Dublins were sent to hospital suffering from the

6th Royal Irish Regt.
8th Corps Troops Supply Column
B.E.F.
France
January 28th 1917.

Dear Mater.

Just a few lines to let you all know that I am quite well in spite of the intense cold that prevails here. The ponds are in great form for skating and the ice is in some cases eight inches thick. A bitter east wind has been blowing for the last week and makes one stick indoors whenever possible. I had a letter from Capt. Smyth this morning and he says he has not seen any of you for a long time but hopes you are all quite well. I got a parcel of cigarettes the other day and I have not the faintest idea from whom they were, at any rate they were all burst and scattered about and damp and quite impossible to smoke. I

effects of the freezing conditions, such as flu, trench fever, trench foot and the like. This outnumbered by nearly three to one the number of men sent to hospital suffering from the effects of war, that is wounded or killed – twenty-nine were wounded in action and two were killed on 12 January.[25] The two men killed were Private Charles C. Watt, nineteen, from Liverpool, and Private Ernest Taggett from Newport in Wales.[26]

Occasionally during this cold period, for safety reasons, men were obliged to bivouac under the stars. (No wonder a high number of men came down with all kinds of cold-related ailments during February.) For some reason or other, artillery units were located near billet areas in reserve and were often the target of German counter-shelling. One battery was set up near the Derry Huts Camp and was regularly a target; consequently, Derry Huts, as the Leinster Regiment historian noted, 'became a doubtful health resort'.[27]

German shelling of Loker began to increase in intensity throughout February 1917. So too did the British response. Over two days in early February German gunners sent approximately 700 rounds of 5.9-inch shells and Rum Jars around Irish front-line positions known as Sandbag Villa and Strong Point 13 (SP13).[28] Being on the receiving end of an artillery barrage was truly horrific. Second Lieutenant O'Sullivan of the 6th Connaught Rangers described some of the terrifying moments he had experienced in the days before his battalion's attack on Guillemont in September 1916, when he was in a damp dugout with only the light of a candle and men groaning in agony:

> Two casualties were slowly dragged groaning into the dugout. One was O'Connell (Martin's batman), and the other an old man, name unknown to me. O'Connell was badly shell-shocked and making horrible twitching, groaning and gibbering; but the old chap had been hit in the stomach and was dying. Murphy got out the morphia and field dressings and had just filled the hypodermic when another shell came with a screaming crash and a tearing draught to extinguish the candle again. The old man was held up during the darkness; but little could be done for him. He was in such agony that we had to lay him flat in the mud alongside the gibbering O'Connell.[29]

During the Rangers' September 1916 attack on Guillemont, O'Sullivan had described an incident where the killing had apparently sent one man completely out of his mind:

> No sooner had I laboriously started off than a little man came running out of a corpse-strewn trench. His hands were holding something cupped in one of those round German fatigue caps, and grinning like a maniac, apparently wanted to share the joke. He came up and showed me the cap – filled and quivering with the owner's brains. Only complete emptiness of stomach spared me further disgust as I retched convulsively and strained to hurry forward.[30]

Even the medics suffered moments of fear when under shellfire. They witnessed some horrible scenes, which deeply affected some of them. Standing in a dressing station after his company commander had given a situation report and details about the attack on Guillemont, O'Sullivan described what happened when a shell exploded at the entrance to the dressing station:

> Whilst binding up a man's leg, a shell suddenly smashed the man to pieces and, fantastically, left Doc unscathed except that a hunk of dirt struck his jaw with terrific force; the dead man's face had been sliced off and stuck like a rubber mask on the side of the trench. Doc caught sight of this suspended face, gazed at it with bulging eyes, put his hands up to his own face, started making noises like a bloody steam engine and took off.[31]

The sight of this man's shattered face may never have left the mind of that doctor.

All men have their breaking points; the only difference between one man's and another's can simply be a matter of time. The stress of being under an artillery bombardment left its mark on the men on both sides. On 4 February 1917, during a freezing-cold frosty night, the bodies of two dead German soldiers were brought in from no man's land facing the Connaught Rangers' sector of the line at Wijtschate. One of the bodies was dressed only in thin underclothes. The poor man's nerves must have simply broken and he must have wandered half-naked into the cold to get away from the shelling. The Irish soldiers buried the two men – Saxons and probably Roman Catholic – at the cemetery in Kemmel. A priest read the last rites over their grave. Colonel Fielding ordered that a noticeboard be shown on the parapet, telling the Germans that his men had given these two German soldiers a proper burial. A few days later, in broad daylight, a German soldier came running across no man's land with his hands up, and was shot from behind by his own men before he reached the wire. The following day, five men of the Connaught Rangers were blown to bits by one of their own shells, which had fallen short during a bombardment of the German lines at their Spanbroekmolen SP.[32] During another of those February German artillery barrages, Corporals Horton and Jones of the 8th Dublins lifted a live aerial torpedo out of their trench. They threw it over the parapet, where it exploded immediately. Both were awarded the Military Medal for their bravery.[33]

During the same month, a direct hit was scored on one of the billets occupied by men of 'C' Company of the Connaught Rangers. In utter panic, the men scrambled out of the billets and were hit again. Three men were killed and eleven badly wounded. The dead were Private James Bannerman, thirty-four, a veteran of the Boer War, from Foley Street in Dublin; Private Owen Treanor, twenty-two, from Emyvale in County Monaghan; and Private John O'Donoghue, seventeen, from Watergate Street, Bandon, County

Cork. All three were buried side by side in Kemmel Chateau Military Cemetery.[34] John O'Donoghue was Bandon's youngest casualty of the war. He came from a family of seven and had been to St Fintan's Boys National School in Bandon. He had first tried to enlist when he was sixteen, but when his mother found out what his intentions were, she went to the local barracks and divulged John's real age, so he was sent home. John went back to the army when he reached seventeen, to Kinsale in south Cork, where he enlisted in the Connaught Rangers.[35] The day after these three men were killed, Private James Hamilton from Drumshambo in County Leitrim died in a field hospital from his wounds and was buried in Bailleul Military Cemetery.[36] A random shell fired by a German artilleryman who sighted his gun many kilometres away with deadly accuracy had killed men from the four provinces of Ireland.

Fortunately for Michael Wall, he was away from the front line when this carnage occurred. However, his hopes of getting home on leave and away from this hell were dashed when his commanding officer, Lieutenant Colonel Edmund Roche-Kelly, issued an order to cancel all leave.[37] General Plumer's plans required all hands to be available for work.

The shortage of leave was a regular theme in Michael's letters. Its absence badly affected the men's morale. Home leave for the ordinary soldier was a rare commodity, and, when it did occur, men often received no prior warning. They were simply notified by a chit detailing 'seven days leave, starting immediately'.[38] Some soldiers would arrive home filthy, infested with lice and exhausted. For much of the war, the average soldier only got ten days' leave for every fifteen months of service. In February 1917 Rowland Fielding applied for twenty-one days' leave to which he claimed he was entitled. This would imply he had served in

France or elsewhere for thirty-one-and-a-half months. In short, Fielding hadn't been home in more than two-and-a-half years.[39] By the summer of 1917 approximately 100,000 men had not had any leave for eighteen months, and roughly 400,000 had served without leave for a year.[40] This was a lot of disgruntled men.

Like Michael Wall, the men who wrote to Monica Roberts knew their letters would normally be read by an officer of middle rank. Regularly mentioning leave in the letters was a subtle way of reminding the officer reading the letters that this issue was very much in the men's minds. Perhaps knowing this, some men would drop the hint in the letter by writing that they had not had leave for more than fifteen months, had been in many battles and were deserving of some leave.

When a soldier was on leave, there was always the temptation not to go back. For some men, the temptation to stay at home was too great. Captain Beater of the 9th Dublins noted in his diary, written in Flanders:

> Corporal Doyle, the best wirer we had and a regular born fighter went home on leave and never returned to this pleasant land of France. The same thing befell Lance Corporal Christy Moore, one of the few remaining original members of my old platoon who went home on 17th of December (1916) and failed to re-join.[41]

Some soldiers believed that even wounded Irish soldiers were not sent to Ireland for rest and recovery because it was feared they would stay in Ireland and not return to their regiment. Instead they thought many were sent to Britain to recover. It was a suspicion held by Private Christy Fox. In a letter to Monica Roberts, he noted:

I think there does be very few of our Irish boys that does be wounded sent to Ireland. They nearly all stop in English hospitals of course they do be well looked after there too I am sure. But I don't think you would beat the Irish people for kindness.[42]

On a more cheerful note for Michael, as he mentioned in a letter home, his job on the railway was going well, and back in Dublin, his former commanding officer, Lieutenant Colonel R. L. Owens in the 3rd Royal Irish Regiment, had been rewarded for his role in putting down the Easter Rising:

> 6th Royal Irish Regt.
> 8th [sic] Corps Troops Supply Column
> B.E.F.
> France
>
> February 8th 1917.
>
> Dear Mater,
>
> Just a few lines to keep your heart up so to speak though I have not very much to say. This job is lasting longer than I expected but it is quite good this weather as there is plenty of work. I am acting as Quartermaster, i.e. looking after rations, clothing and boots and by the time I do my other duties I don't have much time to myself. I got the "Weekly Irish Times" and "Sunday Independent" yesterday. My C.O. at home in the 3rd Batt. has been made a Brevet Colonel in recognition of his services during the Rebellion. Has Doyle been to see any of those demonstrations with the Motor Ploughs yet. According to the "Irish Times" everybody seems to have "got the wind up" in Ireland over the new tillage arrangements. If the ground is as hard as it is here there won't be much of it done. By the way

could you send me out a "baccy" pouch ... Auntie's parcel has not come yet. Love to all.

Your fond son
Michael.[43]

6th Royal Irish Regt.
8th Corps Troops Supply Column
B.E.F.
France

February 8th 1917.

Dear Mater.

Just a few lines to keep your heart up so to speak though I have not very much to say. This job is lasting longer than I expected but it is quite good this weather as there is plenty of work. I am acting as Quarter Master, i.e. looking after rations, clothing and boots and by the time I do my other duties I don't have much time to myself. I got the "Weekly Irish Times" and "Sunday Independent" yesterday. My C.O. at home in the 3rd Batt. has been made a Brevet Colonel in recognition of his services during the Rebellion. Has Doyle been to see any of those demonstrations with the motor Ploughs yet. According to the "Irish Times" everybody seems to have "got the wind up" in Ireland over the new tillage arrangements. If the ground is as hard as it is here there won't be much of it done. By the way could you send me out a "baccy" parcel like the one I have as it is napaick. No more news at present. Auntie's parcel has not come yet. Love to all.

Your fond son
Michael

9

'I stick to my rosary'

By mid-February Michael's job with the supply column had come to an end and he was back with his battalion. They were in billets at Doncaster Huts outside Loker. He took the time to write a somewhat emotional letter home to his mother, and he also wrote and told Joseph not to 'worry about Germany's new mad dog policy'.[1]

> 6th Royal Irish Regt.
> B.E.F.
> France.
>
> February 11th 1917.
>
> Dear Mater,
>
> You will see by my address that I am back again with the Regiment and ready for another tour in the line. As usual I only got a few minutes' notice to come back. ... I know you would be more pleased if my job had lasted longer, but as I always say, don't worry as I know I will get through alright. I know both your prayers & Auntie's and of all at home will not go unheeded. I stick to my rosary as you have always told me and I know I shall be safe and please God that "bright day" in your life will soon appear and I shall pay you back a hundred times as every mother expects. Perhaps you will wonder at my sudden outburst of sentiment, but there is one thing that all the teaching and preaching about minding one's religion has not near the effect that a couple of

months out here has. No one out here gets much time for writing or day dreaming but I am always thinking of you all no matter where I am, more especially on a Sunday afternoon … I have written to Fr Gleeson several times but have not had an answer. I am enclosing a cheque in this letter. Hope you will get it all right.

Your fond son,
Michael.[2]

Theoretically, the battalion may have been resting; in practice, however, in preparation for the great offensive, they began periods of intermittent tactical-training exercises that would last up to the end of May. On 13 February 1917 the 6th Royal Irish war diary made reference to the battalion practising a 'new battalion formation', which was in essence a tactical formation of men used in attacking German trenches.[3] The infantry tactic most battalions used on 1 July 1916 at the Somme was that of a wave formation of companies attacking. Described as 'a vast, complicated parade ground movement, carried out in slow motion', the wave tactic was presented in 4th Army Tactical Notes issued in May 1916 from GHQ.[4] The failure to remove German machine-gun strong points on 1 July along the Somme front had resulted in devastation for the wave tactic used by the British infantry battalions on that dreadful day.[5] Commenting on the wave tactic under the heading 'Formations adopted in moving to the assault', the 86th Brigade (1st RDF) post-Somme battle report noted:

> During the very few days training allotted to the brigades, companies had been trained to move forward across no man's land in lines of platoon columns in file ... machine gun fire was however so intensive that formations were quickly broken up and men struggled forward to the first available cover.[6]

However, by February 1917, based on lessons learned during the Somme campaign, the wave system of attack had been refined, whereby, instead of using companies in wave formations of attack, smaller, specialised, platoon-size assault units – such as Bombers and Lewis Gunners – would be used in the future.[7] According to John Lee, 'in July 1916 the company was the main infantry formation around which the attack was organised. By November it was the platoon, now transformed into four sections of highly interdependent and effective specialists.'[8] Chris McCarthy noted the BEF's tactical doctrine was thus 'shaped by the realisation that it was fighting a platoon and section commander's war'.[9]

Consequently, it was this 'new battalion formation' tactic that Michael's battalion began training with in February 1917. The travesty of the Somme campaign of 1916 had taught the British Army many valuable lessons on topics such as tactics, equipment, infantry–artillery co-operation and the use of aircraft, communications, logistics and treatment of the wounded.[10] Historians such as Peter Simkins and Gary Sheffield have used the concept of the learning curve as a tool for analysing and explaining the improved performance of the BEF after the Somme campaign.[11]

During the few days that Michael's regiment spent practising the new formation, both British and German artillery were very active, firing on each other's batteries behind the front lines. The war diary of the 6th Royal Irish for 16 February 1917 recorded: 'Trenches. Doctor's House. Commencement of Corps artillery bombardment. Very little retaliation on our trenches.'[12] The noise didn't seem to upset Michael very much. He had grown accustomed to it by now:

> 6th Royal Irish Regt.
> B.E.F.
> France.
>
> February 16th 1917.
>
> Dear Mater,
>
> Just a line to let you know that I am quite well and that the trenches are not too bad, at any rate this heavy frost has dried every place up. We bagged a plane (Bosche) yesterday. Leave is off just now so there is no chance of getting away yet awhile …

We will soon be out for a rest again. News is very slack as I never hear from anybody. Love to Auntie and all.

Your fond son,
Michael.[13]

A few days later Michael wrote home again:

6th Royal Irish Regt.
B.E.F.
France.

February 19th 1917.

Dearest Mother,

Thank you ever so much for your parcel containing the socks and tobacco pouch … The trenches are just as muddy as ever after the thaw worse luck but still it is not so cold and there is no need to wear a coat when going round the trenches either day or night. Have you heard that Charlie Adams of Malahide is missing. I saw it in the Times last week. … Best love to all at home.

Your fond son,
Michael.[14]

6th Royal Irish Regt.
B.E.F.
France.

February 19th 1917

Dearest Mother

Thank you ever so much for your parcel containing the socks and tobacco pouche. I was very pleased indeed to get the socks although the others are as sound as the first day. The pouche was A.1. but how did you manage to send them all out so quickly. Did you get my letter with Regde. I sent it last Sunday week. The trenches are just as muddy as ever after the thaw worse luck but still it is not so cold and there is no need to wear a coat when going round the trenches either day or night. Have you heard that Charlie Adams of Malahide is missing I saw it in the Times last week. I must ask you to excuse this short note also pencil. Best love to all at home.

Your fond son
Michael.

On the morning that Michael wrote this letter, three parties of the 6th Connaught Rangers, consisting of nine officers and 190 other ranks, under the cover of fog and a smoke barrage – after 'cheerfully tucking green miniature flags into their caps or button holes' – raided the German trenches facing them at Maedelstede Farm and Spanbroekmolen.[15] All forms of regimental identification had been removed before the raid. This was a common practice used by British raiding parties in order to prevent the Germans identifying the unit from which the raiders came and thus revealing the battle formation of the British in the opposing trenches. The Connaughts raiding party threw all the bombs they were carrying but failed to break into the German line and had to fall back. Naturally, Michael could not write home about this raid, but the war diary of the 6th Royal Irish recorded:

> 19 February 1917. Trenches. Fort Victoria. Raid by the 6th Connaught rangers accompanied by discharge of smoke at 7:15 a.m. Not a success. Germans helped to dress our wounded in no man's land. 2 OR. wounded in 'B' Coy. One of them Sgt. Morrissey, since died of wounds. Buried in Locre [Loker].[16]

When the Rangers returned to their jump-off point, which was on either side of Suicide Road, one of the Rangers, Private P. Collins, insisted on going out into no man's land and bringing in the dead and wounded, despite German fire. Private Collins was awarded the Distinguished Conduct Medal (DCM) for his bravery, but died of wounds on 9 March 1917.[17] At about 9.15 a.m. the Germans offered an armistice so the wounded and dead from both sides could be collected. Three officers and eight men were killed, two officers and seventeen men were wounded, and one officer and six men were reported missing, presumably captured. The Germans insisted that the men who were assigned the duty of collecting the wounded and dead should not come out armed. However, Second Lieutenant Gordon Ralph either ignored, or was not aware of, the German conditions, and consequently he was taken prisoner.[18]

The divisional commander, General Hickie, disapproved of this temporary armistice arranged by the Germans, as it constituted a breach of the order which forbade fraternisation with the enemy. Hickie warned that if it occurred again disciplinary action would be taken. In future, the wounded were to be left in no man's land until after dark, when they would be picked up. Presumably the only way to find these unfortunate men in the dark was to locate where the groans were coming from.

As a sign of things to come, towards the middle of February 'heavy guns' were seen passing through Loker on their way to new locations near the front line.[19] The sight and news around Loker of these guns moving into new positions gave some of the Dublins a bit of a morale boost. Private George Soper wrote to Monica Roberts back in Dublin. He told her a few white lies, which the censor approved:

> I am quite certain we shall finish off the Germans this year. We are taking some of his ground day by day. He never gets any peace whatsoever, if it is not the artillery shelling him it is the infantry raiding his trenches so you can understand the life he is getting … Yes I think the war will finish this year.[20]

Michael wrote home, as usual, just before he returned to the trenches for his turn of duty on 21 February 1917. However, this particular letter portrayed a lonely man fed up with war. It is perhaps the longest letter he wrote home, comprising four pages of beautifully handwritten script in which he refers to lots of things from home:

people, places, home activities. It seems that the constant strain on his nerves with these periods in the front line and the random killing from the shelling were beginning to tell. The letter presents the inner thoughts of a young soldier who had been at the front a little over three months and had become completely disillusioned with the war. As he wrote the letter, the Germans were firing 'Whizz Bangs' on his front line, as the war diary of the 6th Royal Irish recorded: '21 February 1917. Trenches. Fort Victoria. Heavy artillery again bombarded hostile back areas. Enemy sent over a few whizz bangs on 'A' Coy's H.Q. (VIA GELLIA).'[21]

> 6th Royal Irish Regt.
> B.E.F.
> France.
>
> February 21st 1917.
>
> Dearest Mother,
>
> I was very pleased to get your two letters dated 11th & 15th respectively. I also got an Irish Times (weekly). I should like to get my leave before March. I am overdue for leave now by a long time. Well I hope you are right when you say that the war is to end in June. The firing line is not too badly [sic] though there is more noise than usual. It rained very heavy last night and every bit of the place is in a thick paste. However this morning it ceased and there was a soft spring mist – a great growing morning – and in the trees not far away a blackbird was piping a few notes of his merry song. It quite reminded me of the early mornings I used to spend after the rabbits. ... I will feel just as strange when I get back to Dublin as I did when I came out here. The money is so simple here, for one thing it is all in Francs. Yes it was very kind of Mrs Nolan to visit,

yes I do like getting letters from the old country. Your two and three letters were more welcome than you can imagine and they give one something else to think of besides this bedamed and beshagglled [*sic*] bit of line. What a pity Jack has strayed, I hope he will turn up again. Yes there was an officer from the Dublins billeted. I have no idea of who the lady was that spoke to you on the tram ... Oh yes, I shall wire from London ... Perhaps you are wondering how I manage to write a long letter like this when I am in the front line, but you see I have your letters to go by and that makes it easy. I am now answering your letter of the 15th. I am glad you got the cheque all right. Please don't worry about me as I put myself in God's hands and I feel quite safe when I trust in him. I will tell you honestly that the best companion and occupation I have when going round the line during the night and sometimes during the day is my Rosary Beads. I know with all your prayers at home and all I can say myself, I will come safely through. Do you ever get Joseph to shoot a few rabbits or does he interest himself to that degree. Bernard is a dear kid. I wish I could hear his loud stammering now. Give him my love and tell him I have a few souvenirs for him when I go on leave. I suppose Charlie Hodgens is as proud as punch now. Remember me to the Willans next time you see them ... I am glad you bought some War loans. I was thinking of doing so myself but it is so difficult out here. Yes I got the tobacco pouch and socks all right thanks. Remember me to Cunningham and Doyle ... Give my love to Auntie and all at home. Cheero [*sic*] and keep smiling.

Always, your fond son,
Michael.[22]

Reading between the lines in this letter home, there is no doubt that Michael's emotions, understandably, suffered highs and lows.

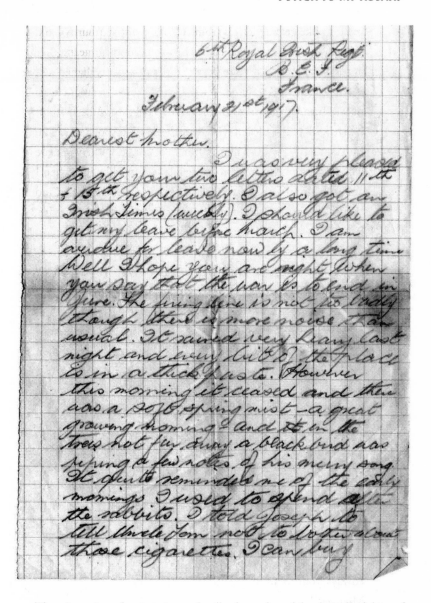

The thought of going into the 'bedamed and beshagglled bit of line' brought him low and made him, naturally, fearful of what lay ahead of him yet again. At such times, thoughts of home and God were his touchstones of reassurance.

145

Despite his regular reminder to the censor, any hopes he had of leave were dashed again. His next chance would not be for another month. Michael's state of mind must have been pretty low at this time. He wasn't the only man feeling down; the cold weather, the lack of movement and constant boredom of trench life – as well as German shelling – drove many men to the brink of insanity. Writing up his diary from his billet in Birr Barracks, Captain Beater of the 9th Dublins felt much the same as Michael. He also felt sorry for the men under his command:

At the present moment I feel that I would give almost anything to be able to leave the infantry for ever and get into something where you would get a good show, get looked after a little better in the way of billets and not to be a sort of labourer for the rest of the army … They actually gave the men a route march on Sunday afternoon, the only afternoon they have a chance of getting to themselves. Heaven knows the poor chaps work hard enough all the rest of the time. It is quite enough to feed anybody up to the neck.[23]

When he came out of the front line, Michael's emotions seemed to perk up a little. The evenings were getting a bit longer and he met a few lads he knew from Dublin, which cheered him up a bit.[24] On the last day of February he wrote home once more:

6th Royal Irish Regt.

B.E.F.

France.

February 28th 1917

Dear Mater,

Just a few lines to let you know I am keeping quite fit. What do you think of the good news in yesterday's paper? It looks as if the war will soon be over. I have met one of the Marchants, he is in the 9th Dublins. You remember they stayed beside us one summer in Howth. We have had a good talk over old times. Young Malone from the North Star Hotel is also an officer in the same Batt[alion]. He has been out here four weeks. I have met fellows out here I knew when I was a kid and although I remember them they don't ken me at all. However we will all be home for Xmas next and fight our battles over again around the log fire. I think the best thing out here when you are out of the line is to listen to a brass band. By jove it makes you feel quite different. I bought an old cornet and it is top hole in the old dug out in the front line. We often hear the Huns playing a tin whistle in their trenches. I had a letter from Cyril the other day & he wants to know when I am getting leave. My platoon Sergt was killed the last time we were in the trenches. I have just written to his mother in Templemore. I was awfully sorry about it as he was very keen & knew his job. Well as far as news goes I have no more. Give my love to Auntie & all at home. By the way I was speaking to Tommy Hughes from Hazlebrook. We were talking about Charlie Adams. Cheero [sic] for the present.

Your fond son,
Michael.[25]

The 'good news' that Michael referred to in this letter and his assumption of the war's ending soon were based on what he had read in the paper. On 6 February 1917 a banner headline in *The Irish Times* read 'America At War In A Week'. Two days later the paper ran an article with the headline 'Senate Approves Break With Germany'.[26] These articles cheered Michael up and led him to believe his homecoming would be brought closer by America's entry into the war.[27]

One of the few morale boosters that Michael found at the front was meeting up with young men from home whom he knew. He didn't feel so abandoned after meeting them. These were his comrades, who shared the same mental and physical deprivations as he did. They had something in common. Charles Stewart Marchant, whom he mentions in his letter as having stayed beside his family one summer when they lived at Glentora in Howth, was a second lieutenant in the 9th RDF.[28]

Michael also met 'young Malone' who worked in the North Star Hotel in Amiens Street, Dublin. He too was a second lieutenant in the 9th Dublins; he had joined the battalion at Loker on the same day as Charles Marchant in January 1917. In fact, not long after they arrived, Charles and 'young Malone' went on a training course together in the 16th Division's school. When Michael met Tommy Hughes from Hazlebrook, they chatted about Charlie Adams – another Malahide man, who was still reported as missing.

Sadly, the usual few casualties occurred during Michael's most recent period of front-line duty and the killing came closer to Michael. Between 19 and 22 February 1917 three members of his battalion were killed. One was his company sergeant major, Daniel Morrissey from Templemore, County Tipperary, whom Michael referenced in his letter above. He died of his wounds on 19 February and was buried in Loker churchyard. On the same day that Morrissey died, Private Thomas Dillon from Glendermott, County Derry was killed. He is buried in Pond Farm Cemetery near Kemmel. Three days later, on 22 February, Private William J. Le Page from Castel, Guernsey, in the Channel Islands, died. He was buried in Kemmel Chateau Military Cemetery.[29]

Over the next week or so Michael had a pleasant surprise. He received a letter from Fr Gleeson, who at that time was back in

Dublin as a curate in the Church of Our Lady of Lourdes in Lower Gloucester Street:

> Church of Our Lady of Lourds [*sic*]
> Lr Gloucester St.
> 2nd March 1917
>
> My dear Michael,
>
> I regret I have not time to write you as long and as newsy a letter as I should like to be able to write you – I had a visit from your devoted and excellent mother yesterday and I can tell you I felt it very much when I realized how I had failed to answer a letter or two you so kindly sent me. But Michael you can realise what mountains of work and worry we priests bear in a hard parish like this with thousands of souls. You will be glad to hear I am going back to the front again, but I cannot say what sector or area yet. I am prepared to go wherever I am most required to help the poor Catholic soldiers to live well and die well. The winter must have been very severe on you, but I am sure you stood it gamely as befits your character. I hope I have the pleasure of [unreadable] I gave you sage councils in my time in Vincents. Your mother is holding up very well and is resigned that you are doing things so well, so [unreadable] and so courageously. I should rejoice very much to be attached to your brave Regiment and Battalion, but I leave all that to those in whose hands I place my services. God knows best the best place for me. Any letter addressed to the above address will always be sent on to me and in fact your mother will always be able to get my address on calling here to the priest. I wish you every success and good luck my dear Michael,
>
> Your sincere friend
> Francis H. Gleeson O.C.[30]

Church of Our Lady of Lourds
Lr Gloucester St.
2nd March 1917

My dear Michael,
I regret I have not time to write you as long and as newsy a letter as I should like to be able to write you — I had a visit from your devoted and excellent mother yesterday and I can tell you I felt it very much when I realized how I had failed to answer a letter or two you so kindly sent me. But Michael you can realise what mountains of work and worry we priests have in a hard parish like this with thousands of souls.

Just like George Soper, who believed they would 'finish off the Germans this year', Michael was convinced that they were going to wipe 'the floor this year with the Germans'. In all his innocence, he imagined himself and his comrades marching up the quays in Dublin and being given a hero's welcome by the folks back home:

6th Royal Irish Regt.
B.E.F.
France.

March 5th 1917.

Dear Mater,

Ever so many thanks for your parcel. I got it yesterday. There was a great difference in the state they were in. A tin box is the only thing to send things out here in. Those small cakes were top-hole. Did you get my watch? I sent it on Saturday by registered post. I want Manning to clean it thoroughly and get it going properly as it has shell shock. Tell him to put a seconds hand on and fix the strap & luminous paint spots. I have had very little time for writing these last few days. A few of us went to a Divisional Concert the other night and it was quite the finest thing I have ever seen. It made you forget all about the war. One song that was sung with great gusto was the latest one 'Take me back to Blighty'. We regard it as a Hymn out here. I expect that all the Irish troops out here will have quite a time of it on Patrick's Day. I got a letter from Auntie yesterday and she wants to know what I want for the 21st. Well I'm going to ask you all not to bother about anything out of the way. The things I want I shall have to wait till I go on leave, whenever that will be I cannot say. One can buy nearly everything out here except boots and clothes. French people alas cannot make boots or military clothes on English lines. One of my jackets at present is all mud and patches and deficient of pieces thanks to barbed wire and other prickly things in this war. I think when it is over I shall have to build a dug out in the pigeon meadow to sleep in. They are quite snug places except of course when it rains and then you know all about it. We had a heavy fall of snow last night and the weather has got quite cold again. Well, we are counting on 'wiping the floor' this year with the Germans. I have accounted for a few already and hope to do another few in the eye before we finish. And then everyone out here will expect a stunning welcome home once again as we march up the Quays from the boat. What! What! Well I must bring my little despatch to a close but hope to send you one soon again. Fondest love to Auntie and all at home.

Ever your fond son,
Michael.

P.S. Cheque enclosed, hope you will get it all right. M[31]

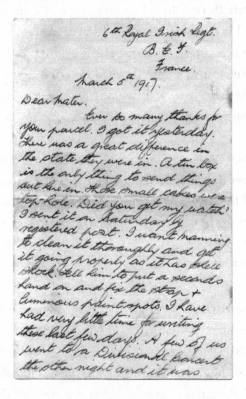

However, by March 1917 some of the folks back home had somewhat changed their attitude to British soldiers.

10

Life in the Reserve around Loker, Kemmel and Dranouter

Much like life in the front line, life in the reserve during those cold and wet early months of 1917 was pretty routine. On average, approximately three-fifths of an infantryman's time was spent in the rear and not in the front lines.[1] Being in reserve was a time and place where a man could have a rest, a bath and a change of clothing. Private Thomas McClure of the 15th Royal Irish Rifles in the Ulster Division found two very hospitable sisters in Neuve Église (Nieuwkerke) who washed his socks and shirts.

> Two sisters used to live in a house in Neuve Eglise, the place was a ruin, but they still stayed there, they washed our socks and shirts and had them clean for us when we came out of the line for a rest. These two were the only civilians I saw in Neuve Eglise, as most of the population were gathered in Bailleul, two miles away, also in Hazebrouck, Cassel and so on.[2]

The reserve was where men like Michael wrote many of their letters home. Once out of the line, when he had some time to himself and was not either working or training, a soldier had few things to do by way of entertainment and few places to visit around Loker or Kemmel. Soccer and rugby matches between battalions were a regular pastime.

The 6th Royal Irish apparently had a good soccer team. On

1 March 1917 they were out of the line in billets at Doncaster Huts and played a football match against their sporting rivals, the 7th Leinsters, on what must have been a very muddy pitch. They beat the Leinsters by ten goals to one.[3]

While in reserve, men were issued wages during what was called 'pay parade'. They would line up in order of rank and march to a desk to receive their wages from an officer. When a man got paid, the most popular places to go were the *estaminets* found in most villages in France and Flanders. Run by local farmers and townsfolk, these were a cross between a pub and a café. For a bit of entertainment, most of the Irish troops serving around Loker or Kemmel went to Bailleul, better known to the Irish soldiers as 'Ballyhooly' after the village in Cork where some of them had trained. It had shops and an ordnance store, a few hotels, restaurants and a club for the officers.[4] Thomas McClure had kind words to say about Bailleul:

> I always liked Bailleul and was content to roam about there and spend any money I had, while some others went to Armentieres to drink. There was a big brewery in Armentieres and while part of this town suffered from shellfire, it was in very good order and not at that period too much destroyed. Shops of every description were open in Bailleul, including the jewellers; the town had a homely appearance. The square in Bailleul always reminded me of Shaftesbury Square [Belfast] entering from the Bedford Street end, our favourite beer houses were Marie's, the Mont des Cats and Rue-de-Falong. At Neuve Eglise, you were held to be in support and it was here that we built the huts that we named Shankill Huts after the Shankill Road.[5]

Due to the loss of friends and the misery of trench life, a sense of humour was vital to keep going. The men put comic names on places around them: a cemetery became a 'rest camp', while going over the top became 'jumping the bags'.[6] The French village of Foncquevillers became 'Funky Villas' and of course Wijtschate became 'Whitesheet'.

As well as going to the *estaminet*, soldiers in reserve towns and villages were entertained by professional as well as amateur concerts they set up themselves. The 16th (Irish) and the 36th (Ulster) Divisions put on divisional concerts during their time facing Wijtschate. Essentially they were morale boosters.[7] This is reflected in a letter written by Michael in March 1917 telling his mother that the concerts he went to in Loker made him 'forget all about the war'.[8]

Sergeant Newman from the 177th Field Battery RFA described a popular act at one of these divisional concerts – a strongman act performed by two men with the stage names of Anthony and Brutus. Their act was the simple sort of stuff performed in any late Victorian or Edwardian circus. Brutus the strongman, played by a friend of Newman's named Dick Bratby, would lift Anthony above his head and, to the amazement of the audience, hold him aloft with one finger (an unseen wire held Anthony from the roof and the audience probably went along with it just for the fun of it). Dick 'Brutus' Bratby would later perform other entertaining feats of strength.[9]

Another source of entertainment in reserve was a cinema in Loker erected by the soldiers. In the middle of February 1917, during a break in training at Butterfly Farm, Private Christy Fox wrote to Monica Roberts that 'we do have concerts out here and also a cinema, there does be a fine sport, we had The Battle of the Somme here on the pictures a week ago.'[10] *The Battle of the Somme*, with scenes of British soldiers being killed and wounded, may not have gone down too well with some of the soldiers who viewed it.

What a charming way to entertain troops: showing them a film of their comrades being shot to pieces by German machine-gun fire at the Somme.

The cinema was often used by officers to present lectures. In mid-February, Lieutenant Colonel Moore DSO (Distinguished Service Order) presented a lecture on the 'Growth of the German Empire'.[11] No doubt it helped to demonise the Germans.

Something that one rarely sees mentioned in a book about the Irish in the Great War is the word 'sex'. Before they went to France, Lord Kitchener issued a written instruction to all his soldiers on 10 August 1914 to treat the women they met with 'perfect courtesy' and stated that they 'should avoid any intimacy'.[12] (Homosexuality was a military offence under Section 40 of the Army Act.) The reality, of course, was quite the contrary. Sexual recreation, whether with a man or a woman, was mainly sought with prostitutes.

Private Edward Casey of the RDF – who has been described as 'an underfed, under-sized and semi-literate Irish cockney from Canning Town' – had left his Irish girlfriend back in Cork. He related his experience with a prostitute after he first arrived at a training camp at Étaples:

> It was at this training camp, I had my second whore. Noticing a long line of soldiers lined-up outside some huts, and making enquiries, I was told it was the camp brothel. The whores were clean and free from the pox. They were examined by our own doctors and not allowed if they were found dirty. After the queue moved slowly forward, I was too interested in the movement of the blokes in front, and for the moment I forgot what I was waiting for. When I was almost at the door, I remembered and by this time I was standing in front of the usual old Lady cock-examiner.

Opening my fly, pulling out my thing, I noticed her hands were dirty. I must have passed the examination. She held up five fingers and said 'francs'.[13]

The officers and NCOs had their own brothels in the same camp. According to Casey, some Irishmen called sex with a woman 'a blow-thru'.[14] There is no record of brothels in Loker. However, Bailleul had its own 'special attraction' for the Irish soldiers. Lieutenant May of the 49th Brigade Machine Gun Company noted:

The special attraction of the town was a girl called Tina. Everyone in the area had heard of her ... she was the best known girl outside Paris ... she was a fine good looking girl and I think a decent girl. She spoke good English and was a barmaid at a café in the town. She had innumerable proposals from English officers including two Generals. Before the attack on Wijtschate, Tina was removed from Bailleul, for it was thought that she had too much knowledge of our troop movements.[15]

Frank Laird knew 'the fair Tina' in Bailleul. He wrote that she became 'enshrined in the pages of the First Hundred Thousand'.[16]

Photographs of nude ladies abounded in the men's billets. Captain Ronald Paul Schweder was an observation officer attached to the 173rd Brigade RFA, which was in turn attached to the 36th (Ulster) Division. He wrote home about some of these pictures in the artillery officers' mess in Dranouter:

The pictures in our mess of nude ladies are much admired. Orr has pinned them on the walls. The one most admired is a picture of a good lady holding up her decks, one in each hand and admiring them in a glass. It is called Egalite.[17]

Despite the rigid Protestant ethos perceived to be within the Ulster Division, the men's sexual adventures were a concern for some of their officers. During their time training at Seaford in East Sussex, for example, some of the Ulstermen found their way to the more colourful houses in London and ended up contracting venereal disease (VD). To try to deal with the problem of VD, Captain Percy Crozier arranged with his medical officer to ensure that all his soldiers 'had access to disinfectants after indulgence in sexual intercourse, free of charge'.[18] The contraction of VD was regarded as a disciplinary offence, as it could technically be considered malingering or a self-inflicted wound.

As early as October 1914 'several cases of Crabs' were reported amongst the 2nd Dublins in France. An investigation found that the cases were mainly amongst the latest reinforcements to the battalion, who came from 'overseas bases'. The commanding officer at the time, Lieutenant Colonel Loveband, recommended that all the men be tested for the disease before they left their overseas base and, if suspected of having the disease, be kept away from his battalion. He reckoned that 'owing to the unsanitary life men are forced to lead when in trenches, any disease of this nature spreads with great rapidity'.[19] One estimate of VD among British troops amounts to as many as 48,000 cases in 1917 and 60,000 cases in 1918.[20] Overall, between 1914 and 1918, there were 153,531 admissions to hospital for VD. In 1918 alone, there was a ratio of 32 to every 1,000 who had some kind of VD.[21] The consequences of contracting VD for the men were terrible enough. However, the consequences for their partners and wives when they returned home must have been devastating.

Although gambling in the army was against regulations, card games of all sorts passed away many a dull hour in the billets around Loker and Dranouter. At the Shankill Huts, men of the

15th Royal Irish Rifles spent the dark hours of late 1916 and early 1917 playing 'House', a game that in essence was a form of Bingo.[22]

Niall Ferguson has suggested that 'without alcohol and perhaps also without tobacco, the First World War could not have been fought'.[23] 'Had it not been for the rum ration,' one medical officer later declared, 'I do not think we should have won the war.'[24] This was an understatement, in the sense that it did not mention the huge quantities of alcohol men consumed when they were not in the front line. Although drinking alcohol in the front line was totally forbidden, ordinary soldiers would get drunk at every opportunity. They had, as one officer in the Highland Light Infantry put it, 'a marvellous talent' for it.[25] Even some of the teetotal Ulster men went over the top on 1 July at Thiepval under the influence of alcohol.[26]

One problem nearly always linked with alcohol and soldiers in the reserve areas was military discipline. When discipline was breached, the actual prosecution of a soldier under the British courts-martial system was a lengthy process with a large number of built-in safeguards. All court-martial cases were subject to scrutiny to ensure that proper procedures had been followed.[27] Army regulations listed twenty-six punishable offences, from war treason down to fraud. Some of the more common offences committed by the Irish regiments were drunkenness and miscellaneous minor offences. Punishments for such offences ranged from field punishment to detention and on to harsher punishments such as hard labour.

There were two basic types of field punishment. Field punishment No. 1 involved the soldier being tied to a gun-wheel or a T-shaped frame and being fed on bread and water and having to remain on public view for a set number of hours each day for five consecutive days, no matter the weather conditions. Although not painful, it was certainly uncomfortable and humiliating.[28] Field punishment No. 2 was less humiliating and involved the soldier running around the billet areas with a full pack and rifle carried over his head as he ran his laps. Some battalion commanders had their own ways of imposing discipline for lapses in regimental standards. For example, when men of the 9th Dublins turned out in the morning looking dirty or unshaven while in reserve around Loker, they were punished with a route march.[29]

On one occasion Colonel Fielding of the 6th Connaught Rangers reported 'an epidemic of crime in the battalion, on a small scale; – insubordination among a few men'. In trying to explain this rise in petty crime, Fielding reckoned that 'scenting danger ahead', some of the men were 'apt to commit some crime, hoping thereby to get imprisonment and so be removed from the firing line'. Fielding called these men 'scrimshankers'. He concluded that the bout of insubordination which occurred was 'one of those cycles which all bodies of men go through at times and will soon pass away'. Consequently, there was a tendency to commute most sentences of imprisonment to field punishment.[30] Another form of 'scrimshanking' was malingering or pretending to be ill. Sick statistics for the 16th (Irish) Division were normal and comparable to other BEF divisions.[31]

One discipline issue wrongly attributed to Irish regiments was political indiscipline. General Maxwell reported that he found it 'very difficult to differentiate between Sinn Feiner and Redmondite. It is merely a question of degree.'[32] Such politically motivated sentiment among the army high command grew in 1917. None of the crimes committed by men of the 2nd and 8th Battalions of the RDF who fought at Wijtschate were of an overtly political nature, such as spreading seditious literature or incitement to mutiny. No members of these battalions were accused of committing the crime of war treason or offences covered under the Defence of the Realm Act.[33] There is no denying, however, that Irish politics were occasionally an issue with some Irishmen in the British Army. In November 1917 men of the Royal Munster Fusiliers held an informal meeting in Ireland declaring that they were 'as good Irishmen and nationalists as any Sinn Feiners. Though they fought for England against the Hun, and would continue to fight till the war was won, their interest in their country was just as SF as anyone else.'[34] However, looking after each other and staying alive were perhaps more important than what was going on back in Ireland.

Many parades, considered good for unit pride, were carried out when in reserve. There were church parades, pay parades (as mentioned), and kit- and billet-inspection parades. Occasionally parades were called to present awards and medals to men. To boost morale in the 16th (Irish) Division, General Hickie created divisional bravery certificates. When battalions were in reserve, it was an ideal opportunity for General Hickie to present his divisional parchment to some of his men. The parchments were known as 'Hickie Parchments'. On 3 October 1916 four men attached to the 8th Dublins received bravery awards while at Loker.[35] On 16 October 1916 Lance Corporal Christy Gallagher from Dublin received his Hickie Parchment. He was subsequently transferred to the 7th Dublins, who at that time were in Salonika fighting the Bulgarians. A little more than fourteen months after he received his award, on 30 December 1917, he was one of seven Dublin Fusiliers who drowned on their way to Egypt following the sinking of HMT *Aragon*.[36]

Some of the officers of the 16th (Irish) Division were lucky enough to be able to return home to receive their awards. For example, Lieutenant Colonel Edward Bellingham, who commanded the 8th Dublins, went home to collect his Military Cross and DSO from King George V on 10 October 1916.[37] In mid-November, Captain J. P. Hunt of the same battalion went home to collect his DSO from the king.[38] However, when Sergeant J. J. Roache received a DCM for his bravery at Ginchy on the Somme, he didn't have the luxury of travelling home to receive his award; he had to stay on in Loker, as the award of a DCM did not merit a home visit.[39]

Back in October 1916, at the closing stages of the Battle of the Somme, a bit of regimental history had been made in the Dublins; the regiment won its first Victoria Cross (VC) of the First World War. It was awarded to a Glaswegian from Springburn, Sergeant Robert (Bob) Downie. Having one of their men win a VC brought a sense of pride to the Dublins in Loker. Private Christy Fox wrote home to Monica Roberts, eager to tell her all about the battalion's hero:

I suppose you have read in the papers of a sergeant getting the VC. Sergeant Downie, he belongs to our battalion. I can tell you he deserves it, he will be going home shortly to get decorated by the King. He has got four medals, the Russian Honour of St George, the French Legion of Honour, the Military Medal and the VC. He won wiping out a machine gun section and capturing their gun. The gun is gone home I expect it will be on view in Dublin. He is a very brave chap; he doesn't care where he goes. It's the first VC that was ever won by the Dublin Fusiliers. There was great rejoicing when we heard he got it and mind you it was time too we got one ... I must now bring my letter to a close. Hoping you will be able to see Sergeant Downie when he arrives in Dublin with his VC. It is about time Dublin got a chance of welcoming home a VC hero. Sincerely. Christy.[40]

Even Lieutenant Colonel Jeffreys, the commanding officer of the 2nd Dublins, was delighted with the news of Downie's VC. He noted in his diary:

> Brigadier Ramsay came round the line with me this morning. He was in the same M.I. [Mounted Infantry] with me in S.A. [South Africa] and we had a very long chat about old days. Downie got the VC. I got a wire from General Lambton this morning congratulating him and the battalion which I thought very nice of him, I am so pleased that he got it.[41]

Bob Downie was awarded the VC for capturing a German machine gun and killing the team that operated the gun. Charging the gunners, he screamed, 'Come on the Dubs.' However, the killing of these men left a mark on the twenty-two-year-old Downie. It must have been a bloody affair, so much so that he rarely spoke about the event to anyone again, not even his own family. Downie returned to Glasgow when his battalion came out of the line just after Christmas 1916. When he returned to Springburn, he was given a civic reception at the Town Hall. In the evening he was given a special reception by the United Irish League and a purse containing treasury notes. He was also presented with a gold watch by his former Catholic school in Springburn, St Aloysius.[42]

While Bob Downie was back at home receiving his award, Private John Byrne of the 2nd Dublins received the Montenegrin Medal for Merit from General Ramsay, a medal for valour presented by the King of Montenegro, Nikola I.[43] John Byrne was indeed a brave man. Christy Fox thought all these awards the Dubs received were great, especially that of Byrne:

> We are still reaping in the honours. We have another man after been

decorated with a medal which they call the Order of the Black Eagle of Montenegro. He is the first man in the British Army to receive it. He got it for devotion to duty in the field. He is a stretcher-bearer; of course they bring in the wounded after a scrap and dress their wounds. He is servant to our doctor and of course he might not go into action at all if he liked, so he says, when there is a battle going on. He is a single man and has no one to fret after so he lets a married man stop behind in his place.[44]

As the months of spring progressed and preparation work for the offensive on Wijtschate intensified, spare time in the reserve for parades or visiting Marie's or the Mont des Cats had diminished. Even the fair Tina had left town.

11

'Curious times'

Michael Wall went back into the front line on 10 March, his battalion relieving the 6th Connaught Rangers.[1] It had been a rough few days in the line for the Rangers. Two days earlier the freezing-hard ground gave the Germans in Wijtschate an opportunity to launch an attack in the form of a large raid on the 16th (Irish) Division's front where the Rangers were located. Late in the afternoon heavy German shelling was reported along the entire front held by the division. The immediate worry for the Irish Division was the entrance to the mine shaft at SP12. At the time of the raid, work was being carried out in the mine, mainly by a party of Dublin Fusiliers under the supervision of the Royal Engineers. Major Smithwick of the 2nd RDF took command of two companies and went out from Rossignol Wood. With the help of some of the miners, Smithwick and his men fought off the raiding party from the mouth of the mine.[2]

Unlike the Rangers' raid earlier in February, however, the German raid was successful. They entered the Irish lines at several points and took twenty-five prisoners and two Lewis guns. The 7th Royal Irish Rifles took the main brunt of the assault and suffered seventy-one casualties. The 9th Corps commander, Lieutenant General Sir Alexander Hamilton-Gordon, demanded a full report. If there was a weak point in the line, he had to know about it. In exoneration, General Hickie reported that the German shelling which preceded the raid had been 'extraordinarily accurate, and consequently many Lewis Guns and their crews were knocked out of action'.[3] The commander of the 48th Brigade, Brigadier General Ramsay, noted in his report of the raid that 'the intensity and concentration of the (German) barrage put on the raided area can only be described as devastating; the trench system within this area has been practically obliterated'.[4]

Having successfully completed the raid, the Germans returned to their lines. As there were no men spared on the Irish side to take their dead men in and bury them, bodies were left in front of the Irish parapet for some time.[5]

Apart from Second Lieutenant Hewitt and Second Lieutenant Laracy being badly wounded while returning from a patrol duty, things quietened down over the next few days.[6] It was quiet enough for Michael to catch up on the news from Ireland in his *Irish Times* and write a revealing letter home:

> 6th Royal Irish Regt.
> B.E.F.
> France
>
> 11th March 1917.
>
> Dear Mater
>
> Very many thanks for your ever welcome letter. I don't know how I managed to write such a long letter except that I suddenly fell into the channel and so carried on. I answered Auntie's letter the other day. I also got a letter from Fr. Gleeson and in it he said he was coming out to France again. We have had four days of wind, rain, sleet & snow but to-day is quite different. It is a lovely soft morning and a few bees are to be seen flying about. I think you were day dreaming when you thought I was coming home on a cycle. Anyway I wish I was. I am hoping to get home soon. I am praying for it too. Yes I got the "Irish Times" and

6th Royal Irish Regt.
B.E.F.
France

11th March 1917.

Dear Mater

Very many thanks for your ever welcome letter. I don't know how I managed to write such a long letter except that I suddenly fell into the channel and so carried on. I answered Auntie's letter the other day. I also got a letter from Fr. Gleeson and in it he said he was coming out to France again. We have had four days of wind, rain, sleet & snow but to-day is quite different. It is a lovely soft morning and a few bees are to be seen flying

"Messenger" OK. What do you think of Laurence O'Neill being made Lord Mayor. By God these are curious times all right. And the paper says that there was a scrap over the election. Does not the conduct of the Irish Party in the House the other day deserve to get all the derision it deserves. No sign of conscription being enforced I suppose. And what do you think the paper said about Major Redmond. It said he looked very war worn and haggard. Well I have seen him and he looks nothing of the sort. Next Saturday is St Patrick's Day and last year I was at home. Do you remember? I was just going to join the regiment. I had a letter from Marjorie Nolan yesterday. I walked a long way yesterday to see a concert and it was quite good. There was a brass band performing and it gave a splendid rendering of selections from 'Carmen' and 'Faust'. It was top hole. Tell Barney I was asking for him. I suppose you have my watch by this time. I suppose Mrs Crawford is very bucked now that the Dr has decided to exert himself to her liking. I had another letter from Cyril on Thursday. I hope you will excuse this short note but I will probably be able to write again soon. We are pretty busy now. Best love to Auntie and all at home.

Ever your fond son,
Michael.[7]

Yet again he mentioned the same old chestnut of leave; he was even praying for it.

The election of a new lord mayor in Dublin seemed to interest Michael. Following a meeting of the Dublin Municipal Council on Friday 23 February 1917, Alderman Laurence O'Neill, who came from Portmarnock (near where Michael lived), was elected to the office of lord mayor of Dublin.[8] A nationalist, O'Neill replaced the unionist incumbent, Sir James Michael Gallagher, who had held the office for two years. It was this change that led Michael to believe he was living in 'curious times'.

The other politically related matter that seemed to interest Michael was 'the conduct of the Irish Party in the House', which he found derisible. This most likely is in reference to the issue of Home Rule for Ireland, which was raised in the House of Commons and was reported in *The Irish Times* on 8 March. The events transpired as follows. At 2.45 p.m. on Wednesday 7 March 1917, the speaker of a packed House of Commons took the chair. Mr T. P. O'Connor, a member of the Irish Parliamentary Party, who had won his seat in Liverpool in the general election of 1885, rose and presented the following resolution to the House:

> That with a view to strengthening the hands of the Allies in achieving the recognition of the equal rights of small nations and the principle of nationality against the opposite German principle of military domination and government without consent of the governed, it is essential without further delay to confer upon Ireland the free institutions long promised to her.[9]

Several speakers of both Ulster unionist and Irish nationalist backgrounds spoke. The debate stretched on into the evening. Shortly after 5 p.m., dressed in the uniform of a major in the 6th Royal Irish Regiment, Major William Hoey Kearney Redmond MP – one of Michael's senior officers in the battalion – rose to his feet. He seconded the motion proposed by O'Connor and made an emotional speech to the house.

Redmond's speech addressed many contemporary topics, such as Ireland's positive response to and participation in the war. However, the main thrust of his speech was his passionate plea for Home Rule to be implemented immediately. On the subject of Ireland's participation in the war, he believed that 'the great heart of Ireland, North and South as well, beats in strong sympathy with the gallant efforts which are being made by the French nation to-day to free their soil from the invader'. Referring to the Irishmen who enlisted in the British Army at the outbreak of the war, he believed they did so in the hope 'that a new and a better and brighter chapter was about to open in the relations of Great Britain and Ireland'. In his plea for Home Rule, he cited the cases of Canada and Australia with their self-governance. In an entreaty to Sir Edward Carson and Ulster unionism to meet nationalists 'half-way', he stated:

> Are we to ever go on the lines of the old struggle of the Stuarts and the Battle of the Boyne? I believe in my soul and heart here today that I represent the instinct and the desire of the whole Catholic Irish race when I say there is nothing that they more passionately desire and long for than that there should be an end of this old struggle between North and South.[10]

Concluding with an appeal for reconciliation between Ulster unionism and nationalist Ireland, he stated:

> It cannot be beyond the wit of men to reconcile the differences of the past. In view of the extraordinary necessities of the time, it surely ought to be the duty of Ulstermen and Nationalists alike to meet each other, and to bring about in Ireland a state of affairs which will bring satisfaction from one end of the United States of America and the English speaking world to the other.[11]

When Willie Redmond sat down, according to T. P. O'Connor, 'you could hear the heavy breathing of the men around you, and I was told by one who was in the gallery that men around him

sobbed and wept unabashed'.[12] Stephen Gwynn later noted that
Redmond was 'an Irish soldier pleading with parliament for Ireland
in the name of Irish soldiers'. He wrote of Redmond's speech:

> There was not a cheer, not a murmur of agreement. As the speaker
> stood there in war-stained khaki, his hair showed grey, his face was
> seamed with lines, but there was in every word the freshness and
> simplicity of a nature that age had not touched. In the usual place in
> the upper bench beside his brother, he poured out his words with the
> flow and passion of a bird's song.[13]

The leader of the Irish Nationalist Party, John Redmond, believed
that the 'Prime Minister was playing into the hands of those in
Ireland who were seeking to destroy the constitutional movement.
If that occurred the Premier would have to rule Ireland by the
naked sword.'[14] John Redmond believed it was pointless for further
debate and, as a mark of protest in the delay on implementing
Home Rule, he led his party members out of the chamber. It was
for this bit of theatre that Michael believed the Irish Party deserved
'to get all the derision it deserves'. At 11 p.m. that night, David
Mason moved the adjournment of the debate. Mr King seconded
the motion and Mr Mason's motion was carried. The House rose
at 11.05 p.m.

A couple of days later, a reporter from *The Observer* interviewed
Willie Redmond, who told him:

> There was no real reason to despair of a settlement for the war has
> erased old hatreds. It has obliterated bitter prejudices because the
> bereavements and sorrows which have resulted from the war have
> been coming to the homes of all Ulster as well as the rest of the
> country.[15]

While all this political wrangling continued, back in Flanders there can be no doubt that more than one young Irish soldier was praying to get home while the war raged on.

12

Paddy's Day at Loker

On 14 March 1917 the 47th and 48th Brigades of the 16th (Irish) Division came out of the line for a rest and a refitting of worn kit and damaged equipment. At 6.10 p.m. they left Loker and marched about eight kilometres eastwards along the frontier to the French village of Berthen, where they arrived at about 9.30 p.m. Michael's battalion was replaced in the line by the 10th Royal Irish Rifles of the 36th (Ulster) Division.[1]

A letter awaited Michael on arrival at Berthen. It was from his young brother Bernard, who wished him a happy birthday. Bernard was nearly nine and put great effort into writing his letter to his brother at the front. Like most little boys who had a big brother, Bernard looked up to Michael and saw him as a hero for fighting in the war. Bernard addressed Michael as Ael and finished with lots of kisses:

Carrick Hill
March 15th 17

Dear Ael,

I hope you are quite well. We are all very well here. I'm writing you this little letter to wish you a very happy birthday and many happy returns of the day. I wish you were at home, it would be much nicer. Sister Rhubert let me off study tonight so that I could write to you, she also gave me this paper. She also gave me sixteen marbles. I like going to school very much. I got into second book this week. I am sending you a sketch of the Tanks. This is the first time I have written with ink. I hope you will excuse it. I am going to get up very early the morning you are coming home which I hope will be soon. I will now close again wishing you a happy birthday.

Your loving brother.
Bernard. xxxxxxxxxx good luck.[2]

Carrick Hill
march 15th 17

Dear Ael

I hope you are quite well. we are all very well here I m writing you this little letter to wish you a very happy birthday. and many happy returns of the day. I wish you were at home it would be much nicer. Sister Rhub_ert let me off study to night so that I could write to you she also gave me this paper. She also gave me

Ever since Queen Victoria had issued the instruction in 1900 that all her Irish regiments were to wear a sprig of Shamrock on 17 March, St Patrick's Day had held a special place in the hearts of all Irish servicemen. St Patrick's Day 1917 in Loker fell on a bright and sunny Saturday. From her home at Stillorgan, Monica Roberts had sent out some shamrock in her latest comforts parcels, and anyone who could get their hands on a bit of shamrock wore it with pride. Corporal Arthur Brennan of the 2nd Dublins wrote to Miss Roberts: 'Everyone that was free attended Mass this morning in remembrance of the great St Patrick. The 17th was well marked out by the great display of shamrock amongst the boys.'[3]

Apart from the obligatory church parades, St Patrick's Day for many of the Irishmen serving at the front meant a few hours of rest and an excuse for celebration. The 1st RDF were billeted near Ville-sur-Corbie, about fifteen kilometres north of Amiens in the Somme department of Picardy. After mass in the morning, football matches between the battalion's companies were played.

The 2nd Dublins were manning the reserve line at Kemmel. They received their mass at Siege Farm and a message from the former Dublin Fusilier Brigadier General H. W. Higginson DSO, commanding the 53rd Infantry Brigade. 'Best wishes to the Old Toughs for St Patrick's Day,' noted Higginson.[4] The 6th and 7th Dublins were still in Salonika fighting the Bulgarians. After mass, the 7th Dublins had a battalion sports day, which included bareback mule races for the men of the Transport Company.[5]

The 7th Leinsters were in billets in the neighbourhood of Flêtre. There is no specific mention of their activities on St Patrick's Day. However, the remainder of their time in March was spent training and with battalion and brigade sports days, which included events such as tug-of-wars, 100-yard and 200-yard racing, and officers wrestling on horseback.[6]

Some of the Ulstermen also honoured St Patrick. Corporal Joseph Glass of the 10th Royal Irish Rifles in the Ulster Division was away at a musketry training course on St Patrick's Day 1917. Whatever celebrations went on with his battalion back in Shankill Camp, one or two also remembered the saint at the Musketry School at Camiers. Corporal Glass claimed that St Patrick's Day was 'no change from any other' day except for the fact that there were a few 'tipsy in the afternoon'. It appears he was one of them, because when he got back to camp two hours after his pass had permitted, he was given a sharp reprimand.[7]

Michael's battalion held a church parade in the morning and a sports day in the afternoon. The following day he wrote home:

> 6th Royal Irish Regt.
> B.E.F.
> France.
>
> March 18th 1917.
>
> Dear Mater,
>
> I hope you are all quite well and have had a pleasant Patricks day. It was a lovely day here and the sun was quite warm. Everything passed off very quietly. Your parcel has not arrived yet. I got a small box of Shamrock from Nellie. The papers contained very sensational news yesterday about Russia. I am enclosing a cutting from the "Daily Sketch", perhaps you have seen it already. However it is one of the chief reasons why I want to get leave almost immediately. I don't know if I can manage it. We are out for a long rest. I feel very drowsy today as it is inclined to rain so I will ask you to excuse a brief note. Give my love to Auntie & all the young folk.
>
> Ever your fond son,
> Michael.[8]

6th Royal Irish Regt.
B.E.F.
France.
March 18th 1917.

Dear Mater.

I hope you are all
quite well and have had
a pleasant Patricks day.
It was a lovely day here and
the sun was quite warm.
Everything passed off very
quietly. Your parcel has
not arrived yet. I got a
small box of Shamrock from
Nellie. The papers contained
very sensational news yesterday
about Russia. I am enclosing
a cutting from the "Daily Sketch"
perhaps you have seen it

already. However it is one of the chief reasons why I want to get leave almost immediately. I don't know if I can manage it. We are out for a long rest. I feel very drowsy today as it is inclined to rain so I will ask you to excuse a brief note. Give my love to Auntie & all the young folk.

Ever Your fond son

Michael.

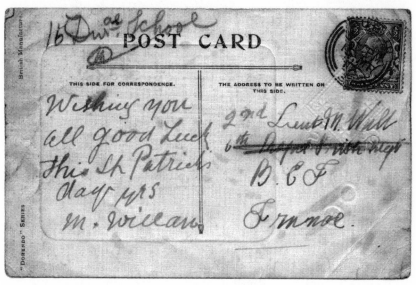

St Patrick's Day postcard from Michael's aunt, Margo Willan,
15 March 1917.

Over the next ten days or so, Michael's battalion remained at Berthen. Whilst there, a nice surprise came in the post – his Aunt Margo had sent him a St Patrick's Day postcard wishing him well. Apart from an inspection on 22 March by General Plumer, who was very satisfied with the turnout, the battalion diary recorded very little activity.[9] It was simply a time for rest, cleaning up a bit and preparing for the next tour of duty. The few days away from the line gave Michael time to reply to some letters he had received from home. It seems that by now that he had resigned himself to the reality that he would never get home on leave, not at least until the war was over.[10]

The weather was turning typically spring-like and the biting cold wind had eased. However, at least when the trenches were frozen, the ground was hard. With a thaw and rain, the mud and collapsing parapets returned. Damp underfoot conditions also brought back bouts of illness in the ranks. During March eighty-six men from the 8th Dublins were sent to hospital suffering from trench fever brought on by the damp conditions.[11] Captain Frankenburg of the 6th Royal Irish was sent to hospital suffering from German measles. He was soon followed by Captain Capel Desmond O'Brien Butler suffering from trench fever. He had been with the battalion for only a little over a month.[12]

It seems quite possible that Michael's commanding officer did not see him as a fighting soldier. Unlike some young officers who were sent on Lewis gun or grenade courses, Michael was sent on a cooking course, which suggests the kind of gentle personality he may have had. He was simply not cut out for combat soldiering. The thoughts of going back into the line this time frightened him so much that he asked his mother to pray for him:

6th Royal Irish Regt.

B.E.F.

France

March 30th 1917.

Dear Mother,

Many thanks for your very nice letter. My watch came alright thank you and it is going alright. We are going into the line tomorrow and perhaps an attack on the enemy. I cannot say where [*sic*] the latter is true or not. I want you all to pray for my safety through the whole thing in case it is on. I may be outstepping the limits of the censor when I say this but I can't help it. I am enclosing a cheque for the usual amount so hope you will get it alright. I hope Fr. Murphy is right. I am about fed up with the war. I wish it would end right now. The weather is still wet and cold here now. I went for a long ride yesterday about 16 miles & I got absolutely soaked. I was sent to see a cooking demonstration of how to make various dainty dishes for the men out of bully & biscuits. Well I must close now. Hope you are all quite well. Give my love to Auntie & all at home.

Ever your fond son,
Michael.[13]

The day after he wrote this frightened letter home to his mother, the battalion moved back to Loker, where they relieved the 2nd RDF in billets at Kemmel Shelters. The front line awaited them.

13

The Swallows Have Arrived

With snow still lingering on the ground, the cold winter of 1917 pushed long into spring. On a bitterly cold 1 April morning, Michael's battalion relieved the 2nd Royal Irish in the front line.[1] The section of trench they were responsible for was situated directly behind the Hong Kong section of the Chinese Wall known as Turnerstown Right. It was in an awful state. The German front-line trenches lay approximately 450 metres straight in front of them. About ninety metres further on was the wood Petit Bois.[2]

The war diary of the 6th Royal Irish recorded for 2 April 1917: 'Trenches. Wijtschate Sector, right sub-section. Sgt. Donnan wounded in the hand. 1 OR killed. Snowing heavily most of the 24 hours. 2nd Lt Blaney re-joined from grenade course.'[3] The one other rank noted as having been killed on 2 April was Private Thomas Donaghy, twenty-two, from 23 Connell Street, Limavady in County Derry. More than likely, he was hit by a sniper. He is buried in Kemmel Chateau Military Cemetery.[4]

At the beginning of April 1917 the 16th (Irish) and 36th (Ulster) Divisions' preparations for the attack on Wijtschate further intensified. To sharpen the men's combat skills and to gain intelligence about the German order of battle, raids were carried out on the German lines facing the Irish battalions. 'Raiding,' according to Nigel Dorrington, 'was an activity that arose almost entirely from the particular conditions created by the stalemate on the Western Front.'[5] The objective of raiding was to improve the morale of the troops, lower the morale of the Germans, secure identifications of German units in their front line, and mislead the Germans as to the location of impending offensives.[6] Moreover, raids were 'a dress rehearsal in miniature for large-scale attacks'.[7] They offered an opportunity to learn about battle planning, tactics, infantry–artillery co-operation, communications and combat skills.[8] However, because raids were carried out in German trenches, killing and maiming was close up. Consequently, raids were not popular amongst the men.

The majority of the men killed in the war were killed by artillery fire; a soldier seldom saw the men who were being killed on the other end of the shell fired. Therefore killing was less personal and easier on the mind. Raids, however, made killing personal; it was one on one. Although Michael Wall had been in the front line on many occasions and faced the hazards associated with it, a trench raid was something totally different. He had never taken part in one. However, rumours of impending raids were spreading through the battalion as they returned to the line. No wonder he was frightened going back this time.

The rumours proved to be correct. With a window in the cold weather, in the half-light just before dawn on 5 April, the 6th Royal Irish carried out a raid on the German trenches. Two days before the raid, 'X' Day as the battalion diarist noted, the 16th Division's artillery had begun a barrage on the German trenches against which the raid took place. The Germans, in turn, replied with a very accurate barrage and hit Rossignol Road just behind the battalion's position at Turnerstown Right. Fearing the raid was a full-scale attack, German miners blew two counter-mine explosions known as camouflets near the Spanbroekmolen mine that faced the Ulster Division. The camouflets caused some damage to the gallery, but not enough to abandon the mine; it was made good soon after.[9]

The raid was a success, and the Royal Irish took forty-one

German prisoners from the 4th Grenadier Regiment from whom 'inestimable information was gained'.[10] The 4th Grenadier Regiment was a unit of the 2nd (East Prussian) Division, which was responsible for the German line from St Eloi in the north to Peckham House in the south.[11] However, the raid was not all plain sailing. On the positive side, along with taking prisoners, the raid was good practice for the men to attack behind a creeping barrage and, no doubt, lessons were learned that would be used in the attack on Wijtschate. On the negative side, however, the battalion suffered many casualties. Although the battalion diary stated that six men of other ranks were killed in the raid, the Commonwealth War Graves Commission records that eleven men of the 6th Royal Irish Regiment were killed in action and two died of wounds on the day of the raid. Two more died the next day, bringing the total to fifteen. The battalion diarist noted that seven other ranks were missing and sixty-six were wounded.

Captain John Edward Day, aged twenty-two, from Newport, County Tipperary, was taken back to Bailleul, where he died of his wounds. His father was a Waterford clergyman, the Very Rev. Maurice Day, who served at Culloden in Bray, County Wicklow. The last time Captain Day saw his family was at Christmas 1916 when home on leave. He had two brothers, one of whom, Lieutenant M. C. Day, had been killed on 3 November 1914 while serving with the Indian Army, 13th Rajputs (The Shekhawati Regiment), in East Africa.[12] On 7 April members of the battalion attended Edward's funeral. He was buried at the British Commonwealth War Graves Cemetery at Bailleul Communal Cemetery Extension.[13] Badly wounded in the same raid was a former student of Castleknock College, Captain Richard (Dick) Burke, aged twenty-five, from Dingle in County Kerry, who had served with the 3rd Royal Irish back in Dublin during the Easter Rising.[14]

On 6 April Michael's battalion was relieved by the 6th Connaught Rangers. It went into Brigade Support at Butterfly Farm. General Hickie and General Pereira visited the battalion to congratulate the men on the raid. The next day, the men washed the mud – and in some cases the blood – from their boots and uniform. They were provided with baths at the Butterfly Farm billets. Afterwards they attended the funeral of Captain Day at Bailleul.[15]

In many regimental war diaries, the loss of men of other ranks was typically noted simply as, for example, 'Killed: 10 OR'. It is a pity these men were reduced by the War Office simply to a nameless number. After all those forgotten years, it would now seem the decent thing to give the men of the 6th Royal Irish who died in this raid their names and restore to them their dignity as human beings, so they are no longer nameless entries on a list. Among those killed were Private Thomas Flood, twenty-five, and Private William Smitheram, thirty, both from St Mary's, Kilkenny. Private Smitheram's body was never found. His name is on panel thirty-three of the Menin Gate in Ypres. Private Michael Casey, thirty-two, and Private Martin Regan, twenty, the youngest casualty of the raid, both came from Cahir in County Tipperary. Acting Lance Sergeant Leonard Carolan was born in Portsmouth, although both his parents, Paddy and Mary Carolan, were Irish. At the time of Paddy's death, they lived at No. 2 New Cottages, Ballysax, County Kildare. Leonard had formerly been a Dublin Fusilier and was twenty-one.[16]

Looking at the list of the men who died with the battalion, it would be reasonable to suggest that the 6th Royal Irish Regiment was a typical 'pals battalion' – a battalion composed of men who enlisted together as pals from communities, villages, workplaces or sports and social clubs. Evidence for this comes from the fact that 'C' Company of the battalion was composed mainly of Derry

National Volunteers who enlisted en bloc, and 'D' Company's men were mainly Guernsey Militia Volunteers. Moreover, two sets of neighbours were casualties of the raid.

From his billet in Butterfly Farm, Michael wrote excitedly to his mother, telling her about the action in which his battalion had taken part, although there is no evidence to suggest Michael himself took part. He was very proud of his battalion, which perhaps is evidence that these raids did in fact boost some men's morale. It seems Charlie Adams had returned to his regiment too. All good news.

> 6th Royal Irish Regt.
> B.E.F.
> France
>
> April 7th 1917
>
> Dear Mother,
>
> Just a few lines to let you know that I am quite alright. We raided the Huns the other night and it was a great success. Our artillery knocked lumps off their trenches and we got a whole bundle of souvenirs. I have quite a number myself. Our men are the best fellas to be found anywhere and they were in great spirits going "over the top". The poor old Huns threw up their hands immediately. We have had congratulations from generals and all the Regiments in the Brigade. I think we could have got through to Berlin if we had the men. ... We are having horrible wet here now, wet and cold as can be. Some parts of the trenches are awful and the water reaches your knees. However I think the war will soon be over now if all the Germans are like we found them the other night. I also had a letter from Kathleen Ward and she says Charlie is back again with his Coy. ... I know this is awful writing

but I am wet and cold so I know you will excuse it. I know you will all have a very pleasant Easter …

Ever your fond son
Michael.[17]

6th Royal Irish Regt
B.C.F.
France
April 9th 1917

Dear Mother,
Just a few lines to let you know that I am quite alright. We raided the Huns the other night and it was a great success. Our Artillery knocked lumps off their trenches and we got a whole bundle of souvenirs. I have quite a number myself. Our men are the best fellows to be found anywhere and they were in great spirits going over the top. The poor old Huns threw up their hands immediately. We have had congratulations from Generals and all the Regiments in the Brigade. I think we could have got through to Berlin if we had the men. I got a parcel the other day, I think it was Thursday

but I don't know who sent it. It came from the stores. I had a letter from Cyril and another from Agatha and she said it did not rain on the day of the concert. Well that must have been because I was away. We are having horrible wet here now, wet and cold as can be. Some parts of the trenches are awful and the water reaches your knees. However I think the war will soon be over now if all the Germans are like we found them the other night. I also had a letter from Kathleen Ward and she says Charlie is back again with his Coy. I had a very nice card from Mrs. Crawford but I don't know her address so I can't answer till I get it. Could you send it on. I know this is awful writing but I am wet and cold so I know you will excuse it. I know you will all have a very pleasant Easter at

Easter Sunday 1917 fell on 8 April and the battalion held a memorial service for Captain Day in Bailleul.[18] It would be nice to think the men also prayed for their other comrades who died following the raid. Always thinking of him, Michael's mother had

189

written to him on 3 April and enclosed some blessed palm for Easter. She had several masses said for his safety and even got the Lord Abbot to pray for him.

Carrick Hill
Malahide
3rd–4–17

My dearest,

I received your ever welcome letter also Bernards he was delighted to get a letter all to himself he would have written to you for Easter & feels very sorry [he has] not been able to do so he is in bed with his old complaint for the past week but is a little better to-day. I hope you are keeping well in spite of all this dreadful weather, it must be very severe in France as we are having very heavy snow storms & hail also east wind that would skin the rats. I had Holy Mass for your intention & had three said some time ago for your safety. I had a letter from the Lord Abbot this morning, he said the community were praying for you. I trust the Lord will hear our prayers in this dreadful time of war. My dear do not bother about long letters as I know you have very little time for writing. I hope you have got your watch by this. I sent you a parcel from the stores for Easter on Friday 30th. You will excuse this short note as I am off to town.

Will write you soon. Wishing you a very Happy Easter.

Your loving Mother.
Theresa Wall.

PS (I enclose a little blessed Palm).[19]

Carrick Hill
Malahide
3rd-4-17

My dearest.
I received your ever welcome
letter also Bernards he was delighted
to get a letter all to himself he would
have written to you for Easter & feels very
sorry not been able to do so he is in bed
with his old complaint for the post week
but is a little better to-day. I hope you are
keeping well, in spite of all this dreadful
weather it must be very severe in France
as we are having very heavy snow storms
& hail also east wind that would skin the
rats. I had Holy Mass for your intention &
had three said some time ago for your
safety. I had a letter from the Lord Abbot
this morning he said the community were
praying for you. I trust the Lord will

In high spirits, Michael's battalion returned to the line facing
Wijtschate on 11 April, relieving the 6th Connaught Rangers.
Nothing very exciting happened on this four-day tour of front-
line duty. Most of the time the battalion worked on cutting gaps
in the German wire defences for raiding parties to get through.
This was extremely dangerous work and was mostly carried out at

night. One of Michael's brother officers, Second Lieutenant Barry, fell victim to the wire-cutting work.

Young Bernard wrote to Michael on the day he returned to the line. It must have been heartbreaking for Michael, perhaps sitting alone in a cold and damp dugout, to read Bernard's letter, the contents of which would have reminded him so much of the home he could not get to. Strangely for mid-April, snow was still on the ground at Carrick Hill:

> Carrick Hill
> 11th April 1917
>
> My Dear Ael,
>
> I was very pleased to receive your very welcome letter, I would have written long before this but I have been ill for some time. I am quite well now and go back to school on Monday.
>
> The weather is very cold, there is snow every day and the rain barrels are full of ice. I hope you are having better weather in France. Cyril told me you had a dog named Butcher, how I wish I could be with you and be your little mascot.
>
> We have very little music since you went away. Mother said she will take me to the pictures when you come home, I hope that won't be long. This old war is too long.
>
> I got a top and can flog it very well. Cyril got two tops also.
>
> Sheps and Toby eat [sic] all the goose eggs that were in the nest. We have three hens to hatch, one eat five of the eggs [sic], there is another hen hatching ducks. When you come home you will find a great number of ducks and chickens, there are about forty lambs. All the men that were from Brooks Thomas are finished, the carpenter mended my wheel barrow.
>
> Cyril made a plot and I am going to mind it while he is away. I have got seven birds' nests but if the weather does not get better

I am afraid I will not find any more. Cyril and I found an Owl in the big haggard, we are getting it stuffed. Doyle's cat has four kittens, we are getting two of them. I will now close as I have no more news to tell you. Hoping you are very well with much love from your loving brother.

Bernard xxxxxxxxxx[20]

Carrick Hill
11th April 1917

My dear Ael
    I was very pleased to receive your very welcome letter, I would have written long before this but I have been ill for some time. I am quite well now and go back to school on monday.
    The weather is very cold there is snow every day and the rain barrels are full of ice. I hope you are having better weather in France. Cyril told me you had a dog named Butcher, how I wish I could be with you and be your little Mascot.
    We have very little music since you went away. Mother said she will take me to the pictures when you come home I hope that wont be long. This Old war is too long
    I got a top and can flog it very well Cyril got two tops also.

It was roughly a year since the rebellion in Dublin had taken place, but it seems debate in the trenches about the Rising hadn't gone away. Michael's feelings towards the Sinn Féiners hadn't gone away either. It was at this time that he suggested that a few frosty nights on the fire step would 'cool their ardour'.

6th Royal Irish Regt.

B.E.F.

France

April 14th 1917

Dear Mother,

Very many thanks for your two letters recently received. The palm was very nice as these Belgian and French people do not use palm but a sort of box wood. We are in the trenches now and we have had some awful weather. One night it snowed very hard while I was on duty in the front line and I have no hesitation in saying that it was the worst time I ever put in anywhere. The men felt it too. What do you think of our latest successes. We feel in great spirits over it and we worry the old Hun with everything we can. I feel quite confident that that [*sic*] the war will be over soon and that I shall see you all again shortly. I have very little time for writing now until I come out and I have still to answer Cyril's and a few more. I really do not know where to start ... Those Sinn Feiners should be sent out here to do a few nights on the fire step, I will guarantee it to cool their ardour. The weather is still cold but it has been dry for the last two days. I got all the parcels thank you. No, I do not get any letters other than your own. If you could send out some small tea cakes they would be better than anything else, but for heaven's sake don't send any eggs as we can get any amount of them here. How are all the crops getting on. Are there any foals yet? I must write to Auntie as soon as I can get time. Give my love to all at home.

Your fond son,
Michael.[21]

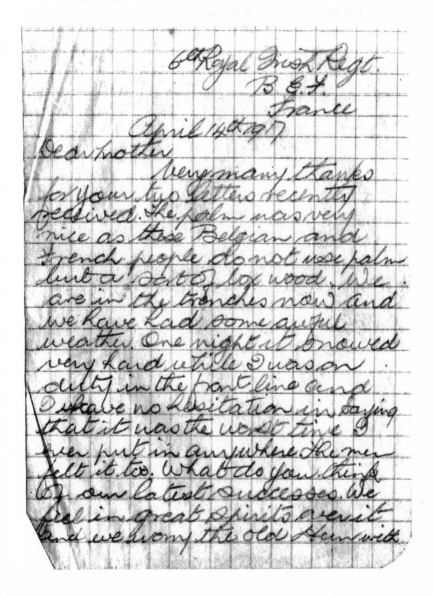

everything we can, I feel quite
confident that that the war will
be over soon and that I shall
see you all again shortly. I
have very little time for writing
now until I come out and
I have still to answer Cryals
and a few more. I really do
not know where to start it. I
had a letter from Jamie Clifford
a few days ago. Louis Carter
must feel fed up at having
to wait so long. Those Sinn Feiners
should be sent out here to do
a few nights on the fire step, I
will guarantee it to cool
their ardour. The weather is
still cold but it has been dry
for the last two days. I got all
the parcels thank you, so I do not
get any letters other than your own.
If you could send out some small
flat cakes they would be better
than anything else. Ask for Scones

Michael wrote home again a week later:

> 6th Royal Irish Regt.
> B.E.F.
> France.
>
> April 20th 1917.
>
> Dear Mother,
>
> Again we are out of the trenches for another rest and thank goodness the weather has got a little warmer and drier. But the noise of our guns pounding away at the old Boche [*sic*] is deafening. The "old push" goes on merrily from day to day and if the weather keeps dry there will be a great many more Germans who will not go back to the Fatherland. Nearly everything we put standing on the table is knocked down by the vibration. However I have got so used to it that it does not prevent me sleeping at night. I got the "Weekly Irish Times" that Joseph sent quite safe. There was not much news in it. I also got Bernard's letter. I forgot whether I mentioned it in my last letter or not. I am sure everybody is talking about the new success we have had and various assumptions being pressed forward as to when the war will be over. Have you heard anything about Jack Fletcher lately? I know there must be a great many anxious parents about relatives at home now especially when such stupendous moves are afoot. When are we going to get those 250,000 men that are eligible in Ireland. I shot two more Bosche last tour in the trenches. By Jove war would be child's play if there were no shells. Being under shell fire is no picnic I assure you because you are always asking yourself "where is the next one going to go." I know when I get home and anything makes a hissing noise near me I will be inclined to "duck" … When you see the postman arriving this morning you will know he has a longer letter than usual.

Good bye for the present and give my love to Auntie and all at home.

Ever your fond son,
Michael.[22]

6th Royal Irish Regt.
B.E.F.
France.
April 30th 1917.

Dear Mother

Again we are out of the trenches for another rest and thank goodness the weather has got a little warmer and drier. But the noise of our guns pounding away at the old Boche is deafening. The "old push" goes on merrily from day to day and if the weather keeps dry there will be a great many more Germans who will not go back to the Fatherland. Nearly everything we

Michael's optimistic hope of getting those 250,000 Irish recruits was never going to be realised. By late April 1917 recruitment in Ireland had fallen off drastically. During the six-month period between August 1915 and February 1916 recruitment in Ireland was 19,801. Between February 1916 and August 1916 it had fallen to 9,323.[23] No doubt the aftermath of the Easter Rising had a negative effect on recruitment.

However, for Michael and the men who were with him, the news in the Irish papers wasn't all bad. After all, there was the 'new success' that Michael wrote about, which was in fact the costly capture of Vimy Ridge on 9–10 April by Canadian and Moroccan troops during the Battle of Arras. The Irish papers were full of the news about the advance at Arras. *The Cork Examiner* reported 'British Great Offensive, Gigantic Battle'; on the same day 'Brilliant Drive by the British, 5,800 prisoners' appeared in the *Irish Independent*.[24] The next day, the latter paper practically doubled its estimate of German prisoners taken: 'Big drive by the British. Over 11,000 prisoners.'[25]

Over the coming few weeks, the 6th Royal Irish would be out of the line at training. The newspapers back home were still talking Irish politics, but at least the winter of 1916–1917 at last began to show signs of fading away. April ended in relative calm for Michael and his battalion. Out of harm's way, training, games of football and the divisional band playing at Clare Camp – about two-and-a-half kilometres north of Bailleul – kept their spirits up.[26] Furthermore, the weather was getting warmer and, amidst the noise and desolation on the Western Front, Michael wrote to say the swallows had arrived.[27]

His last letter of April 1917 was to his aunt. In it he referred to many men he knew from home who were serving in France or elsewhere in the war. It may seem a trivial point, but it is interesting nonetheless to note the number of men from the Portmarnock/Malahide area of north County Dublin who were in the forces, in one way or another. They included Bertie Christie, Louis Carter, Tom Perkins, Charlie Adams, Tommy Hughes, Charles Marchant and many more mentioned in previous letters. This is a simple example of how this terrible war in Europe had penetrated down to a small rural community in Ireland.

14

Training and Away from the Guns for a While

The routine trench life that the Irish regiments facing Wijtschate had experienced up to now was over. In fact, from the middle of March to the middle of May, the buzzword around the 16th and 36th Divisions' headquarters was training. Serious preparation had begun for the upcoming offensive on the Messines Ridge.

The guiding principles for General Plumer's staff were the 'Three Ts': Trust, Thoroughness and Training.[1] To facilitate training for the planned attack on Wijtschate in June, a brigade rotational operational scheme was established whereby one brigade in the division was in support, one in the line and one at training in the 2nd Army training area at villages around the town of St Omer. Having been replaced in the line by a battalion from a relieving brigade, battalions scheduled for training would first carry out company-size and specialised unit training around Kemmel, Loker, Dranouter or Bailleul, before moving to brigade-size training in villages near St Omer. Over two months or so, every brigade in both divisions would spend an average of two to three weeks at the 2nd Army training camps, carrying out brigade-size training exercises.

One of the first brigades of the 16th (Irish) Division to come out of the line for brigade training was the 48th Brigade, which contained the 2nd, 8th and 9th RDF Battalions and 7th Royal Irish Rifles. They came out of the line on 19 March and were replaced by the 49th Brigade. The Dublins spent the next two weeks in Loker carrying out company tactical training and platoon-size training as Lewis gunners and bombers.[2] The tactical lessons learned from the Somme were now on the training curriculum.

At the end of their company training around Loker or Dranouter, there was time off for a bit of relaxation before they marched to St Omer. Most battalions played football matches, and the 16th Division band was on hand to cheer things up a bit around Loker too. The day before the three Dublin Fusilier battalions left Loker for St Omer, which was 'on the Saturday before Palm Sunday', that is 31 March 1917, their officers played a rugby match against the 16th Divisional Train (Transport). The match was played at the Curragh Camp. Just for the record, the Dubs were beaten by thirteen points to nine.[3] Over at Clare Camp, the 6th Royal Irish played a soccer match against the RFC. The Royal Irish won by two goals to one.[4]

Led by their pipes and drums, the 48th Brigade marched out of Loker on 31 March 1917 for their brigade training. At the end of the column, like some regimental trophy of war on display, came their German prisoners.[5] One can only assume these prisoners were used as labourers and carrying parties. Because of losses and the fall off in recruits, many of the battalions were at roughly half their normal strength. For example, the 8th Dublins had thirty officers and 573 men when they marched off from Loker to Zouafques, a little village about eighteen kilometres north-west of St Omer.[6] Nonetheless the men's spirits were high on leaving the war zone behind them for a while. On the day the Dubs marched out of Loker, Private George Soper, who had read in the newspapers that the Yanks were coming, wrote to Monica Roberts:

I thought we were going to see America in along with us according to the papers, but they have changed their minds and sent a note. Again, what a pity there is not a paper shortage in America. I wonder what they would do for notes then. Well, we can carry on without them.[7]

With several stops along the way in Bailleul, Strazeele and Hazebrouck, it took the column three days to march the seventy-five kilometre journey to the 2nd Army training area around St Omer.[8] Fr Willie Doyle SJ, who accompanied the Dubs, described the pace as being 'slow' and 'no joke'.[9] The first day the men marched thirty kilometres with a heavy rifle and full pack. Fr Doyle's destination was the village of Nordausques, some fourteen kilometres north-west of St Omer. On Sundays, Fr Doyle served mass and gave benediction in the church at Nordausques. He became friendly with the village curate.[10] The 48th Brigade was billeted in farmhouses around the villages of Nordausques and Zouafques.[11]

Large training areas were laid out where each battalion could conduct dummy attacks on its particular objective of the German line. Replicas of the German trench system at Wijtschate were constructed so attacking units would be familiar with what they might face on the day of the attack. German pillboxes and machine-gun positions were marked with location boards and flags of different colours.[12] According to Fr Doyle, the Dubs' morning training sessions were 'given up to various exercises, one of which was the storming of a dummy German trench to the accompaniment of fearful, blood-curdling yells, enough to terrify the bravest enemy'. The afternoon was 'spent at football and athletics sports'.[13]

The curriculum for all infantry battalions training around St Omer was in accordance with the training doctrine outlined in

Stationery Service training manuals, many of which were issued following the Somme campaign of 1916.[14] Improved cohesion between infantry units of neighbouring brigades and divisions in the line of attack, and between infantry and artillery, was a particular lesson learned from the Somme campaign; the key to the success of this cohesion was good communications. Consequently, communication systems were practised in both these modes of attack at brigade-size training grounds around St Omer.

The tactical dispositions or tactical attack formations of the infantry troops in training were identical to those that would be used in the battle to take Wijtschate, even to the exact distance of the objectives. To achieve harmony and understanding between flanking or adjacent infantry units on either side along the line of the infantry attack, officers from flanking battalions attended each other's training exercises at the 2nd Army training camp. For example, officers from the 9th Royal Welsh Fusiliers – which would be the flanking battalion of the 19th (Western) Division – attended training exercises of the 7th Royal Inniskilling Fusiliers, their flanking battalion in the 16th (Irish) Division. In late May, during a practice attack carried out by the 47th Brigade at Alquines, the GOC of the 109th Brigade, Brigadier General A. St Q. Ricardo, accompanied General Pereira, GOC 47th Brigade.[15] These two Irish brigades would attack Wijtschate side by side.

To achieve cohesion between attacking infantry and artillery batteries, Captain O'Brien Butler of the 6th Royal Irish, for example, went to A/180th Battery of the RFA to review and appraise the demonstration of the creeping barrage, which was simulated by a line of flag-waving soldiers advancing to the accompaniment of side-drummers. Developed during the Somme campaign by British and German artillery, the creeping or lifting barrage was an artillery-barrage tactic used whereby the area being hit by artillery shells would, at specific times, be moved forward to a new target area – typically one hundred metres beyond the previous target area – behind which the infantry would advance. In essence it was a protective curtain of shellfire for the advancing soldiers. These creeping barrages in training were simulated by flags set across the lines of attack.[16] When the artillery attack on Wijtschate came, it would be Captain O'Brien Butler's men who would be behind, and in some cases under, this creeping barrage, when it would no longer be a training exercise.[17]

Field companies of engineers also trained with infantry battalions in the supervision of consolidating SPs when taken. For example, under the supervision of the 157th Field Company of the Royal Engineers, assault sections from Michael's 6th Royal Irish practised consolidating a captured German SP.[18]

Finally, in keeping with Plumer's philosophy on thoroughness, back near Kemmel models of the Messines Ridge were provided for officers to study. On the slopes of Scherpenberg Hill, between Loker and De Klijte, an elaborate model of Messines Ridge – with all its trenches, forts, roads and woods – was constructed by the Corps of Engineers attached to 9th Corps. It was surrounded by a wooden gallery and trench boardwalks, so that at least a company of men could examine it at one time.[19] It was regularly updated as new German trenches were spotted by aeroplanes or old ones were smashed by the artillery.

Aerial reconnaissance was particularly important in gaining up-to-date information, but was not without its cost. On 5 May a British aeroplane was shot down over the Irish front line. The plane came down in the section of line occupied by Michael's battalion.[20] Despite the odd setback, the RFC supplied 300 aircraft, which outnumbered their German counterparts by two to one. The 53rd Squadron, which had a battle strength of twenty-one aircraft and was stationed at Bailleul, was attached to 9th Corps and patrolled the skies over the Irish lines.[21] In addition, further observation of the German lines was obtained from the 2nd Kite Balloon Wing of the RFC, which flew eight captive balloons at 2,500 metres high from between 2,700 metres and 4,500 metres behind the front line.[22] Just outside Bailleul, the British and Germans each had their own small grassy aerodrome where their balloons looked out over no man's land 'spotting for their respective artilleries'.[23]

At the end of all the training exercises, training conferences to analyse the exercise were held at which suggested improvements were made. Relevant adjustments were then made to the emerging plan.[24]

Occasionally, terrible accidents occurred during the training exercises. In mid-February, for example, Sergeant Stephen Francis Ward, an instructor attached to the 2nd Dublins, was burned to death at the 16th Division's training school at Saint-Jans-Cappel. The circumstances of his death are not recorded. He was given a military funeral and buried after mass on Sunday 18 February in the Loker churchyard. Sergeant Ward was thirty-one when he died. He was born in Dublin but lived in Springburn in Glasgow, where he enlisted. It is possible that he and Sergeant Bob Downie VC would have known each other.[25]

Another unfortunate incident occurred during the 47th Brigade training exercise at Alquines in late May. A local civilian was shot dead by a soldier from Michael's battalion. Interestingly, Michael never referred to it in any of his subsequent letters home. The soldier who committed the act was a Private Kenny. Amid great scenes of emotion from the townspeople, Kenny was identified by the daughter of the man shot.[26] The story behind the death of this local man is not recorded in the battalion diary. However, on 14 June 1918, a Private J. Kenny of the 6th Royal Irish was tried at a field general court martial for murder. He was deemed to be insane and no sentence was passed.[27] The trial was held a little over a year after the tragic death of the local man. It may have been that the military court was waiting to see if Private Kenny's mental state would improve so that he could stand trial.

Towards the end of their brigade training at Nordausques, the Dublin Fusiliers battalions held their sports days. These consisted of six-mile route marches, football matches and cross-country races for the 'good of the men's health and morale'.[28] The 8th Dublins seemed to have a good football team. In the final of the brigade competition, they beat the Royal Irish Rifles by two goals to nil.[29] Later they held an intercompany cross-country running competition. Private James Hughes from 'C' Company was the first runner home. Despite his obvious level of fitness and cross-country running abilities, this young man would die of wounds on 7 August 1917 near Frezenberg Ridge.[30]

While brigades of the 16th (Irish) and 36th (Ulster) Divisions were at training, back at the front and support lines, battalions from both Irish divisions worked long hours improving the defensive infrastructure of the lines. They strengthened and constructed shell-proof dugouts to withstand the expected artillery duels; dug trenches for the network of telephone cables; dug and widened communication trenches; laid light railways; built and stocked casualty-clearing stations for the wounded; and stocked dumps with ammunition and stores. Officers closely studied aerial photographs and intelligence reports gathered through the aerial reconnaissance carried out by the RFC.[31] The build-up impressed Michael. In a brief note home he noted to his mother, 'By Jove there are shells here for old Fritz.'[32]

Two days later he wrote home again:

6th Royal Irish Regt.

B.E.F.

France

May 4th 1917

Dear Mother

I hope you got my last letter alright as it had a cheque enclosed. I had a letter from Cyril and a paper from Joseph. The weather out here is extremely hot at present and if you only stir you feel as if you were doing a devil of a lot of work. I see in the paper that they propose keeping the wounded in France now so a "blighty" is not much use. I will soon have to go and see the dentist as my teeth have got into a rather bad state and give me a rotten time, in fact sometimes I can't take the slightest interest in my work, but on the other hand one has to report sick for anything like that and I don't like it as it is not, as it were, playing the game. I was at a very good sports this afternoon given by the R.E. [Royal Engineers]. The programme of events is enclosed. We go into the line tomorrow and I must close now. Give my love to all at home.

Your fond son
Michael.[33]

Michael's battalion, along with the other battalions of the 47th Brigade, came out of the line for their company training on 25 April and moved into 'very poor accommodation' at Clare Camp.[34] On 5 May they returned to the line, where they relieved the 9th RDF, who had returned to their billets at Kemmel Shelters from their brigade training at St Omer. There was definitely no chance now of his returning home, even if he received a 'Blighty'.[35] Wounded men were now being kept in hospitals in France. One

> 6th Royal Irish Regt.
> B.E.F
> France
> May 4th 1917
>
> Dear Mother
>
> I hope you got my last letter alright as it had a cheque enclosed. I had a letter from Cyril and a paper from Joseph. The weather out here is extremely hot at present and if you only stir you feel as if you were doing a devil of a lot of work. I see in the paper that they propose keeping the wounded in France now so a "blighty" is not much use. I will soon have to go and

must admire Michael's sense of honesty and commitment, which says something about the man's character. Despite his toothaches, he didn't want to report sick. He felt if he did so at this important time he would not be 'playing the game'.

The first couple of days back in the line for Michael were noisy enough. German gunners targeted British rear areas, dumps, roads and camps, which they knew were troop-concentration areas. They also knew that this massing of material around the western regions of the Wijtschate–Messines Ridge was some form of build-up for an eventual attack. The artillery duels began in earnest on 1 May and continued on and off with increasing intensity over the next month. Although the British had an overwhelming superiority in artillery in the sector, when artillery duels did open up, German retaliation was at times fierce and accurate. So too was that of the British. On Monday 7 May the battalion diarist of the 6th Royal Irish noted: 'In punishment for hostile shelling of back areas, all the 2nd Army guns and Howitzers bombarded the enemy lines for five minutes, firing at a rapid rate.'[36]

Kemmel Hill, which overlooked the Germans in Wijtschate, was, according to Frank Laird, 'honeycombed with gun positions and underground galleries'.[37] During the previous few weeks the work of hiding these artillery pieces was carried out under the supervision of Captain J. O'Sullivan, Royal Engineers. On completion, elaborate green camouflage netting was draped over the guns. In that great old Irish tradition of turning tragedy into comic verse, the image of this green netting presented some Irish minstrels in Flanders with the subject matter for a song, sung to the tune of 'The Wearing of the Green':

Oh! Paddy dear an' have you heard the news that's goin' round?
Our guns are hid, just where we're bid, by diggin' underground.
A camouflage so fine and large, prevents their bein' seen,
For they're hangin' nets, with trimmin' up, a wearing of the green.

I met with Gen'ral Hickie, and I took him by the hand,
And I said, 'How's our artillery?' 'Sure,' said he, 'they're doin' grand.'
With guns in pits, all makin' hits, with shell – dumps in between,
Get fine disguise, from pryin' eyes, by wearing of the green.

They love the ould Division in the land the boys come from,

And they're proud of what the boys have done at Loos and on the
Somme.

So if by chance we all advance to Whitesheet and Messines,

They'll learn our guns that strafed the Huns were wearing of the
green.[38]

On Monday 7 May, the day the entire 2nd Army artillery hit back at their German counterparts, Field Marshal Haig communicated the satisfactory results of the Paris Conference to his army commanders in the field and indicated what the future roles of their armies would be.[39] The attack on the Wijtschate–Messines Ridge would begin in one month, to the day.[40]

Back at the coal face, the quest to gain local intelligence on the German order of battle in Wijtschate intensified as the day of the attack drew closer. On the night of 9/10 May a 'small enterprise' was carried out by Michael's battalion when Second Lieutenant Dunne and Second Lieutenant Turner, with twenty-five other ranks, led a raid on the German lines in the Petit Bois salient. Dunne and Turner's men entered the German trenches and took one prisoner alive from the 33rd Infantry Regiment, 2nd Division. They killed three others.[41] All the raiders were accounted for after the raid; however, two men later died from wounds they received, one of whom was Lance Corporal William Doherty from Tuighboyne, County Donegal.[42] The next day they were relieved in the line by the 2nd Royal Irish Regiment. Lieutenant Dunne was later awarded the Military Cross for his work during the raid.[43] Young officers like Dunne and Turner were groomed and tested for their leadership and combat skills. Men like Michael lacked such skills and consequently took no part in raids.

Following this raid, Michael's battalion came out of the line for about two weeks.[44] It was their turn now to head over to the brigade training grounds around St Omer.[45] While on the march, Michael had the job of bringing up the rear and gathering the stragglers. They met Portuguese troops as they marched through Wizernes.[46] In an act of defiance, the Connaught Rangers made a large green flag with a yellowish harp, but without the crown above it that was part of their usual emblem, which they carried on the march and hung over their billets.[47]

On 12 May, Michael wrote home:

> 6th Royal Irish Regt.
> B.E.F.
> France
>
> May 12th 1917.
>
> Dear Mother,
>
> Many thanks for yours of the 6th inst. ... I don't think you are quite right when you say the birds ought not to sing. I think they ought to, it makes us forget sometimes. The other morning two cuckoos were having a conversation – one behind our line and the other behind the Hun's line. I heard some Huns fighting like a lot of cats behind their line. Well I hope the dentist will make a good job all right. My teeth are not very good now. I must close now as the post is going out. Love to all at home.
>
> Your fond son
> Michael.[48]

Michael's mother must have suggested to him that the birds shouldn't sing in such a place. One must wonder why. Perhaps she saw the war as being linked to the destruction of nature and therefore not a place for the beauty of birdsong. She was right.

Michael's brigade training came to an end on Saturday 26 May. At 8 a.m. the next day – which incidentally was Whit Sunday – the men went to mass. The 6th Connaught Rangers had mass in an orchard, where the padre preached a short sermon in the course of which he invited the men to join in the singing and not to be embarrassed or ashamed of men on either side hearing them. 'God didn't mind if we could sing in tune or not,' he reckoned. Moreover, no matter how bad the Connaught Rangers were at singing, nobody, in his opinion, could surpass the Munsters for their singing. They were simply awful.[49]

Michael must have dreaded going back to the line. This time it was going to be very different. The attack on Wijtschate was getting nearer and he knew it. He sent some of his kit home. Perhaps, in some odd way, doing so gave him a belief that at least some part of him was getting out of this war and going home.

15

'We'll hold Derry's Walls' – Relations between the Irish Divisions in Flanders

The order of battle set out by 9th Corps for the attack on Wijtschate would pitch the two infantry divisions from Ireland side by side on the day. In reality this was the closest the army came to the formation of an 'Irish Corps' containing all the Irish divisions, 'something that John Redmond had lobbied for in the early part of the war but was denied by Kitchener'.[1] The significance of this was not lost on nationalist politicians. Earlier in May an article written by Major Willie Redmond had appeared in *Irish Life*. The theme of the article was Redmond's pet subject: Irish unity in Flanders and Ireland:

> If the people of Ireland, North and South, could but see the Irish troops from North and South in the field, what a splendid thing it would be and how much good it would do ... For the two Irish Divisions – undivided in their splendid devotion to the cause they believed to be just – there will ever be gratitude and honour in Ireland, no matter what may be said to the contrary. It will, indeed, be a happy event if a sense of brotherhood and mutual forbearance should spread in Ireland, leading at long last to concord and liberty in the Empire. For this there are few Irishmen who do not yearn, and for this there are a few things that have done more than the calling into being, side by side, of the Irish Divisions.[2]

Soon after his final return to the front, Willie Redmond wrote to a friend in Ireland on the same theme:

> I wish I had time to write you all I have seen out here. My men are splendid and are pulling famously with the Ulster men. Would to God we could bring this spirit back with us to Ireland. I shall never regret I have been out here.[3]

Irish newspapers and others wrote in agreement with Redmond's sentiments. The mainly unionist *Irish Times* noted the coming attack on Wijtschate, stating that a 'very pleasing feature of the battle is the fact that the Ulster regiments are fighting in the most friendly rivalry side by side with southern Irish battalions'.[4] The Great War historian Liddell Hart wrote that the two divisions fighting side by side was 'a feat of symbolic significance'.[5]

The actual interface of the two divisions for the attack on Wijtschate would come along the divisional boundary at a point along Suicide Road. On one side was a battalion that had a component of Derry nationalists, that is the 6th Royal Irish Regiment; on the other side was a battalion with a component of unionist-minded Donegal and Fermanagh Ulster Volunteers, which became the 11th Royal Inniskilling Fusiliers on the formation of the 36th (Ulster) Division.[6] Some of the men from the two battalions were probably neighbours in Ireland. Irishmen from north and south would indeed fight side by side and, sadly, die side by side. It was the symbolism of that reality that lay behind Redmond's political rhetoric in his *Irish Life* article.

It was no coincidence that these divisions were put beside each other for the attack on Wijtschate. The decision to place them in this way ultimately came from the GOC of the 2nd Army, General Plumer. It was made some time around the middle of

September 1916. The arrangement may well have been politically motivated – an attempt to improve Irish recruitment. By October 1916 it was clear to senior officers in the 16th (Irish) and 36th (Ulster) Divisions, and indeed politicians back in Ireland, that Irish recruitment was declining.

In late September 1916 Adjutant General to the Forces Sir Nevil Macready stated that the Irish infantry units were 17,194 men below strength.[7] Recruitment had dropped off drastically all over Britain, and Ireland was no different in that regard. From 4 August 1914 to 1 August 1916 recruitment in Ireland dropped from 50,107 to 9,323. By February 1917 it had fallen further to 8,178.[8] By January 1917 large-scale drafts of English recruits began to fill the ranks of the service battalions in both the 16th (Irish) and 36th (Ulster) Divisions, a consequence of which was the decline in the Irish nature of the divisions. John Redmond believed that the fall off in Irishmen joining the 16th (Irish) Division was due to the fact that drafts for the Irish Division had been sent to other units and that wounded men from this division were not being sent back to their Irish battalions.[9] Whatever the reason, the reality was that non-Irishmen filled the gaps in the Irish battalions. For example, on 24 November 1916 the 6th Royal Irish Regiment received a draft of fifty-eight men of other ranks, who were mostly Englishmen taken from the surplus of RFA recruits.

A further example of the decline in Irishmen and rise of Englishmen in the 16th (Irish) Division can be seen in the 2nd RDF. In December 1914 Irishmen made up 87.3 per cent of the 2nd RDF, and Englishmen 9.1 per cent. By August 1917 the percentage of Irishmen in the battalion had fallen to 46.6 per cent, and Englishmen had risen to 47.9 per cent.[10] However, it would be wrong to assume that all the replacement drafts into Irish battalions were not Irish. On 21 December 1916 the 8th RDF received a draft of 116 men, all of whom were 'RDF men'.[11]

In the 36th (Ulster) Division, the proportion of Irishmen in the infantry battalions, though reduced, still stood at around 60 per cent in early 1917. When supporting arms were taken into consideration (the divisional artillery was not recruited in Ireland), the overall proportion of Irishmen in the division had fallen to 50 per cent.[12] One of the consequences in the fall-off in the 'Ulster' composition of the division was the possibility of the division losing its 'Ulster' title. However, following a lobbying campaign and General Nugent's report to his corps commander in which he outlined his officers' desire to retain their Ulster title, GHQ agreed to drop the proposal and the title was retained.[13]

Whatever the causes for the decline in Irish recruitment were – and one can only assume the obvious one being the loss of so many lives at the front and possibly the effects of the Easter Rising in Dublin – the reality was that Irishmen were no longer coming forward to enlist and the Irish nature of both divisions was declining sharply in 1917. Something had to be done to stem the tide of men turning away from the recruiting offices in Ireland. General Macready presented five possible solutions: the introduction of conscription; the amalgamation of the 16th (Irish) and 36th (Ulster) Divisions; the reinforcement of Irish units with English conscripts; allowing the divisions to waste away; or the transfer of Irish units from non-Irish to Irish formations. The Army Council opted to amalgamate the 16th and 36th Divisions.

During the debate on this proposal, however, politics raised its head again. John Redmond came to the conclusion that amalgamation was unnecessary, whereas Edward Carson proposed that the 36th (Ulster) Division should be amalgamated with the Scottish 51st (Highland) Division. General Nugent thought the amalgamation of the two Irish divisions would work, but in the end it did not take place as a compromise solution was reached. This stipulated that men recruited in Ireland would go to regular Irish battalions, while English drafts would be used to maintain Irish service battalions.[14] Moreover, Irish battalions in non-Irish divisions would be transferred to the 16th (Irish) Division.

At a 2nd Army meeting of corps commanders held on 3 October 1916, General Plumer stated that volunteers had been asked for from other units to join the 16th (Irish) Division. The volunteers must be Irishmen.[15] Consequently, some weeks later, in mid-October, the 2nd Royal Irish Regiment was transferred from the 7th Division to the 49th Brigade of the 16th (Irish) Division, and, in mid-November, the 2nd RDF was transferred from the 10th Brigade in the 4th Division to the 48th Brigade of the 16th (Irish) Division.[16] The 1st Royal Munster Fusiliers merged with the 8th Munsters, resulting in a battalion with a strength of forty-eight officers and 1,069 other ranks.[17] Bringing the Dublins' battalions together went down well with most of the men. It was a move that boosted regimental morale at the front. Private Christy Fox stated: 'We are now belonging to the 16th (Irish) Division, we have a Dublin Fusiliers Brigade, and the 2nd, 8th, 9th and 10th Battalions are together.'[18] The 1st RDF was in France with the 29th Division. The formation of a Dublin brigade was something John Redmond had wanted. On October 1916 he had written to the adjutant general suggesting such a brigade for the 16th (Irish) Division.[19]

It seems reasonable to conclude that, due to the fall-off in Irish recruitment, the measures taken by GHQ in October 1916 were designed to restore a sense of Irish/Ulster pride and identity in both Irish divisions. It seems likely that it was hoped this would have a positive impact on recruitment back in Ireland. It is in that context that the placement of the two Irish divisions side by side facing Wijtschate must be seen.

The idea may have worked, up to a point. In 1915 the number of men recruited in Leinster was 14,204. In 1916 it dropped to 5,767. That is a drop of 59.4 per cent over that twelve-month period. In 1917 some 4,041 men were recruited in Leinster, which is a drop of 29.9 per cent for a similar period. Although the overall trend in recruiting was downward, the rate of decline had slowed down during 1917.[20]

Regardless of what was going on back in Ireland, in Flanders the reality of war brought these Irish divisions into the countryside around the Flemish villages of Loker, Kemmel and Dranouter. The sentiments expressed by Willie Redmond on the relationship between men from the two Irish divisions working, and eventually fighting, side by side against a common enemy in the field were becoming a reality. The fact that there is little mention of the 36th (Ulster) Division in the battalion diary of the 6th Royal Irish Regiment, or any other Irish regiment, is not an indication of the level of interdivisional encounters that occurred. It must be remembered that the nearest 'Irish' regiment to the Ulster Division in the coming attack was Michael Wall's battalion. The censor would never have allowed important details such as battle order to be written about in letters. Therefore Michael could not have made any reference to the Ulster Division in his letters home, even if he had wanted to do so.

There were many instances and cordial occasions when men from both divisions came together in small numbers, at training exercises and around the villages of Loker, Kemmel and Bailleul. For example, on Saturday 26 May 1917 the band of the 16th (Irish) Division put on a concert in Loker for all to attend; many of the 14th Royal Irish Rifles who were in 36th's Divisional Reserve in Doncaster Huts in Loker at the time attended the show. They would have had to mix with men from the 16th (Irish) Division at the concert.[21]

Large-scale social get-togethers were rare and only came about at occasions such as football matches. On the afternoon of Saturday 21 April 1917, the 9th Royal Irish Fusiliers (The Faughs), a battalion of the Ulster Division's 108th Brigade, played a football match against the 2nd RDF in Loker. The Faughs must have been a good side, because they beat the Dubs by seven goals to nil. Four days later they beat the 6th Connaught Rangers two goals to nil.[22] On 29 April the 6th Connaught Rangers played another football match against what Rowland Fielding described as a battalion 'of the Carson (36th) Division'.[23] The team they played was in fact the same 9th Royal Irish Fusiliers.[24] Both matches were played in Loker.

At the 29 April match, which was unusual for the Ulstermen insofar as it was played on the Sabbath, a crowd of up to 3,000 was reported to have turned up to watch the match. The large attendance gave concern to Colonel Fielding. Such a concentration of troops, if spotted, offered a prime target to German artillery. However, knowing something about the politics of Ireland and the interest this match had developed, Fielding allowed his heart to rule his head on this occasion and permitted the match to take place. He would have been a brave man to cancel it. German artillery or not, this match was going to proceed. During the game, a man on the Ulster side was heard to say: 'I wonder if we shall get into trouble for fraternising with the enemy!'[25] The Faughs again beat the Rangers by two goals to nil.[26]

Irish historian Tim Bowman has suggested that 'relationships between men of the 16th (Irish) and 36th (Ulster) Divisions were not all that satisfactory'.[27] However, there were examples of both good and bad relationships between the divisions.

Taking the good relationships first: on 5 December 1916 the 47th Brigade of the 16th (Irish) Division relieved the 109th Brigade of the 36th (Ulster) Division, taking over the northern sector of the Spanbroekmolen salient. It remained in this sector for approximately three months until 12 March 1917.[28] In his book *Ireland in Ten Days*, Captain Stephen Gwynn, an officer with the 6th Connaught Rangers and a nationalist MP, recalled the following incident. As part of the handover, a piece of the sector facing Wijtschate was being handed over by Ulstermen to the 16th (Irish) Division and an officer was sent to inspect the lines before taking over. The colonel of the occupying Ulster battalion showed him around the communications trenches, which they had made or remade, and told him the names – 'Limavady Junction' and so forth – all of which belonged to Ulster. At last they came to a strong point. This was the head of a mine-shaft surrounded with ring after ring of sandbag breastworks. Here the colonel paused and said, 'We call this place Derry Walls, but I suppose your people will be changing all these names.' 'Colonel,' answered the nationalist officer, 'we'll hold Derry's Walls for you as long as one of us is standing.'[29]

The originator of Captain Gwynn's report was Lieutenant Colonel Macrory, the commanding officer of the 10th Royal Inniskilling Fusiliers, the Londonderry Regiment of the Ulster Volunteers. He had great praise for the 16th (Irish) Division and longed for the day when politicians on both sides of the political and religious divide in Ireland would set aside their narrow-mindedness and come to some form of agreement on Ireland's future:

All honour to the gallant 16th Division ... here's to the day when narrow-minded and self-seeking politicians will no longer be able to prevent two such brave and chivalrous peoples from living in the truest friendship in their own home country, as they lived – and died – in friendship in a foreign land.[30]

On St Stephen's (Boxing) Day 1916, Gwynn wrote to his cousin Amelia, 'We are alongside the Ulster Division and making great friends with them – which is well.'[31]

Another incident was recounted by Second Lieutenant Percy McElwaine of the 14th Royal Irish Rifles when they were in the line at Wulverghem in the winter of 1916. It was taken as no more than a bit of harmless banter:

> On one occasion there was a slight adjustment of our front near Wulverghem. A battalion of the Dublins 16th (Irish) Division took over from one of our battalions. I think indeed from the YCVs. As the Dublins came in, one of them remarked, 'Glory be to God will you look at the Carson's Boys.' From whom there was a reply. 'Get the Hell out of that you bloody Fenians.'[32]

Walter Collins was a Londoner who served in the 9th Royal Irish Rifles. Like a lot of English folk, Walter had little knowledge of Ireland's religious and political divisions. In a fine bit of political correctness, he referred to his battalion being with the 'Irish (Ulster) Division (36th)'. On the theme of Irishmen sticking together to fight a common enemy despite their religious differences, he noted in his diary:

> For identity in the field we wore a shoulder flash, an orange-shaped symbol or tab to denote our association as Orangemen ... I was very much the odd man out with my comrades at that time being a lone Londoner among so many Irishmen, but I was very much taken on my face value and I had a very happy association with them. Being

practically politically unconscious at that time I found it very difficult to understand their antagonisms of religious belief etc. which at times boiled up, but if they fought each other on occasion there was never any doubt whose side they were on in relation to the common enemy or of their courage in action whatever part of Ireland they came from.[33]

It is not directly related to the Irish at Wijtschate, but in the context of Irish soldiers from the north and south of Ireland working together in harmony, one Dublin Fusilier's experience in working alongside men from the Ulster Division is worthy of note. On Friday 20 November 1915 Private Joseph Elley of the 2nd RDF wrote home to Monica Roberts, thanking her for the latest food parcel. The weather then was freezing hard:

> Well, we are having a time, it's simply heart-breaking to see such strong and good boys getting frost bitten … We have the Ulster Division with us at present and fine good lads they are, good old Ireland again. The Dublins get on with all the regiments, especially the Jocks and on the whole it's great to be out here knowing you are defending your own at home.[34]

In early December Elley wrote to Miss Roberts again:

> I suppose you saw in the papers about Redmond's visit to the front. I might say he spoke to the Ulster men and there is no bad feeling amongst us fellows out here and I think it will end such feelings forever.[35]

There were times, however, as can be seen from Rifleman Collins' account above, when the mood was not so convivial between men from both divisions. An example of this can be found in the book *Trekking On* by Lieutenant Colonel Deneys Reitz, the commanding officer of the 7th Royal Irish Rifles of the 48th Brigade in the 16th (Irish) Division. In this he recalled how he and his adjutant had prevented a fight between some of his men and 'the bloody Orangemen' from the Ulster Division:

> In the course of the evening I sent a fatigue party to fetch supplies for our canteen from the Ulster depot. Soon after their return I heard a violent commotion in the marquee where we kept our stores. There was the sound of breaking crockery, mingled with oaths and shouts, and, rushing up to enquire, I found that the men were busy wrecking the place. When I demanded the reason, several of them angrily flourished bottles in my face, to the accompaniment of threats and curses against the bloody Orangemen. To me the bottles seemed harmless, for they contained only soda water, but, when I asked for enlightenment, it appeared that the root of the trouble was the labels, which bore the title 'Boyne Water'. The men started off in a body for the Ulster Division to avenge what they considered a mortal insult. I had heard of The Battle of the Boyne, but it conveyed no political implications and I thought the men had gone crazy. Fortunately I was able to telephone through to the Ulster headquarters, who hastily turned out several hundred men to surround the malcontents; and with tactful assistance of our Adjutant, young Hartery, who understood Irish politics, we managed to get our men back to camp without bloodshed.[36]

It seems that it took little to offend some members of the 7th Royal Irish Rifles, if all they needed to fight the Ulstermen were the words 'Boyne Water' written on a bottle label.

In September 1917 the 2nd Royal Irish Rifles, in a further move motivated by politics/recruiting, were transferred from the

25th Division to the 36th (Ulster) Division. This particular battalion of the Royal Irish Rifles was a regular battalion with a large component of Roman Catholic soldiers from Cork and Dublin. Fr Henry Gill noted that the move 'came as a surprise and a disagreeable shock almost to everyone'.[37] The feelings expressed to Fr Gill by men of the Ulster Division on the arrival of his battalion were, as he noted in his diary, 'most uncomplimentary'.[38]

There is no doubt that some good relationships were struck between the men from both Irish divisions in Flanders. However, it is important to point out that these relationships were not as cordial as Willie Redmond and others made them out to be, and were, as Bowman suggested, 'not all that satisfactory'. Yet the reality was that in May 1917, whether they liked it or not, the two divisions from Ireland were side by side and would need each other for their survival more than ever.[39]

16

'God grant that I come through ... we have let Hell loose'

Friday 1 June 1917 was a wet day in Loker. Michael Wall's battalion was in Clare Camp; the men were cleaning their equipment and preparing to leave for a brief duty in the front line. The only trouble they had was from a German naval gun mounted on a canal barge that had fired off during the previous night. It had forced men out of their billets and to bivouac instead in surrounding fields to avoid its shells.[1] Before he packed up his kit and moved off, Michael wrote a quick letter home. He told his mother that they were going to finish the war this month and to have a bath ready for him:

> 6th Royal Irish Regt.
> B.E.F.
> France
>
> June 1st 1917.
>
> Dear Mother,
>
> Our rest is finished and once again we are back again in the sound of the guns. I expect we shall soon be in the trenches again and in the thick of it. Well, God grant that we may come safely through. Fancy this being the first of June and being out here. I have just received your letter of the 27th inst. We are too busy to be thinking of going to such people as dentists, we are going to finish the war this month so have a bath ready for me on the

first of July. Well you can see we have our tails up and as far as Fritz goes, we don't mind him or even his whiz[z] bangs. Well I wish we were marching back to Blighty. Did anything arrive with my coat? I sent home a German gas helmet and I am anxious to know if it got home safe. What a pity the weather spoiled the bazaar. We had sports on last Sunday and we had an officers wrestling on horse-back competition and it was a great rag. I was pulled off second last. There were some torn shirts after it and to make things better, as I was galloping along the road back to the billets, I ran over a French hen. By jove rabbit shooting would be rather tame sport after France ... Well, strenuous times are ahead of us shortly and we will need all your prayers more than ever. I am sending this letter and cheque in a registered envelope for safety and I am including the cost of kit (11 shillings). Well, I must close now for want of news. Give my love to Auntie and all at home.

Ever your fond son
Michael.[2]

The wrestling on horseback must have been a great bit of fun for Michael and his pals. It is very easy to forget that many of these men were young; some, like Michael, were still only teenagers.

Michael and his battalion were indeed back again to the familiar sound of the guns. During 1 June British artillery opened a barrage along the entire 9th Corps front, the purpose of which was, according to the war diarist of the 2nd RDF, to deceive the Germans 'into thinking that an attack was to be made and make him put on his barrage so that we could observe the portion of our line likely to be barraged when our attack came off'. The barrage 'lasted for ten minutes and the enemy made no immediate reply. Later on he put a few heavies into strong points.'[3]

The British shelling that day was part of a continuous period of shelling that had, in fact, begun on 21 May. As well as conning the Germans into returning a counter-barrage and revealing their artillery positions, the main purpose of the barrage now was – like most previous barrages in the war – to demolish the German wire defences before the infantry attack.[4] However, this concentration of firepower was unprecedented. Between 21 May and 6 June – using 2,266 field guns and howitzers – the British fired off 3,561,530 shells into the German defensive zone of some 17,000 yards (15,500 metres) long.[5] By rough comparison, the British fired 1,732,873 shells during the opening barrage of the Somme campaign in June 1916 over a 25,000 yard (22,800 metre) front, using 1,537 similar artillery weapons.[6] A German soldier of the 4th Grenadier Regiment facing the 16th (Irish) Division at Wijtschate wrote in his diary:

> 1st June 1917. For a long time we have supposed that the enemy offensive from Arras would extend north – the time appears to have come – today is now the 13th day on which our trenches and the ground behind us have been exposed to heavy fire, which very often increases to drum fire. All the trenches are smashed in, no more shelter is to hand, battery emplacements up to two metres thick are completely destroyed, and even six metre deep galleries are not safe from guns of heavy calibre – thus we are forced into the open without any protection and have to submit to the passing over of iron hailstones – our losses consequently are very heavy – each day we must thank God that we are still alive.[7]

On this occasion the German wire was comprehensively cut in front of the Irish line of advance. Unlike the chalk-laden soil along their Somme trench systems, which allowed the Germans to build deep, well-protected dugouts, the waterlogged soil of Flanders prevented them – and indeed the British – from digging similar dugouts. Hence most of the defences were above ground and exposed to artillery. German trench lines were thus smashed in, and what was left of the villages of Wijtschate and Messines was reduced to rubble. By Friday 1 June retaliatory German artillery fire began to slacken.[8]

On 2 June Michael and his battalion left Clare Camp and moved closer to the action. They left the Dublins and the rest of the 48th Brigade, who had relieved them back at Clare Camp and were making their own preparations. Before the 8th Dublins arrived at Clare Camp, Private George Ryland 'being found under age was sent to England and struck off the strength of the battalion'.[9] It is not known for certain what George's age was when he was sent home to what was then Kingstown in Finglas, north County Dublin.[10] To have been sent home, he must have been under the minimum regulation age of eighteen. Assuming he spent a year or so in training, it is more than likely he was only seventeen when he enlisted. It would be interesting to know how his commanding officer found out his age – possibly from a letter from a worried mother back home.

Like Michael Wall, George was another Irish youngster smitten by this terrible war. When he got home to Ireland, George re-enlisted in the army and joined the 7th Royal Irish Regiment. He returned to France and was promoted to sergeant. On 4 October 1918, at eighteen years of age, George Ryland died of wounds when his battalion were in the front line opposite the Flemish village of Wervicq.[11]

To the officers and men who would soon attack Wijtschate, Sunday 3 June was designated V Day.[12] The British bombardment and German retaliation carried on, even though it was the Lord's day. Michael's battalion had arrived at Renmore Lines near Loker. Second Lieutenant Jones and twenty-five other ranks, who had been away carrying out some last minute work on the light-gauge railway lines, rejoined the battalion.[13]

That night some 2,000 British incendiary oil drums were fired on the Bois de Wijtschate (Wijtschate Wood). The drums were filled with a mixture of aluminium powder and magnetic oxide of iron, which, on the bursting of the drum, combine to form a combustible material. The burning produces a temperature high enough to melt steel and rain a glittering cascade of white-hot, molten metal on anybody or anything that happens to be near it.[14] This terrifying projectile was devised by the Royal Engineers and used to flush out German machine-gun posts in the Bois de Wijtschate.

Back in his billet at Renmore Lines, Michael wrote a note home. Reassuringly he told his mother that he had met Fr Gleeson:

> 6th Royal Irish Regt.
> B.E.F.
> France
>
> June 3rd 1917.
>
> Dear Mother
>
> I know you will be very pleased to hear that I met Father Gleeson yesterday. He is with his old Regiment again and I am going to see him again this evening as we are going "over the top" in a few days. I tell you there is going to be some row. So pray hard for us all.
>
> I have very little news except there is an awful row going on, but we are not in the trenches yet. I hope everybody at home is quite alright. Rest assured I shall come through this show quite

safe. Give my love to everybody at home and keep the bright side out.

Ever your fond son
Michael.[15]

6th Royal Irish Regt.
B.E.F.
France
June 3rd 1917.

Dear mother

I know you will be very pleased to hear that I met Father Gleeson yesterday. He is with his old regiment again and I am going to see him again this evening as we are going 'over the top' in a few days. I tell you there is going to be some row. So pray hard for us all.

I have very little news except that there is an awful row going on, but we are not *in the trenches yet. I hope everybody at home is quite alright. Rest assured I shall come through this show quite safe. Give my love to everybody at home and keep the bright side out.*

Ever Your fond Son

Michael,

Monday 4 June was W Day. A conference was held for the commanding officers of the 47th Brigade. The final plans for the attack were discussed and any unforeseen problems were ironed out. Thoroughness was now a fine art. Michael's battalion moved up into a reserve position near the Chinese Wall. One chap from Michael's battalion, Private John Fraher from Kilfinnane in County Limerick, was killed – possibly by a sniper – while working near the wall of sandbags.

To gain some last-minute intelligence on the German line and to examine the effect of the barrel bombs, 250 men of the 6th Connaught Rangers went on a night raid on the German Nancy Support and Nancy Switch Trench system in the Bois de Wijtschate. Apart from losing three officers – two dead and one blinded for life – the raid went well for the Rangers. They returned in rags, their clothing torn to shreds by the broken German wire. It would seem there were some survivors of the barrel bombs. The Rangers brought back seven prisoners, one of whom was wearing an Iron Cross.[16]

As this raid was going on, the nuns at the convent in Loker laid on a dinner organised by the officers of the 7th Leinsters.[17] In attendance were officers from the 16th and 36th Divisions, along with French and Belgian officers. It is unlikely any of the junior officers such as Michael were invited to sit at such a high table. 'The last supper' would be an appropriate description for this gathering. For some it was indeed so. It was at this dinner that Willie Redmond 'prayed for the consummation of peace between North and South'.[18]

Tuesday 5 June was termed X Day. From early morning, German artillery was active over the Irish lines. From 3.45 a.m. to 11.30 p.m., both SP12 and Hong Kong Trench, which were occupied by Irish troops, were shelled with 5.9- and 8-inch shells. Surprisingly, the Rangers who occupied the line that day suffered few casualties.[19]

Back in his divisional headquarters at the convent in Loker, General Hickie issued the 'Order of the Day' to his men in the 16th (Irish) Division:

The Big Day is very near. All our preparations are complete and the Divisional Commander wishes to express his appreciation and his thanks to all the officers and men who have worked so cheerfully and so well. The 16th Division is fortunate in having had assigned to it the capture of the stronghold of Wijtschate. Every officer and man – Gunners, Sappers, Pioneers, RAMC, [R]ASC and infantry of historic Irish regiments – knows what he has to do. Let all do their best, as they have always done, continuing to show the same courage and devotion to duty which has characterised the 16th (Irish) Division since it landed in France and it will be our proud privilege to restore to Little Belgium, the 'White Village', which has been in German hands for nearly three years.[20]

During the day, 'A' and 'B' Companies from Michael's battalion packed their kit and prepared to move to their jump-off positions near their front line facing Maedelstede Farm. They moved up to relive 'B' and 'D' Companies of the 6th Connaught Rangers. Michael and his men marched up late at night and began the changeover at 1 a.m. on Wednesday 6 June. By 4 a.m. the change-over was complete. On their way up they were briefly shelled by gas shells, but there were no reports of casualties.[21]

The same sort of operation occurred for thousands of assault troops who moved into position for Zero Day up and down the British and Anzac front line. Before he set out, Michael wrote a very emotional and reassuring letter home to his mother. He never made it over to see Fr Gleeson, but, knowing Michael, he had made his peace with God.

> 6th Royal Irish Regt.
>
> B.E.F.
>
> France
>
> June 5th 1917
>
> Dear Mother,
>
> In a short time we shall be going "over the top" and you probably will not hear from me until it is over. God grant that I come through for your sake. It is going to be an awfully trying time for everybody. I sent home some more kit the other day. I hope it will get home like the last. Perhaps I shall be home by this day week myself, who knows. One thing out here is that the weather is awfully hot and our guns are making it hotter still for the Hun. They are giving themselves up freely and they ask us if we have let hell loose on them. Well, look out for startling news soon. We are going up to the line tonight. I was at the altar this morning

and I feel quite confident although between you and I, my nerves are nearly gone and it will take a long rest before I feel up to the mark. However, once we get into it I shall not mind but I hate the suspense of waiting for these shows. One thing, the men are in great form. I could not get over to see Father Gleeson the other evening and I was very disappointed. Well, I hope you will excuse me now as I want to drop a line to Auntie. Best of love to you all and pray for my safety. Hope to see you all in a week or two.

Ever your fond son,
Michael.[22]

6th Royal Irish Regt.
B.E.F.
France
June 6th 1917.

Dear Mother,

In a short time we shall be going 'over the top' and you probably will not hear from me until it is over. God grant that I come through for your sake. It is going to be an awfully trying time for everybody. I sent home some more ~~————~~ but the other day. I hope it will get home like the last. Perhaps I shall be home by this day week

On Wednesday 6 June, Y Day, as the sun rose, a German aeroplane flew unopposed very low up and down the British line, firing on the gathering men in support and jump-off trenches.[23] Michael and his men were now in their jump-off trench facing the Germans in the right subsection of the line between Maedelstede Farm and Petit Bois. They stayed there for the next twenty-four hours or so. It was a familiar place for Michael to be amid the terror and noise of the front line. But, no matter how many times he was there, each occasion must have stripped a piece of his nerve ends away. Waiting around for so many hours to hear that whistle blow and go over the top must have brought him and many others to the edge of madness. This time, however, he reckoned it was going to be different. He believed that this attack was going to end the war once and for all, and that a hero's welcome awaited him and his men back home in Dublin. The constant bombardment had indeed let hell loose on the men in the opposing trenches. Later on during the day 'C' and 'D' Companies moved up, and the whole battalion was now ready for the final whistle.

Back in the 2nd Army headquarters at Cassel, General Haig paid General Plumer a visit and wished him and his staff the best of luck for the next day's attack. There was an air of confidence amongst Plumer's men.[24] General Tim Harrington, Plumer's chief of staff, briefed the gentlemen of the Press Corps about the forthcoming battle. The journalists William Beach Thomas and Philip Gibbs of the *Daily Telegraph* were in attendance. Harrington was asked whether he thought tomorrow's battle might help change the course of the war. He smiled, thought for a moment, then answered: 'Gentlemen, I do not know whether we shall change history tomorrow, but we shall certainly alter the geography.'[25] Nice to see some of the so-called 'donkeys' had a sense of humour.

During 6 June Willie Redmond, accompanied by his commanding officer Lieutenant Colonel Roche-Kelly and Major Charles Taylor, went to each company of the 6th Royal Irish and spoke 'encouragingly to all'.[26] Major Taylor recalled that Redmond 'spoke to every man'.[27] It would be nice to think that Redmond and Michael shook hands and wished each other well. For the previous three nights, Redmond had slept in a cellar under the chapel at the Hospice in Loker. His room-mate, Fr Edmond Kelly, chaplain to the Royal Irish Fusiliers, asked Redmond to speak to his men. Redmond obliged and spoke to the men of the Faughs for about a quarter of an hour.[28] He also had time to speak to the men of the 7th Leinsters, who were the other spearhead battalion of the 47th Brigade in the attack.

The theme that ran through all of Redmond's words of encouragement was, yet again, the symbolism of men from the north and south of Ireland fighting together. Colonel Roche-Kelly, a regular officer with the Royal Irish Regiment and twenty years younger than Redmond, who was fifty-six, did not want Redmond to go over the top with his men in 'A' Company. However, after threatening to disobey Roche-Kelly's wishes or resign his commission, Redmond was finally given permission to go.

Later on in the evening, while Michael and his men were at their front-line jump-off positions, the second wave of troops to be used in the attack moved up into their positions. At about 9.30 p.m. the three battalions of the Dublin Fusiliers left Clare Camp and began their march up to their assembly trenches behind the leading battalions. At roughly 2 a.m. on 7 June, the Dubs took their position along Watling Street Trench and the Chinese Wall. They would not move out until around midday on 7 June.

During the night of 6/7 June, oddly for that month, the heavens opened with a thunderstorm, and torrents of rain fell on the men waiting to go over just before dawn. The British bombardment had slightly slackened. The Germans seemed to fear that the ease-up might merely be the precursor of the storm, so they sent up signals calling for a barrage, thus continuing the artillery duel for a while longer.[29]

Amidst all the noise, the rain, the mud, and the fear, sweat and anxiety amongst men waiting for the unknown, could be heard the voice of an Irish Jesuit priest. At about 1 a.m. on 7 June, Fr Willie Doyle SJ, accompanied by Fr Frank Browne SJ, offered mass in a temporary sandbag chapel at the rear of the Dublins' trenches. Before the mass they had a rest on two stretchers, which would no doubt find use the next day. At 2.30 a.m., after they had said mass, the two chaplains put on their battle kit and headed for their respective First Aid posts.[30] At that hour the countryside around Wijtschate began to quieten down.

17

'Come on the Royal Irish'

Thursday 7 June, Z Day. By 3 a.m. Michael Wall's men had fixed their bayonets. The British guns stopped firing and an eerie hush fell over the countryside. Men spoke in whispers to each other. As if Mother Nature wanted to let the men know she still existed in this terrible place, nightingales were heard singing in what was left of Rossignol Wood.[1] The countdown to Zero Hour began. Minutes passed away slowly; even the final few seconds of waiting for the signal to charge the German front line seemed to drag.

What must have run through Michael's mind in those final few moments of silence as he shivered with nerves and stood waiting to go with his men? His mother, family and Carrick Hill? A hero's welcome marching with his men up the Dublin Quays? That hot bath he would have? Maybe he thought about how, when all this was over, he would meet a nice girl and get married. No doubt a word with his God passed away those last few seconds. It was during these last minutes that the Dublins in their reserve trenches took out their rosary beads and prayed for the German soldiers who were about to be vaporised.[2]

The overall objective that faced both General Hickie and General Nugent was to remove the Germans from Wijtschate and push them back behind a predetermined line beyond the ridge near the village of Oosttaverne on the eastern side of Wijtschate. The plan to take the objective was set to proceed in three stages throughout the day, with a specific objective at each stage. To make sure all units knew what their specific objective and tasks were, and in order to have all units singing from one hymn sheet, every combat unit was given a detailed set of Operation Instructions in the days before 7 June.[3]

The tactics used to take and consolidate Wijtschate by both Irish divisions would be similar. These tactics had been practised on brigade training grounds in villages around St Omer back in April and May. Under a creeping barrage of artillery and machine-gun fire set to lift at specific time intervals, each brigade and each battalion in that brigade was assigned a specific section of German trench to take according to a specific time schedule. Contact aeroplanes used to observe the fall of British artillery shells would fly over the battlefield at specific times throughout the day and communicate with artillery batteries below on the accuracy of their firing. When each section of German trench was taken, support units such as the Royal Engineers and Pioneers would advance to the captured line and consolidate the gains that were made. Field artillery would also move up to new lines and assist the assault on the final objective. A limited number of tanks would be available to assist the advancing infantry.

In an effort to keep the element of surprise intact and to stop the planned time of attack – 3.10 a.m. – from falling into the hands of raiding Germans before 7 June, Zero Hour was deliberately kept from the men for as long as possible. It had been carefully chosen as one-and-a-half hours before dawn, and a visibility of a hundred metres had been estimated as the first light glimmered on the eastern horizon.[4] The half-light before dawn at 3.10 a.m. was seen as an advantage to the attacking Irish troops. The guiding principles for General Plumer and his staff officers of 'Trust, Training and Thoroughness' would be put to the test.

The rain had stopped and an almost full moon shone in a clear sky.[5] At seven seconds before Zero Hour, the first of Empire Jack's mines went up – the Trench 127 mine at the southern end of the front facing the Australians at St Yves.[6] Within seconds, the rest exploded. The time officially recorded between the firing of the first and last mines along the front line was nineteen seconds.[7] Standing on Mount Kemmel, Philip Gibbs from the *Daily Chronicle* looked on with amazement at this display, on the morning that it seemed as if hell had broken through the surface of the earth. It was, he said:

> The most diabolical splendour I have ever seen. Out of the dark ridges of Messines and Wijtschate and that ill-famed Hill 60, there gushed out and up enormous volumes of scarlet flame from the exploding mines and of earth and smoke all lighted by the flame spilling over into mountains of fierce colour, so that all the countryside was illuminated by red light. Where some of us stood watching and spellbound by this burning horror, the ground trembled and surged violently to and fro. Truly the earth quaked.[8]

The 36th (Ulster) Division had in front of them one of the strongest sectors of the German front line. The knoll of Spanbroekmolen and the fortified points at Kruisstraat and Peckham were on each flank of the advancing Ulstermen. The mine in front of the division was named the Spanbroekmolen mine. Dug by the 171st Canadian Tunnelling Company and packed with 91,000 pounds (41,277 kilograms) of ammonal explosive charge, it had been discovered by German counter-mining in late April and almost destroyed.[9] However, it had been saved and recharged with explosives.

Right up to Zero Hour, there was an element of doubt as to whether or not Spanbroekmolen would explode. In the days leading up to the attack, German tunnelling units had blown damaging camouflets near the mine, and consequently a new tunnel was driven through a tract of gas-drenched ground (which cost three brave men from the 171st Tunnelling Company their lives), past the section blown in by the camouflets, to reach and save the charge just hours ahead of Zero Hour.

In the end the mine went off fifteen seconds after Zero Hour. The Corps Standing Orders noted that if a mine did not go off following a wait of fifteen seconds after Zero Hour, it was to be assumed that the mine was not going to go off, and so the men were to advance to the German lines.[10] This was Russian roulette. When the mine did explode, huge mounds of clay the size of farm carts were thrown into the air, forming a crater 130 metres in diameter.[11] The Royal Engineers had estimated a period of twenty seconds for the mine debris to fall back to earth.[12] In reality the dust did not settle for two hours.[13]

Following the blasts, many of the leading assaulting troops found it impossible to see more than a few metres ahead of themselves, as the air was thick with dust, smoke and panic. Visual and oral communications were near impossible. In the haze, units crossed each other, but as the fog of dust began to settle, the leading platoon and company commanders reorganised and brought some level of order back to the chaotic infantry assault.[14]

Some of the leading Ulster battalions had begun their advance just after Zero Hour and were in no man's land when the Spanbroekmolen mine went off. They had used this tactic on 1 July when they had faced the Schwaben Redoubt in the Somme. However, some of the 14th Royal Irish Rifles were caught by falling debris from the mine explosion and were killed. They were buried practically where they fell, at the British Commonwealth War Graves cemetery named Lone Tree Cemetery, behind the Spanbroekmolen crater known as the Pool of Peace.[15]

The shock wave resulting from the explosion of 874,200

pounds (396,530 kilograms) of ammonal along the front led local people to believe they had experienced an earthquake. Similarly, Professor Barrois of the Geology Department at Lille University, twenty-four kilometres away, also thought an earthquake had occurred.[16] In the same town, German garrison troops ran panicking through the streets. Their comrades who had been at the receiving end of the explosions were literally blown to pieces. Fr Willie Doyle SJ, standing well behind, wrote:

> Not only did the ground quiver and shake, but actually rocked backwards and forwards, so that I kept my feet with difficulty … Later on I examined one of the mine craters, an appalling sight, for I knew that many a brave man, torn and burnt by the explosion, lay buried there … I can't share the general sentiment that 'they deserve what they get and one better.' For after all, are they not children of the same loving saviour who said: 'Whatever you do to one of these my least ones you do it to me.' I try to show them any little kindness I can, getting them a drink, taking off the boots from smashed and bleeding feet, or helping to dress their wounds, and more than once I have seen the eyes of these rough men fill with tears as I bent over them, or felt my hand squeezed in gratitude … I shall make no attempt to describe the battle field. Thank God, our casualties were extraordinarily light, but there was not a yard of ground on which a shell had not pitched, which made getting about very laborious, sliding down one crater and climbing up the next, and also increased the difficulty of finding the wounded …
>
> I came across one young soldier horribly mutilated, and all his intestines hanging out, but quite conscious and able to speak to me. He lived long enough to receive the last sacraments and die in peace.[17]

Bob Grange from Ballyclare, County Antrim, was a sergeant with the 12th Royal Irish Rifles, who were assigned to the second wave of attack at the time the mines went up. He had been promoted to sergeant after the Somme. When the mine at Spanbroekmolen went off, he had to claw at the sides of his trench to keep himself upright. Later that day, when a German-speaking officer of his battalion questioned some prisoners, he was told that a party of some 300 men had gathered directly over the mine in preparation for a raid on the Ulster lines at 6 a.m.:

> They were all packed into Spanbroekmolen, getting ready for the raid, and unfortunately for them we started ours at 3:10 a.m., so they all went up in the air. I never saw carnage like it in such a short space. There wasn't a human body intact lying around the place ... just bits and pieces, arms, heads, feet, legs. Terrible mess.[18]

Second Lieutenant Arthur Glanville of the 2nd Dublins also experienced the mine explosions. He was only 475 metres from the Maedelstede Farm mine when it went up:

> I both heard and felt the whole nineteen of them when they went up instantaneously. The ground swayed in an alarming manner and the trench rocked like a boat on a sea, but as for the noise of the explosions, it was completely drowned in the simultaneous burst of the hundreds of guns which were concealed behind us in every nook and corner.[19]

Immediately after the last mine exploded, some 2,266 various guns of British artillery opened up on what was left of the German defences and battery positions along the ridge. The noise level was deafening. Glanville noted:

> The noise of our own guns was so great that two men in our battalion got very bad shell shock. They are both in England now. I wish I

could be affected thus! Even the German guns have not succeeded in upsetting me.[20]

Standing almost wheel to wheel alongside each other, the 18-pounder guns fired off at their maximum rate of fire ahead of the advancing infantry to create a creeping barrage. In tandem with these came a standing barrage using 18 pounders, 4.5-inch Howitzers, medium and heavy Howitzers and machine guns, whose targets were German trench lines and strong points in front of the advancing Irish battalions.[21] The historian of the 7th Leinsters noted:

> The barrage which broke out at Zero Hour and covered the advance of the troops was unexampled in its intensity in any previous engagement of the war. Every machine gun on the front was pouring its hail of lead over the heads of the attackers … The many trench mortars were busy too on selected objectives.[22]

Fr Edmond Kelly also described the bombardment: 'Our artillery was so terrific that I heard several of our men express compassion for the enemy who were holding the trenches opposite.'[23]

As the last mine exploded, like a distress signal from a sinking ship, flares shot up from the German side signalling to their artillery that the battle had begun and to expect the British infantry to come. Their counter-barrage opened, and one of their shells burst outside the battalion headquarters of the 7th Leinsters, located at Lunette Dugouts, which was at the top of one of the mine shafts facing Petit Bois. Inside was the commanding officer Lieutenant Colonel Thomas R. A. Stannus; the Adjutant Captain E. L. L. Acton; the 47th Brigade trench mortar officer attached, Captain James Roche; Captain J. A. J. Farrell, acting second-in-command; two artillery liaison officers; and four other ranks used as runners for carrying urgent messages. The bursting shell killed Captain Roche, the two artillery officers and the four other ranks. Lieutenant Colonel Stannus and Captain Acton were very severely wounded; Colonel Stannus later died from his wounds and Captain Acton was crippled for life.[24]

Three nights earlier, Colonel Stannus and Captain Roche had attended the dinner in Loker that the nuns presented for the officers of both the 16th (Irish) and 36th (Ulster) Divisions. James Roche was a very well respected and reliable officer. He was a native of Caherciveen, County Kerry, but lived with his parents in Monasterevin, County Kildare. Before the war he had been a solicitor. Colonel Fielding wrote of Roche that he was 'one of the wittiest raconteurs I have ever met, and as brave and ready a soldier as I have ever seen. As Brigade Trench Mortar Officer, he was a genius. In conversation he was remarkable.'[25] Tom Stannus left behind a wife, Lilith Graydon-Smith, and two young daughters.[26]

The leading assault battalions of the 16th (Irish) Division's 47th Brigade were the 7th Leinsters and Michael's 6th Royal Irish Regiment. On their left flank came the 49th Brigade and on the right flank of the 6th Royal Irish came the 109th Brigade of the 36th (Ulster) Division. These units began the first stage of the operation and attacked the first objective, which in the case of Michael's brigade was a section of the German front-line trenches named Nancy Trench and the woods Petit Bois and Bois de Wijtschate on the western edge of Wijtschate. Under the storm of steel and falling dust from the mine explosion at Maedelstede Farm, 'A' and 'B' Companies from the 6th Royal Irish advanced into no man's land, passing the crater that by now was the grave of many an unfortunate dead and mutilated east Prussian. Falling debris, earth and stones rained down for minutes after the mines exploded and it was almost impossible to advance in a straight line. The worst effect of the explosion was the fumes, which caused a large number of the advancing Irish troops to vomit. Confused, high on adrenaline, blinded and choking with dust, they battled their way across no man's land to their first objective.

At approximately 3.30 a.m., twenty minutes after Zero Hour, Major Willie Redmond of 'A' Company of the 6th Royal Irish Regiment was fatally wounded by shell fire. He received these wounds somewhere between the mine crater at Maedelstede Farm and the Nap Support Trench. A small piece of shrapnel entered his left forearm below the elbow and another entered his calf. His men, believing him only slightly wounded, moved on without him. John Breen, who had joined the 2nd Royal Irish in 1911, had been posted to the 6th Royal Irish. He was a member of Redmond's 'A' Company and spoke of advancing with him:

> Before we went over the top that morning he was with us: all he said was Come on the Royal Irish. I don't know where he was killed. I didn't see him after we got over the top, because, I needn't tell you, we were looking out for ourselves.[27]

Redmond was found by Private John Meeke of the 11th Royal Inniskilling Fusiliers, from Brevarden, Ballymoney, County Antrim. Private Meeke, who was later awarded the Military Medal, remained with Redmond until a stretcher bearer from the Ulster Division arrived to take him back to their dressing station.[28]

The resistance encountered by the leading companies of the 6th Royal Irish and 7th Leinsters in their advance into Petit Bois and Bois de Wijtschate came from men of the 4th Grenadier Regiment and 33rd Fusiliers. Some of the Grenadiers were killed by Leinster bayonets. The fortunate ones who surrendered were taken prisoner.[29]

Taking the attack on to the second stage, as per their operation instructions, with the aid of a tank – which turned out to be the only one working – came the 1st Royal Munster Fusiliers. They were accompanied by four officers and a hundred men from the 6th Connaught Rangers used as 'moppers', that is small units of men attached to attacking infantry whose objective was to capture or kill any German soldiers who had been left behind by the main body of attacking troops. Many of the bewildered Germans the Munsters and Rangers encountered were either killed in their dugouts or taken prisoner by the moppers. As many as twenty-five to thirty prisoners were taken on the Wijtschate to Oosttaverne road. One dead German soldier found by the Connaught Rangers was reported as being chained to his machine gun.[30] The Munsters and Rangers passed through the ranks of the 6th Royal Irish and 7th Leinsters shortly after 5.50 a.m. – getting a great cheer as they did so; they took the second objective, which ran through the eastern side of Wijtschate.[31] In their enthusiasm to get forward, one group of Munsters advanced beyond the line of their own creeping barrage and suffered casualties as a result. One of the Munsters' officers, twenty-one-year-old Second Lieutenant Edmund T. Hussey, was killed by what might be termed today as 'friendly fire'.[32]

The Munsters and Rangers pushed on, and by 8 a.m. the two objectives had been taken and the field guns of the 59th and 113th Brigades, RFA, were brought up near the new front line.[33] At around midday, the three battalions of the RDF and 7th Royal Irish Rifles of the 48th Brigade came into the fray for the third stage of the operation; they were used to carry the advance on to the final objective, attacking a site known as Oil Trench near the village of Oosttaverne.

The 8th Dublins set up their headquarters at what was called

Sonnen Farm and the 9th Dublins set up their headquarters at Torreken Farm.[34] Using pack mules to carry up wire, munitions such as grenades, and water, the occupied line was consolidated. Both farms were about three-quarters of a kilometre beyond Wijtschate. This was where the Irish advance stopped. Within six hours of the first assault, parties were already at work making roads through shell holes across the mutilated zone and even laying water pipes to get drinking water up to the new front line.

However, late in the evening of 7 June, tragedy hit the 33rd Brigade of the 11th (Northern) Division, a reserve brigade attached to the 16th (Irish) Division. Battalions of this brigade that were out beyond Wijtschate suffered casualties from their own artillery due to the slowness/breakdown of communications round the battlefield. It was self-inflicted carnage. Their casualties reported at 11 p.m. on 7 June amounted to twenty-four officers and 423 other ranks killed, wounded or missing. This was 40 per cent of the casualties suffered by the entire 16th (Irish) Division between midnight on 6/7 June and midday on 9 June, the total being 1,183 officers and other ranks killed, wounded or missing.[35]

Over the next few days, roads and light railways were advanced across the battered wilderness; little locomotives were puffing their way over land where, a few days previously, no man could show his face.[36] The battle to take Wijtschate had come to a successful end, and Irish troops from the four corners of Ireland had captured the little 'White Village', which by that stage was a mere mound of rubble. Fielding wrote to his wife telling her of the destruction:

> You can just distinguish where the roads were. You can recognise what was the chief outstanding feature – the Church – only by tracing its position from the map. But you cannot recognise the square. All is dust and rubble. We visited the famous Hospice, which caps the

ridge and used to be most prominent during the long months when we occupied the breastworks in the swamp below. The highest bit of wall remaining is eight to ten feet high. The only structures that have resisted our bombardments are the steel and concrete emplacements built by the enemy among the foundations of the village, several of which have withstood the racket fairly well and if the garrisons had stood their ground they could have given a lot of trouble.[37]

The British front line had advanced three kilometres east when night fell on 7 June. Some 5,650 German prisoners were taken along the entire frontage during the attack. The German losses were estimated to be almost 20,000, of whom half were missing. 2nd Army casualties on 7 June were fewer than 11,000.[38] The 16th (Irish) Division placed eight German officers and 674 men in their holding camps and passed on 300 to 400 others to neighbouring divisions.[39] The 36th (Ulster) Division captured a total of thirty-one officers and 1,208 other ranks.[40] The diarist of the 6th Royal Irish Regiment, writing from the Nap Support Trench, thought that the 'attack was a complete success which even exceeded the wildest dreams of the General Staff'. However, the exploding mines 'nearly spoiled the show'.[41]

In a letter home to his mother on 9 June, Second Lieutenant Glanville of the 2nd Dublins wrote in a rather exaggerated tone about the taking of Wijtschate:

As you may imagine, we have been having a very exciting time, but as far as fighting goes, we had little to do as the Germans, i.e. those who had no time to escape, were only too willing to surrender. We took hundreds of prisoners. There is no use telling you the results as you must know them better than we do. I will tell you more about it when I have time and write a decent letter. The 16th Division were chiefly instrumental in taking the most difficult bit of ground including several ridges and two villages ... The men are all in splendid spirits but rather tired as they have not washed or slept for days. We hope to be relieved soon but at present we are very busy consolidating our new positions.[42]

When things had quietened down a bit, Glanville wrote a more detailed letter home to his mother on Sunday 15 June, when the 2nd Dublins were out of the line in Tatinghem, France:

I wonder if you got the letter I wrote during our last tour in the trenches when we took the valuable Wijtschate/Messines Ridge from the Germans. I was in it all right but our battalion had a minor part to play, partly because we had done very valuable work in a raid previous to the attack. We had to take over the new positions on the night of the attack but the Germans were so beaten that they did not trouble us with anything like a counter attack.

The whole advance was a wonderful affair. We had practically no casualties, thanks to our artillery which really was responsible for the success. The German trenches and small dugouts were battered out of all recognition. The large dugouts were battered in. The Germans had fled from or were caught in the others. Our artillery must have buried hundreds of the Germans during the show and the preliminary bombardment I need hardly tell you, the place shrieked like nothing describable. Dead everywhere, mostly buried; as those who managed to escape our artillery were only too glad to become prisoners. The thing was splendidly organised. A few hours after the show started our field guns were moved up, our pack mules were right into the old German lines with supplies and we had even German prisoners carrying up ammunition and consolidating material to the lines as we took them. They worked very willingly too. One guard to about twenty prisoners was sufficient. We also made them carry down our wounded. Between work and submitting themselves to the never ceasing searches of our men for souvenirs, they did not get much peace. I got a Mauser pistol as a souvenir myself ...[43]

The number of casualties suffered by the 16th (Irish) Division at Guillemont and Ginchy in September 1916 during the later phases of the Somme campaign was a total of 4,330 killed, wounded or missing.[44] In contrast, the casualty figures for the division between midnight on 6/7 June to midday on 9 June at Wijtschate were nine officers killed and fifty-six wounded,125 men of other ranks killed and 844 wounded, with 149 missing: a total loss of 1,183.[45]

The regiment within the 16th (Irish) Division with the highest death casualties was the 2nd Royal Irish Regiment. Twenty-five men of other ranks and one officer were killed. They came in on the second assault wave to take the second objective about 350 metres beyond the buildings of L'Hospice at the northern end of Wijtschate. L'Hospice was a ruined hostel and a German strong point, which put up a stubborn defence in the initial assault by the 7th/8th Royal Irish Fusiliers, who, in fact, bypassed it. It was later used as a dressing station where their chaplain, Fr William Fitzmaurice, was awarded the Military Cross for tending to his wounded men whilst himself being wounded and under shell fire. One young man killed with the 7th/8th Royal Irish Fusiliers was Private Jimmy Halfpenny, a Belfast Catholic who had originally enlisted in the Connaught Rangers. On 12 July 1912 Jimmy, as a 'weedy boy', had been one of many Roman Catholic Belfast shipyard workers who were run out of the Queen's Island yards following a clash between Home Rulers and Orangemen at Castledawson in County Londonderry.[46]

Losses to the Ulster Division between midday on 6 June and midday on 9 June at Wijtschate were sixty-one officers and 1,058 other ranks killed, wounded and missing, which was a total of 1,119.[47] The 14th Royal Irish Rifles suffered the highest loss of men of any battalion in the Ulster Division on 7 June: forty-one of their men were killed.[48] On 1 July 1916 losses to the Ulster Division at Thiepval had been 5,104.[49]

Despite the human sentiments expressed by Fr Willie Doyle in his attitude towards his fellow human beings, that is the German prisoners, soldiers from both sides inflicted equal doses of terror on each other. Nobody had the monopoly on battlefield virtue. Yes, there were moments of humanity shown, but a soldier named Private W. D. Gallwey, serving with the 47th (Queensland Tasmania) Battalion, 4th Australian Division assigned to take Messines, presented the darker side of what men could do in times of war. Private Gallwey's division was engaged at the southern end of the Wijtschate–Messines salient. When called upon, they were used as a reserve assault division. As they lay waiting to advance towards the Oosttaverne Line, they were heavily shelled by German artillery and suffered appallingly. As they moved forward, Gallwey's section came under machine-gun fire from a German blockhouse:

The gun in this blockhouse was now silenced by our machine guns so we moved on again. Walked right up to the place and a couple of men went into the entrance where the gun crew was found all huddled up inside. They evidently had been wounded and killed by our fire. No time was lost here however, our men fired point blank into the group. There was a noise as though pigs were being killed. They squealed and made guttural noises which gave place to groans after which all was silent. The bodies were all thrown in a heap outside the block house to make sure all were dead. There were five of them together. Nearly all were young men. It is an impossibility to leave wounded Germans behind us because they are so treacherous. They all have

253

to be killed. Too often after an advance, our men have been shot in the back by the wounded they left in the field. Now to obviate such a thing, we have what is called a 'mopping up party'. This consists of a small number of troops and [they] despatch any of the enemy who might have been passed over in the first rush. Sometimes in our hurry we leave a wounded man and then the duty of the mopping up party is to finish him. Their work would be light today for we are determined to kill every German we come across.[50]

'Despatch' was an interesting word chosen by Private Gallwey for the act of murder.

The Australians were not the only ones who carried out such atrocities. The Irish battalions who took Wijtschate had their own mopping units.

By 8 p.m. on 7 June the 6th Royal Irish Regiment had set up their headquarters in a captured concrete dugout in the north-east corner of Petit Bois. Exhausted and mentally drained, they settled into an obliterated muddy German trench and slept through a noisy night. They hadn't had much rest since they had entered the line at 1 a.m. on the previous Wednesday morning, which was roughly forty-three hours earlier.[51]

On the morning of 8 June their headcount began. There were thirty-one men who didn't answer the call: four officers and twenty-seven men of other ranks. The four officers were Major Willie Redmond, Captain Capel Desmond O'Brien Butler, Second Lieutenant Robert Hewitt and Second Lieutenant Michael 'Al' Wall.[52] It is not known for certain at what time during the attack or where exactly Michael was killed. However, since he was a member of 'B' Company and they, along with Redmond's 'A' Company, were involved in the attack on the first objective, it seems likely to have been during that operation. It would not be too far off the mark to assume that he was killed sometime between 3.10 a.m. and 3.30 a.m. and somewhere in the short distance between Maedelstede Farm and Nap Support Trench, not very far from where Major Redmond was fatally hit. There is every possibility that both men were hit by short-falling shells fired from their own side when the creeping barrage began.

Michael was nineteen years, one month and seventeen days old. He had been with the battalion at the front for 228 days, a little over seven months. Although he died in a soldier's uniform, Michael Wall was not a soldier, certainly not a combat soldier. He did not partake in any other major combat operations that his battalion undertook. What would this gentle young man have done had he been confronted by a Prussian Guard in Wijtschate? Killing would have been difficult for him.

Perhaps because of the death of his father, Michael was devoted to his mother. His regular letters to her testify to that. She never forgot him and kept all his letters and his cap badge. His siblings lost their big brother; they must have cried bitter tears when they got the bad news. As his teacher in St Joseph's, Brother O'Farrell, predicted, Michael did turn out to be a fine man, but sadly God did not spare him as O'Farrell had wished. He was a bright young man on his way to University College Dublin when war broke out. He liked his *Irish Times* and smoking his pipe. He had no time for the politics of Sinn Féin. Like many young men at the outbreak of the war, he was smitten, almost seduced, by the thought of adventure in a foreign land. The war was just a means to fulfil that quest for adventure. However, within weeks of his arrival in the war zone, he realised he had made a mistake in enlisting. He became disillusioned and angry at those who were not with him in mind and body. But there was no way out. His death at Wijtschate deprived him of his future. He would never have the opportunity of loving a woman, perhaps having children and telling his grandchildren about the day his regiment took Wijtschate from the Germans. His death and the deaths of those young men who died with him – be they Irish or Prussian – deprived the world of great potential. Redmond's death deprived Ireland of a reconciling nationalist voice at a time when it was needed. What could these men have contributed to a post-war Ireland and Europe had they lived? Tragically we will never know.

Although Willie Redmond died that day, there were signs that his gospel of Irish reconciliation had not fallen on deaf ears. During the late afternoon of the attack on Wijtschate, like many of the unit commanding officers who took part in the attack, Major J. C. Boyle of the Ulster Division's 150th Field Company took a walk on the front to inspect the work his men were doing in consolidating a part of the line the infantry had captured. He found his men working beside and in co-operation with some Munster Fusiliers. Major Boyle didn't miss the political significance of men from the Munsters working together with men from a Field Company of Engineers attached to the Ulster Division. He noted the following in the war diary:

> Number 1 Section I found had not been able to start work owing to hostile shelling. Lt Thorne was just starting them in conjunction with 16th Division Royal Munster Fusiliers. So Ulster and the South of Ireland consolidate a position. The Orange and Green working together and blended well.[53]

Rev. John Redmond was a Church of Ireland chaplain attached to the 9th Royal Inniskilling Fusiliers on the day of the attack. Again on the theme of men from both Irish divisions working together, he wrote:

It was impressive to see what a feeling of security before the battle the Ulster Division had in having the 16th Irish on our left flank and that the 16th Division had in having our Ulster Division on their right flank. This feeling of goodwill and confidence between the two divisions had been growing for some time. I wish the entire north and south that they represent, could participate in the same spirit.[54]

Colonel H. C. Wylly CB added similar sentiments to those expressed by Rev. Redmond and Major Boyle:

Messines was distinguishable in the current account as an 'Irish Day'. The Wijtschate end of the ridge was taken by Irish battalions, in which were Ulster men and South of Ireland men, men who take different sides in the religious and political controversies which separate Ireland, but who take a common view as to the necessity of ending the German threat to civilisation.[55]

Over the next couple of days, Michael's body and those of his comrades who had died on the battlefield with him were gathered and brought back to Kemmel for identification and burial. Willie Redmond was buried in the garden of the nuns' convent at Loker at 6.30 p.m. on 8 June. Troops from the 10th Royal Inniskillings of the Ulster Division and the 2nd Royal Irish Regiment from the 16th (Irish) Division provided the Guard of Honour. On hearing of Redmond's death, Rowland Fielding wrote home to his wife:

How one's ideas change! And how war makes one loathe the party politics and condone and even approve when his opponents revile such a man as this! I classify him with Stephen Gwynn and Harrison – all three, MEN – Irish Nationalists, too, whom you and I, in our

Tory schooling, have been brought up to regard as anathema! What effect will his death have in Ireland? I wonder. Will he be a saint or a traitor? I hope and pray it may teach all – North as well as South – something of the larger side of their duty to the Empire.[56]

When Michael's battalion got back to the safety of their billets at Renmore Camp, the battalion headquarters was visited by journalists William Beach Thomas and Philip Gibbs. Beach Thomas wrote that the death of Willie Redmond in an Ulster Field Ambulance had 'exercised almost a mystic influence on many of the troops, as I know from the lips of officers and soldiers of his unit. It symbolised mystically the value of his sacrifice and softened the shock of his death.'[57]

Captain O'Brien Butler, an ex-Belvedere College boy, had been killed trying to take a German concrete bunker. Which bunker is not recorded; it may well have been the one in which the battalion set up its headquarters, or it may have been the one on the southern end of Petit Bois, part of which is still there. He is buried at Kemmel Chateau Military Cemetery, not very far from where he died.[58]

Second Lieutenant Hewitt was twenty-nine when he died. He came from Bognor in England. His body was found on 9 June and was buried in Kemmel Chateau Military Cemetery along with Michael, Captain O'Brien Butler and two other men.

Michael's battalion seemed to attract a lot of attention on 9 June. Not only was it visited by two eminent journalists, but the men were 'cinematographed going into the canteen' at Renmore Camp.[59] Sadly, however, Michael Wall wasn't with them.

18

One Haversack
and Six Religious Medallions

One summer's day during Michael Wall's childhood in Howth, he had played in the local fields facing their house with the boy next door. That boy was Charles Marchant, whom Michael had mentioned in the February 1917 letter to his mother: 'met one of the Marchants, he is in the 9th Dublins. You remember they stayed beside us one summer in Howth.'[1] Later in their lives, these two young men had met again, but in fields neither as playful nor as happy as those of their childhood back in Howth. There were no seagulls flying about, no scurrying rabbits; the smell was not of freshly cut grass. These instead were the fields, as Tom Kettle once wrote, where 'tired men sigh, with mud for couch and floor'.[2]

On 4 June 1917 the 9th Dublin Fusiliers were camped in Clare Camp near Bailleul, preparing for their part in the battle to take Wijtschate. The German naval gun mounted on the canal barge had its sights well set on Clare Camp.[3] As a safety precaution, the Dublins were ordered not to sleep in their tents, so had to sleep under hedges in the fields near the camp. Second Lieutenants Charles Marchant and Edmund Cooney were in an old farmhouse at the corner of the camp when one of the shells from the barge fell nearby, obliterating the building and killing both young men outright.[4]

Could anyone, watching those two boys playing together in a field in Howth, have foreseen that they would die together in a terrible war within a week of each other?

Charles Marchant came from 2 Greenmount Road, Terenure in Dublin. Educated at the High School, Dublin, he was only twenty-one when he was killed. *The Irish Times* noted on the death of Marchant: 'Clontarf Cricket Club has lost another of its most prominent members.'[5] Edmund Cooney came from Harmony House, Donnybrook, also in Dublin. He was twenty-seven when he died alongside Charles. Both men are buried in Loker Church-yard British Military Cemetery.[6]

Every spare minute of every day that Michael was away, he must have flashed through his mother's mind. What was he doing? Where was he? Was he safe? Did he get to mass? Back in Carrick Hill, his bed was still made up, cold and untouched. There had been no music in the evenings since he left, just silence.

Not long after he had gone to France, the postman had delivered the first of Michael's many letters to his mother. He was alive and safe. Over the next few weeks and months, he regularly wrote home. Often he had little to write about, but the letters were important and served a purpose. Theresa kept all of them in a folder. Like any mother, she wanted to protect her son as much as she could. She had a mass said for him. She brought his mind home by telling him all the local gossip and chat. She sent him *The Irish Times*, his pipe, sweets and cakes. She looked forward to the postman coming with Michael's regular letters. All seemed well.

Then one day the postman arrived with a different-coloured envelope, a very official-looking envelope. Written over the top were the words 'Telegram. No Charge for Delivery'. It wasn't Michael's handwriting. Sitting down, heart racing and hands trembling, Theresa opened the envelope. The office stamp read 'Portmarnock, Ju 12 17'. Written in dark pencil were the words:

OHMS

War Office London

To Mrs. Wall, Carrick Hill, Malahide, Co Dublin.

Deeply regret to inform you 2nd Lieut M. T. Wall Irish Regiment was killed in action June 7th. The army council express their sympathy.   Secretary War Office[7]

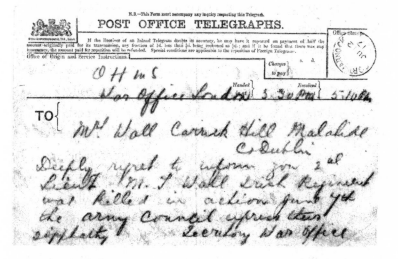

Not long after Michael's mother read that wretched telegram, she received two very consoling letters from Flanders. One, dated 11 June 1917, was from Michael's commanding officer, Lieutenant Colonel Roche-Kelly:

Dear Madam,

I very much regret to have to inform you of the death of your son, 2 Lt M. T. Wall in action on June 7th, during the battle in which the Irish Division did so well. I wish I could have been the bearer of better news, but it may be some consolation to you to learn that he died at the head of his men & that he suffered no pain, death was instantaneous. We buried your son in the military cemetery at KEMMEL a short way behind the battle field, with two officers of the Battalion, where his grave will be well looked after. The Revd Fr Wrafter S.J. officiated at the burial.

With deepest sympathy from all members of the battalion.

I remain,
Yours truly,
E Roche-Kelly
Lieut. Colonel
6th Bn Royal Irish Regt.[8]

The second letter, dated 12 June 1917, came from Michael's company quartermaster sergeant, Sergeant Henry Kellard:

Dear Madam,

You will probably have read of the great success of our troops in the capture of the strong positions on the Wytschate–Messines Ridge, and I am sorry that your joy in learning of this success should be clouded by the grief which this success has cost you. The bearing of sad news is always unpleasant, and how many mothers are there who daily dread that news? For in that great success, your son, whom we all loved so well as a gentleman and one ready to aid all, laid down his life not far from the spot where Major Willie Redmond was hit, and thus he sacrificed his all for the cause. He showed inspiring courage and coolness, and considerably helped in the success of the day.

Your son was ready for the sacrifice, and I hope you may accept also with reconciliation the cross laid upon you as one before has borne a heavier.

The N.C.Os and men appreciated very highly his worth as

an officer and a real gentleman, and with me they join in assuring you of their condolence and warmest sympathy.

I am, yours respectfully,
Henry F. Kellard
C.Q.M.S.
'B' Coy. 6th Royal Irish Regt. B.E.F. France.[9]

Dear Madam,

12th June 1917

You will probably have read of the great success of our troops in the capture of the strong position on the Wytschaete Messines Ridge, and I am sorry that your joy in learning of this success should be clouded by the grief which this success has cost you. The bearing of sad news is always unpleasant, and how many mothers are there who daily dread that news for in that great success, your son, whom we all loved so well as a gentleman and one ready to aid all, laid down his life not far from the spot where Major Willie Redmond was hit, and thus he sacrificed his all for the cause. He showed inspiring courage and coolness, and considerably helped in the success of the day.

Your son was ready for the sacrifice, and I hope you may accept also with reconciliation the cross laid upon you as one before has borne a heavier.

The N.C.Os and men appreciated very highly his worth as an officer and a real gentleman, and with me they join in assuring you of their condolence and warmest sympathy.

I am, yours Respectfully,
Henry J. Kellard C.Q.M.S.
B Coy. 6th Royal Irish Regt. B.E.F. France

Mrs. Wall

A few days later, on 17 June, the standard telegram arrived from Buckingham Palace:

> To Mrs Wall, Carry [sic] Hill, Malahide, Co Dublin

> The King and Queen deeply regret the loss you and the Army have sustained by the death of your son in the service of his country. Their Majesties sincerely sympathise with you in your sorrow.   Keeper of the Privy Purse.[10]

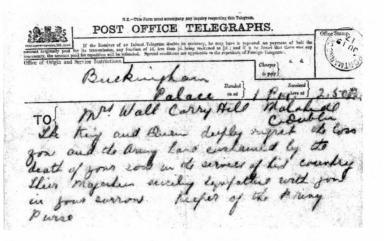

One must wonder: did the 'Keeper of the Privy Purse' even know Michael's name? These formal telegrams seemed cold, faceless and matter of fact. They didn't even have a name on them. Who was the 'Secretary of the War Office'? Who was the 'Keeper of the Privy Purse'? Who cared? Could the faceless sender of such terrible news not have the decency and respect to even write his or her name? Perhaps when one has written thousands of such telegrams day in day out, names and faces become irrelevant.

With a sad bit of irony, notice of Michael's death appeared in the Monday 18 June edition of his favourite read, *The Irish Times*:

'Second Lieutenant Michael Wall, Royal Irish Regiment son of the late Michael Wall of Hollybrook Road, Clontarf, was killed in action on the 7th inst.'[11]

On 25 June a staff captain from the War Office's Graves Registration and Enquiries section at Winchester House, St James's Square, London, wrote to Michael's mother informing her that her son had been buried in Kemmel Chateau Military Cemetery.[12] His grave reference was X.73. Later she received a card from the Imperial (later Commonwealth) War Graves Commission with a photograph of Michael's grave, which had a wooden cross planted in the earth under which Michael was buried.[13]

W2805—R1706 20,000 5/17 HWV(P923)   G17/385

The number below should be quoted on any further communication on this subject	The Director of Graves Registration and Enquiries,
17/23276	WAR OFFICE, Winchester House, St. James's Square, LONDON, S.W.1.

25 JUN 1917

Madam,

I am directed to inform you that a report has been received which states that the late 2nd Lieutenant M. T. Wall, 3/att. 6th Irish Regiment is buried in Kemmel Chateau Military Cemetery, S. W. of Ypres.

The grave has been registered in this office, and is marked by a durable wooden cross with an inscription bearing full particulars.

I am,

Madam,

Your obedient Servant,

[signature]

Captain, Staff Captain,

D.A.A.G. for Brigadier-General,

Director, Graves Registration and Enquiries.

Mrs. Wall,
   Carrick Hill,
      Malahide,
         Co. Dublin.

The Vice-Chairman
Imperial War Graves Commission

Begs to forward as requested a Photograph, taken by
the Director - General of Graves Registration and
Enquiries, of the Grave of :—

Name _____ *Wall*

Rank and Initials _____ *2nd Lieut M.T.*

Regiment _____ *Royal Irish Regt*

Position of Grave _____ *Kemmel Chateau*

Military Cemetery

All communications respecting this Photograph should quote the
number ⟨763/14/20924⟩ and be addressed to :—
IMPERIAL WAR GRAVES COMMISSION,
82, Baker Street,
London, W. 1.

Owing to the circumstances in which the photographic work is carried on, it is
regretted that in some cases only rough Photographs can be obtained.

[M1366] 86361/Wt11 12m 8/21. G & S. E. 7297.

**Michael's grave at Kemmel Chateau Military Cemetery, Kemmel,
Flanders.**

Over the remaining summer months and early autumn of
1917, Theresa set about obtaining the few possessions Michael
had had with him when he died. It is not known for certain who
gathered up Michael's personal effects after he had been killed, but
it may well have been Sergeant Kellard. It was the responsibility
of his commanding officer to see that these effects were forwarded
to the War Office in London, which, in turn, handed them over
to a shipping agent named Messrs Cox and Co., Shipping Agency
Ltd, based at 16 Charing Cross, London. It was this agency's
responsibility to deliver Michael's effects to his mother at Carrick
Hill.[14]

On 27 June Theresa signed 'Army Form 126A – Effects', which essentially was an agreement between the 'Executor of the Late Officer's Will' – that is the deceased officer's father, mother or widow – and the Army Council to undertake 'to pay or secure the payment of any public or preferential claims that may exist against his estate'.[15] Although a man might have died for his country, his country was not prepared to pick up any bad debts he left behind. Within the War Office there was an office called 'The Standing Committee of Adjustments'. One of its jobs was to go through the personal accounts of deceased officers and present a report to the Secretary of State for War on each deceased soldier's financial affairs. The report it presented on Michael showed that he did in fact have a servant and that the servant was due eleven shillings in wages. After receiving a credit of two pounds and one shilling, and taking out the servant's wages of eleven shillings, the report concluded that a balance of one pound and ten shillings was now in the hands of the paymaster and, being part of Michael's estate, was due to Mrs Wall.

The following were items of Michael's personal effects:

1 Box of writing paper and envelopes.

1 Small package for posting (addressed to Miss H. O'Connor, The Grove, Celbridge, Co. Kildare.)

1 Envelope containing sample letters, greeting cards and religious cards.

1 Tobacco Pouch.

2 Compasses in case (1 with sling.) One of the compasses had the initials R.B. Knox inscribed on it.

1 Haversack.

2 Note cases.

1 Whistle lanyard.

6 Religious medallions.

1 Identity disc.

2 Railway Time Tables.

1 Tie pin.

1 Inch tape.

Francs 1.50.[16]

When Michael's mother received the package of his belongings, there were in fact some items missing. On 30 July she wrote back to the War Office:

> Carrick Hill,
> Malahide,
> Co. Dublin.
>
> Sir,
>
> With reference to the death in action on June 7th 1917 of Sec. Lt M. T. Wall 3rd attached 6th Royal Irish Regiment, I beg to inform you that there are some of his belongings which I have not yet received. These comprise a wrist watch, fountain pen (Waterman), a pair of field glasses, a new tobacco pouch, brandy flask, bunch of keys and a silver cigarette case. I would feel deeply grateful if you would kindly inquire about them and let me know if it is possible to trace them.
>
> I am Sir,
> Your obedient servant,
> Theresa Wall.[17]

Theresa received a response to her letter from the War Office, dated 7 August 1917. It informed her 'that no further effects of the late Second Lieutenant M. T. Wall, 3rd attached 6th Battalion, Royal Irish Regiment, have yet been placed at the disposal of this

Department'.[18] Theresa never did get the missing items. They may seem trivial, but such things are dear to a broken heart.

Theresa was now left with three children. There was Joseph, who was seventeen; Agatha, fifteen; and Bernard, nine. Living with her sister at Carrick Hill, Theresa had little or no personal income to support this family. She thought that, since the death of Michael deprived her of a potential wage earner, a letter to the War Office might improve her lot. She asked one of her relations to write on her behalf:

> 41 Kenilworth Park,
> Rathgar,
> Dublin
>
> 19th September 1917.
>
> Dear Sir,
>
> I am writing to you on behalf of Mrs T. Wall, Carrick Hill, Malahide, to know if there is any money due to her son the late 2nd Lt M. T. Wall who was killed in action about July 9th last. He joined the service in February 1916 and went to France the following October. There is £8–6s–4d showing in his account at Cox and Co. His banking number is T.2 369/4993. I believe a gratuity under Royal Warrant for pay is given to relatives and if same is sent to Mrs Wall it would be a great help to her.
>
> She is a widow with four children, 2nd Lt Wall being the eldest and the only one who contributed to her support, needless to say he was a great loss to her in every way. Mrs Wall who is in reduced circumstances is at present living with her sister but leaving her very shortly.
>
> Yours truly
> (Miss) L. G. Willan

PS. 2nd Lt M. T. Wall was in the 3rd Royal Irish Regt. He made no will he being under age.[19]

In early October 1917 Theresa paid a visit to Fr Robert Carrick, the parish priest of Peter and Paul's Church, Baldoyle, County Dublin. They were good friends. Fr Carrick had said a couple of masses for Michael. When Michael had wanted to enlist in November 1915, Fr Carrick had signed a character reference form for him. Now, under much sadder circumstances, he had to act as a witness and sign a written statement in Theresa's presence, the Army Effects Form 107, which stated that Michael had left no will.[20]

Whatever Theresa was entitled to and whatever she got from the War Office, nothing could ever compensate her for the loss of Michael.

19

Remembrance

By November 1927 Michael Wall was ten years dead. In a kind and humane act, Theresa's sister Margo had allowed Theresa and her young family to remain on at Carrick Hill after his death. It was there that Theresa reared and educated her three remaining children the best way she could. On Thursday 3 November 1927 plans for the coming war-remembrance weekend services in Dublin were advertised in the public-notice section of *The Irish Times*. That year, Armistice Day fell on Friday 11 November, and the annual remembrance parade was to take place to the temporary Irish Cenotaph in the Phoenix Park, Dublin.

Opposition appeared to the commemoration on the night before the parade, when a public meeting was held by the Anti-Imperialist Association in Foster Place, Dublin. Its secretary, Mr Ryan, essentially told the gathering that they, that is the anti-imperialists, 'were in the majority now and whether the Imperialists liked it or not they would have to abide by it'.[1] After the meeting they marched off towards O'Connell Street, and a few 'roughs' amongst the marchers resorted to 'poppy snatching' – ripping the poppy from the lapel of the wearer's coat. At Westmoreland Street the police moved in and broke up the marchers with 'commendable firmness'.[2]

Antagonism towards remembrance parades in Dublin often manifested itself in the form of poppy snatching in the days leading up to Remembrance Sunday. Even then, the flower had become divisive and, to some, a symbol of British imperialism. On one occasion, poppy snatchers got an unpleasant surprise when they tried to grab the poppy from the collar of a little girl named Jane O'Reilly, who remembered walking with her father along the north quays in Dublin to the Phoenix Park. Her father, Jimmy O'Reilly, was a Dublin Fusilier who had survived the war and who worked at the *Irish Independent* newspaper. Jimmy used to put a pin behind the poppy on Jane's little coat, so that if anybody tried to grab it, they would get a pin stuck in their hand.[3]

Poppy sellers also became a target for Irish republican anger, as did poppy depots. The house of Mr Tom Barry from Carrigtwohill, County Cork was raided by three armed and masked men who burnt his store of poppies and stole his typewriter.[4] However, despite the bands of poppy snatchers who roamed the streets of Dublin in 1927, the Flanders flower was worn in Dáil Éireann. *The Irish Times* reported:

There were poppies in the Dáil yesterday. A godly bunch bloomed on the Government back-benches; they were scattered here and there amongst the Independents; two or three flowered in the Press gallery and a few were visible up aloft where a dozen or so of the general public watched the proceedings. In all, seventeen deputies wore the Remembrance emblem, among them being Mr Heffernan (Parliamentary Secretary for Posts and Telegraphs), Messrs Osmond Esmonde, Cumann na nGaedheal Government TD for Wexford, Alfred Byrne, Independent TD for Dublin North, Mahony McDonagh, Cumann na nGaedheal Government TD for Galway and P. W. Shaw, Cumann na nGaedheal Government TD for Westmeath (always active in the interests of the ex-Servicemen). George Wolfe, Cumann na nGaedheal Government TD for Kildare (an ex-Cavalry officer and has an unmistakable Cavalry bearing), Jasper Wolfe, Major Bryan Cooper, Government TD for Dublin County, Captain Redmond, National League Party TD for Waterford, John Good, Independent TD for Dublin County,

E. H. Alton, Independent TD for Dublin University, W. E. Thrift, Independent TD for Dublin University, Sir James Craig and Major Myles who wore his military medals including the Military Cross.[5]

Armistice Day in Dublin in 1927 was cold, bright and sunny. The ex-servicemen assembled in Beresford Place facing the Customs House at 9.30 a.m. They formed up in fours facing Butt Bridge in accordance with the branch of the British Legion of which they were members. The branches that lined up that day were Bachelor's Walk, Rathmines, Insurance, 5th Lancers, 8th Royal Irish Hussars, Mountjoy Square, Great Northern Railways, Kingstown, Old Comrades, Killester, Jacob's, and Trinity College OTC. Veterans who were members of the Irish Transport and General Workers' Union also marched in the parade. Bringing up the rear was the Irish Guards Club.

Early in the morning, the Killester ex-servicemen travelled by train from Killester to Amiens Street Station. Their train journey was free of charge, compliments of the Great Northern Railway. Their leader was an ex-Royal Inniskilling Fusilier, Captain J. C. De Lacy MC. At Amiens Street they laid a wreath at the memorial in the train station to the members of the Great Northern Railway who had died in the war. Following the wreath-laying, the men walked down the inclined road from the station and by the Custom House to Beresford Place.[6] There was a great hum around Beresford Place with hundreds of men in conversation, smoking and generally shuffling about in the cold, sunlit air. Over the hum of the voices came a familiar loud and commanding roar from Major W. Nolan to form up.

At 9.45 a.m., in companies of 200 strong under the command of Major Nolan, the parade marched off in military formation via Eden Quay up the northern line of the city quays. Leading the parade was the brass band from the Bachelor's Walk Branch of the Royal British Legion. There were two other fife-and-drum bands in the parade. In behind the Bachelor's Walk band came the leaders of the British Legion in the Irish Free State, who included General Sir William Hickie KCB, Major Bryan Cooper, Captain Redmond and British Legion area councillors. Next in line came the Bachelor's Walk Branch, and so on through the ranks of branches down to the Irish Guards Club at the rear.

On they marched in quick time up the quays to cheers from well-wishers and sneers from others. For 364 days of the past few years, the majority of the men who marched that Friday morning through Dublin were nobodies. However, on 11 November they put on their medals, polished their boots and marched in their finery through Dublin with their chests out and heads held high. *The Irish Times* reported:

> In the measured beat of the marching ranks there was no hint of the broken boots that scarcely kept the hoar frost from some feet, weary with their fruitless search for work. The swing of the straight shoulders held no apology for the coat that might be threadbare; and above the shining medals were eyes that looked ahead, yet held a proud realisation of the crowds who stood and watched.[7]

One prominent figure amongst the men was Fr Newcombe, who had once been chaplain in the 1st, 51st and 61st Divisions. At the head and rear of the procession were two large Union Jacks. Smaller Union flags were carried here and there in the parade and on some of them were the words 'Honour the Dead'.

Strangely tagged onto the parade was a group from the Irish fascists organisation. 'Bareheaded, wearing black shirts and carrying their banner', they 'were a distinctive section of the procession'.[8]

Quite a number of women, young and old, who were relatives of men who had fought in the war, also took part. General Hickie estimated that 18,000 people marched through Dublin that day to the Phoenix Park.[9] Police estimates for the following year put the number of ex-servicemen who paraded at 20,000. A further 10,000 witnessed the ceremony in the Phoenix Park. So Hickie's estimate seemed reasonable.[10] Traffic along the quays was held up as the parade moved along.

They passed Collins (Royal) Barracks, from which some of the men would have marched out on their way to Gallipoli or France, or indeed to fight against the Irish Volunteers in 1916. Just before 11 a.m. the parade entered the Phoenix Park by the main entrance at Parkgate Street. As they passed through the gate, the band struck up 'The Old Brigade', and the men on parade proceeded to take their place around their Cenotaph – which was in fact the wooden Ginchy Cross brought back from Guillemont.

Railwaymen from Harcourt Street, Inchicore, Westland Row (Pearse Street) and Kingsbridge (Heuston) Stations earlier in the morning had laid a wreath at the memorial in the railway station at Kingsbridge. The memorials at Amiens Street (Connolly) and Kingsbridge Stations list the railwaymen who were killed in the Great War, and are still there, cared for by Iarnród Éireann (Irish Rail). In the Law Courts at Dublin Castle, members of the Bar assembled at the Bronze Memorial and laid wreaths in memory of their fallen colleagues.[11]

Following their wreath-laying service at Kingsbridge Railway Station, other men from the Great Southern Railway Branch of the British Legion – and from suburban branches from Inchicore, Phibsborough, Palmerstown and Guinness Brewery – marched into the park and in turn took up their positions around the Ginchy Cross.

The ceremony took place at the foot of the Wellington Monument. The Ginchy Cross was temporarily erected about seventy metres away from the foot of the eastern side of the monument. In the form of an amphitheatre, an estimated 30,000 people gathered around the cross. The band took its place on the northern end of the cross; directly facing it on the southern side of the cross were the officers of the Royal British Legion in Dublin. Like a scene from the Catholic shrine at Lourdes in France, on the eastern side of the cross were located the invalid veterans from the Blackrock Military Pensions Hospital. Earlier in the morning about 300 patients in their blue uniforms, with civilian overcoats and hats, had paraded in the hospital grounds and those who could marched to the church of St John the Baptist in Blackrock, where mass was celebrated by the Rev. Fr O'Gorman, CF. After mass, the men paraded in Carysfort Avenue and then boarded three special tram cars, which brought them to the entrance of the Phoenix Park, where they took up their positions at the cross. Some sixty limbless patients who were ex-servicemen were conveyed to the park in charabancs (a kind of open bus) and cared for at the cross by members of the Queen Mary Army Auxiliary Corps and nurses from the hospital. Distinguished visitors were issued with a ticket that allowed them to bring their cars into the park near the cross.

As the crowd assembled and everybody took their appointed places, the band played Chopin's funeral march. At 10.59 a.m. precisely, the last post was sounded by a bugler, and two minutes of silence followed.

The Irish Times, eloquent as ever, portrayed the scene:

The Last Post pierced the morning air and a great hush fell on the multitude that had gathered to pay homage to the fallen. Away in the distance a siren hooted mournfully; the hum of an aeroplane, glittering in a brilliant sky, faded into oblivion and for those two poignant moments there was silence.[12]

At exactly the same time back in the city, outside Trinity College, students held a service of remembrance by observing a two-minute silence. With the exception of buildings such as Trinity College, the Bank of Ireland, the Ulster Bank, the Royal Bank of Ireland and Kingsbridge Terminus, there was little or no display of flags in the city centre or indeed of the two-minute silence. Perhaps reflecting the duality of allegiance that existed amongst the people of Dublin in November 1927, the Union Jack was flown alongside the Irish Tricolour over Trinity College.[13]

Across the road, in Foster Place, a rival crowd from the Anti-Imperialist Association held a rally in opposition to the students holding their meeting. Following the two-minute silence, the students began to sing 'God Save the King'. Immediately the Anti-Imperialists began singing 'The Soldiers' Song', the anthem of the Irish Free State.

Meanwhile back in the Phoenix Park, at precisely 11.02 a.m., the silence was broken with the sound of reveille. There then followed a wreath-laying ceremony. First up was General Hickie, who laid a wreath made from poppies in the shape of a cross. He was followed by the Irish writer Katherine Tynan Hinkson, and so on, until all those who wished to lay a wreath had done so. Soon the base of the wooden cross was hidden under a pile of colourful wreaths.

As the procession of wreath-layers marched past the cross, the band played suitable tunes such as 'Brother, thou are gone before us'. *The Irish Times* reported:

Company after company, bearing their standards and wearing their shining medals, the ex-Service men marched past the cross that is the headstone of fifty thousand Irish graves. Bands crashed out the old wartime tunes that we all knew so well, while the men who fought and lived marched back to their jobs in factory, workshop and office ... hundreds of sad-faced women, mothers, sisters and wives of the dead, formed a pitiful procession round the cross.[14]

It was only those who were employed who 'marched back to their jobs'. Many who marched had no jobs and lived in near destitution. Moreover, there were veterans who could not physically march in the parade: men who had been crippled and left to look after themselves, and men left insane and ruined by the effects of shell shock and alcohol abuse from depression and loneliness. There were also men who were disillusioned and, as a matter of principle, would not march in the parade.

As the contingents of ex-servicemen and British Legion branches marched past the cross, General Hickie took the salute, after which the 'National Anthem was sung by thirty thousand voices. Generals, privates, peers and labourers stand to attention as in days that are gone.'[15] The national anthem, according to *The Irish Times*, was of course 'God Save the King'. The *Irish Independent* suggested a mixed reaction to this: 'A section of the crowd began singing God Save the King. A large number of people wearing poppies began to leave when this was in progress and at its conclusion there were outbursts of cheering.'[16]

When the march past and ceremony were finished, the companies of men marched off in the direction of the Islandbridge Gate and out of the park, continuing along Conyngham Road and the northern quays to the centre of Dublin. General Hickie and a few others – such as Sir Simon Maddock, the ex-governor of the RHMS – travelled over to lay a wreath at the Celtic Cross War Memorial in the grounds of the RHMS. It was from this same school that Michael's friend R. W. Smyth had written to him in 1915 about the chances of getting a commission.[17]

As the parade from the Phoenix Park proceeded back to the city centre, scuffles broke out between marchers and a group of men from the Anti-Imperialist Association. At Ormond Quay, a fight began when men from the association tried to take a Union Jack that one of the marching women was waving. 'The encounter developed into a large scale boxing match. Dozens of young men could be seen exchanging blows.' The police moved in and broke up the fight.[18] Ten years earlier, many of these veterans had stood their ground against German and Turkish shell fire; the last thing they were going to run away from was a boxing match with a few individuals.

It should be no surprise that such aggravation was seen around the city. The fascists in their black shirts and tightly cropped hair marched back from the park waving the Union Jack as well. In many ways it was disingenuous of the organisers of the remembrance services to parade this flag in Dublin at such an unstable time in the fledgling Irish Free State. There were consequences, and the Irish government imposed conditions on the British Legion in the holding of future parades throughout the state.

By 1.15 p.m. Dublin had returned to normal. Along the route back to the city centre there were – as there still are – plenty of watering holes. No doubt, in the snug of these public houses the First, Second and Third Battles of Ypres, along with the landings at Gallipoli, were fought all over again.

In the rest of Dublin, life went on as usual. In the afternoon The Waratahs, a touring rugby team from New South Wales, beat Ireland in a rugby match by five points to three at Lansdowne Road. They too had a representative who laid a wreath in the Phoenix Park. Apart from a few scuffles in Grafton Street, the night was relatively quiet by the previous year's standards. For those who could afford it, *Smiling Irish Eyes* was on stage at the Theatre Royal. The poppy snatchers and the poppy wearers had gone home to hang up their banners for another year. The Ginchy Cross in the Phoenix Park stood in silence and total darkness. Around it lay approximately seventy wreaths of all shapes and sizes, put there by people from all strands of Irish society. But, for the first time in ten years, and indeed for the last time ever, one wreath under that famous cross had this simple note attached: 'Mrs Wall of Carrick Hill, Malahide (son)'.[19]

20

Michael's Belated Funeral – a Personal Reflection

In 1966, like most Irish schools during that year, Michael Wall's old school, St Joseph's CBS in Dublin, celebrated the golden jubilee of the 1916 Easter Rising. A booklet was produced containing details of the twenty-four past pupils who had fought in the Rising. On 22 April 1966 the staff and students attended a special mass in the Church of the Visitation in Fairview. On their return to the school, a short ceremony was held, which included an address to the pupils by the principal, Brother McCaffrey, on the subject of the Rising. There then followed a reading of the Proclamation and a raising of the national flag by Matthew Connolly, brother of Captain Seán Connolly, a past pupil who had been killed during Easter week fighting with the Irish Citizen Army. Afterwards an exhibition on the Rising, organised by the students, was opened in the school. Particular emphasis was placed on the role of past pupils and on revolutionary activity in the Fairview–Marino area of Dublin during the Rising.[1]

June 1967 would have been the golden jubilee of Michael Wall's death. However, his death and the circumstances in which he died were not commemorated by Brother McCaffrey or any of his staff. There were no exhibitions about the 16th (Irish) Division or the 6th Royal Irish Regiment at St Joseph's in 1967. The political atmosphere in Ireland at that time was a lot less tolerant of such history than it is today. Things were different then. In defence of

Brother McCaffrey, it is possible that neither he nor any of his staff knew anything about their past pupils who had died fighting with the Royal Irish Regiment in the Great War or fighting against their own schoolmates during Easter 1916. It would be nice to think that if he was aware of Michael, being a man of the cloth, he might have kept a prayer in his heart for Michael's soul as well as Seán Connolly's.

On a sunny Tuesday morning thirty-three years later, 5 September 2000, fifty-nine members and friends of the RDFA stepped off their touring bus, parked just off the Wijtschatestraat (the Suicide Road) outside Maedelstede Farm. Eighty or so metres along the road towards Wijtschate stands the Celtic Cross memorial to the 16th (Irish) Division. The group walked past the Maedelstede Farm mine crater blown early on the morning of 7 June 1917. Many of the tour party took photographs of the crater, which looked so peaceful surrounded by lush green grass and cattle grazing, and is today a quiet place where local people fish.[2] Swallows zipped through the air.

Earlier that morning I had guided the group on a battlefield tour and had told them what had happened to Michael Wall, Desmond O'Brien Butler, Willie Redmond, Robert Hewitt and many more Irishmen who liberated the village of Wijtschate on 7 June 1917. We walked on round the bend in the crater and tried to establish the exact spot from which Michael and his men took off on that June morning. Amongst the group were three brothers who were related to Michael: Andy, Dermot and Michael Kavanagh. These three men were accompanied by their wives, Rosemary, Aileen and Anne respectively. All six had come to Wijtschate for one reason, which was to give their long-forgotten, distant relative Michael Wall a belated family funeral.

Our group stopped at the place where we thought it was most

likely that Michael died. We just stood there quietly. Nobody said a word. The silence, broken only by the chirp of the odd swallow fluttering above us, brought a lump to my throat. I had got to know so much about this young man that his death was almost personal to me. Getting off the bus, I had had a feeling this would happen. I had thought to myself that these would be the hardest few minutes of our trip.

The silence and the sadness of Michael's story got to many of the individuals who stood together on that roadside. Some folks just wandered off – embarrassed, perhaps, to show their emotions. After a few moments, I told the gathering all I knew about this young man, about him writing to every girl he knew back home, about his pipe, his *Irish Times*, his initial sense of adventure and how it gradually turned into dejection and regret. Most of all, I told them about his mother and the letters he wrote to her. Like many of us, Andy's wife, Rosemary, was a bit upset when she spoke of Michael. We gathered some poppies and wild flowers growing around the spot where Michael and his comrades had died – something to bring home and remind us of our few minutes of silence.

We walked back to the bus and headed along the Wijtschate-straat towards the village of Kemmel, and on out to Michael's grave. We gathered round his headstone and Dermot began our service of remembrance. In a very broken and emotional voice, speaking on behalf of his family, Dermot told us about his forgotten distant cousin. He thanked all who stood around him for giving him and his family the opportunity to finally lay Michael to rest with the dignity he so rightly deserved. We said a decade of the rosary for Michael and the men who lay beside him. His mother would have liked that. We laid a wreath of poppies upon which was stapled a copy of the last letter Michael had written to his mother. Some day before I join him, I hope to place a bit of Carrick Hill over his grave.

Our group left the Kavanagh family at Michael's grave for their own private moment. The rest of us wandered around Kemmel Chateau Military Cemetery. There was very little talking. From my own point of view, I felt totally drained of emotion. This young man had been part of my life for the previous two or three years. Writing his story, I just didn't want to get to the part where he died. So long as he was alive in my story, he was alive in my heart and mind. I kept putting off having to write about 7 June. Visiting the place where he died and being with his family at his graveside was an honour and privilege for me. It was where I would end my story.[3]

That night our committee had booked a restaurant named En De Wolf near the village of Westoutre. It was our last night in Flanders. We invited some Belgian friends: Erwin Ureel and his wife, Mia, and Trees Vannesste and Johan Vandelanotte (RIP), who were members of the tourist office in Kemmel, without whom our successful tour simply would not have happened. Following our meal, Trees offered a very short speech. In my opinion, her few words told us something that, as Irish people, we had never really appreciated or heard before. For those in Ireland who thought and still think that Michael Wall, Willie Redmond, Tom Kettle and thousands more Irishmen like them died in vain or for the wrong cause, or were dupes of British militarism, in reply to their accusation, I offer the following words of a Flemish woman who lives in Wijtschate: 'Dear Irish Friends, it is a pleasure to see you here tonight. We thank you for visiting our region and commemorate your Irish relatives, friends and acquaintances who *fought for our freedom*. Thank you.'[4] The italics are mine because I want to highlight the fact that many years after Michael's death, people in Flanders, if not in Ireland, still appreciated the ultimate sacrifice that Michael and thousands of other Irishmen made for *their* freedom.

In the autumn 2000 newsletter published by the past pupils of O'Connell CBS School, North Richmond Street, there appeared an article entitled, 'On the Somme and in Flanders Fields'. The article was written by Andrew Kavanagh. His brothers Michael and Dermot also contributed to it. All three men, like their relative Michael Wall, were past pupils of this Christian Brothers school. It seems that, like the rest of Irish society, one of Michael's old schools remembered him at last.

**Farewell Michael, rest in peace my son,
Ireland didn't forget you.**

Endnotes

Preface

1   In 1999 the Dublin Civic Museum at 58 South William Street, Dublin, was the postal address of The Royal Dublin Fusiliers Association (RDFA). The RDFA presented public lectures and exhibitions at the Civic Museum. Rosemary's letter was addressed to Mr Tom Burke, Chairman, The Royal Dublin Fusiliers Association, c/o The Dublin Civic Museum, 58 South William Street, Dublin 2.

2   Out of no disrespect to my Flemish friends, I use the term 'Messines' throughout this text, and not 'Mesen'.

3   This volume of work is now in the archive of the RDFA in Dublin City Library and Archive, Pearse Street, Dublin.

4   It was from this work that I produced a travel guide on the Battle of Wijtschate and Messines entitled *The 16th (Irish) and 36th (Ulster) Divisions at the Battle of Wijtschate–Messines Ridge, 7 June 1917*. It was published by the RDFA in Wijtschate in June 2007.

5   Michael's letters in this text are transcribed exactly how Michael wrote them. The transcriptions include his punctuation and spelling.

1 Innocence

1   The house is still there and lived in to this day.

2   The census of 1901 noted him as being an accountant. See http://www.census.nationalarchives.ie/reels/nai003675795/.

3   Theresa's marriage certificate, dated 25 May 1897, noted her father's occupation as being a 'Car owner'.

4   McBrierty, V. J., *The Howth Peninsula: Its History, Lore and Legend* (North Dublin Round Table, Dublin, 1981), pp. 62–63. In 1899 a new church, the Church of the Assumption, was consecrated. After the opening, the old church became the parish parochial hall. It is now apartments named 'Renaissance House'. An interesting artistic feature on Renaissance House is the sculpture of two granite wagons, which were carved on the wall of the old Catholic church as a mark of

gratitude to the men of the local Kilrock quarry who helped build the church in 1814.

5   School records of Michael Wall, Glentora, Howth, County Dublin from St Joseph's CBS, Fairview, County Dublin.

6   Corcoran, M., *Through Streets Broad and Narrow: A History of Dublin Trams* (Midland Publishing, Leicester, 2000), pp. 47 and 72. In those days the Dublin United Tramway Company ran the tram line from the East Pier Terminus in Howth to Nelson's Pillar, which stood in Sackville Street (now O'Connell Street) in the centre of Dublin.

7   'Wall, 2nd Lieut Michael, 6th Royal Irish Regiment', RDFA Archive, Dublin. Letter from St Mary's College, Marino, County Dublin, 2 June 1906. (At that time, the place of residence for the Christian Brothers was St Mary's College in Marino and a pathway led from St Mary's down through the fields of Marino to St Joseph's School at Fairview.)

8   Brockie, G., *St. Joseph's C.B.S. Fairview 1888–1988* (St Joseph's CBS, Dublin, 1988), pp. 30–33.

9   It is not known why they moved from Howth, but Clontarf was much closer to Michael's school. In fact, Michael could walk to St Joseph's from his new home in about fifteen minutes.

10   Not much is known about Sir Percy after his departure from Carrick Hill.

11   Kennedy, T., *The Velvet Strand: A History of Portmarnock* (Confidential Report Printing, Dublin, 1984), p. 134. The fields were called the Sea Field, the Peafield, the Ten Acres, the Seven Acres and Martello Field.

12   Conversation between author and Mrs Margaret Flood, granddaughter of Margo Willan, Dublin.

13   'Irish Census', 1911, Dublin District 14/11, National Archives, Dublin. The census of 1911 presented the population of Portmarnock and surrounding townlands as being 120 people made up of twenty-three families, the majority of whom were Roman Catholic. The village and surrounding townlands occupied an area of 386 acres.

14   *Ibid.*

15   *Ibid.*

16   Conversation between author and Mrs Bride Lowry, daughter of Tommy Cunningham, Portmarnock, 2001.

17   Portmarnock Youth Project Team, *Portmarnock: A Closer Look* (Wolfhound Press, Dublin, 1985), p. 120.

18 *Ibid.*, pp. 109, 113 and 114. Beyond Carrick Hill House lay Beechwood, a late eighteenth-century country house and home to Nathaniel Trumbull, a prosperous Dublin tobacco merchant.

19 Kennedy (1984), pp. 132–133.

20 Osborne was friendly with another artist, Nathaniel Hone the younger (1831–1917), who lived in Malahide, a parish near to Portmarnock. Both men painted local country scenes such as cows grazing in the fields and meadows. Hone's painting *Pastures at Malahide* portrays a summer scene of cattle relaxing in pastures around Malahide. Hone donated more than one hundred of his paintings to the National Gallery of Ireland (in Merrion Square, Dublin), where *Pastures at Malahide* can be seen in the Irish Artists' room.

21 Portmarnock Youth Project Team (1985), pp. 46–48.

22 'Wall, 2nd Lieut Michael, 6th Royal Irish Regiment', RDFA Archive. Letter from St Mary's College, Marino, 2 June 1906.

23 Minutes of Dublin County Council meeting of 17 June 1915, p. 223. Eleven young people applied for the 1915 scholarship but only nine were granted scholarships. Of those nine, only five went on to study at UCD. The previous year the Scholarship Committee had awarded a scholarship grant to a J. J. Murphy from Grove, Fethard, County Wexford. He had turned down the offer because he was awarded a commission in the army.

24 'Wall, 2nd Lieut Michael, 6th Royal Irish Regiment', RDFA Archive. Letter from Principal Walker of O'Connell's CBS, 26 November 1915. Another pupil whose path through the Christian Brothers from St Joseph's in Fairview to O'Connell School in North Richmond Street was John A. Costello. He reached the pinnacle of public life by becoming taoiseach twice, from 1948–1952 and 1954–1957. See Brockie (1988), pp. 24–25. Costello was one of two ex-Joey's boys to reach the office of taoiseach; the other was Charles J. Haughey.

2 Smitten by War

1 *The Catholic Bulletin*, No. 7, April 1917, p. 256. Fr Gleeson had volunteered to serve as a chaplain to the Irish troops on 10 November 1914.

2 'Wall, 2nd Lieut Michael, 6th, Royal Irish Regiment', RDFA Archive. Letter from Fr Gleeson to Michael Wall, 14 March 1915. Roughly two

months after Fr Gleeson wrote to Michael, on 8 May 1915, the evening before the Battle of Aubers Ridge, the 2nd Battalion of the Royal Munster Fusiliers marched through the Rue de Bois about one mile out from the French town of Neuve Chapelle. They halted near a wayside shrine and, moving off the road, formed up in their companies. In front of each company was a green flag with the Irish harp and the word 'Munster' embroidered on it. It was here that Fr Gleeson gave General Absolution to the men of Munster before they went into action. The scene was captured by the famous war illustrator Fortunino Matania. The painting was destroyed in the London Blitz, but fortunately some prints have survived to remind us of that poignant moment. Fr Gleeson survived the Great War. He carried on his chaplaincy work in the Irish Free State Army. He became parish priest in St Catherine's Church in Meath Street, Dublin; by the time of his death in 1959 he had progressed to the status of canon.

3   Paris, M., 'Boy's Books and the Great War', *History Today*, Vol. 50, No. 11, November 2000, p. 44.

4   Paris, M., *Over the Top: The Great War and Juvenile Literature in Britain* (Praeger Publishers, Westport, CT, 2004), p. xiii.

5   Muller, S., 'Toys, Games, and Juvenile Literature during the First Wold War in Germany and England: A Comparison', paper presented at 'Uncovering the First World War', a conference held in Trinity College, Dublin, 23–25 September 2005.

6   'Wall, 2nd Lieut Michael, 6th Royal Irish Regiment', RDFA Archive. Letter from R. W. Smyth to Michael, 21 September 1915. Smyth referred to the boys of The Royal Hibernian Military School (RHMS) spending the previous month (August) at Carrick Hill. The RHMS was built in 1769, the funding of which came from a society of wealthy ladies and gentlemen for the education of the families of soldiers who were living in poverty. The school catered for ninety boys and fifty girls. Some 215 ex-pupils fought in the Crimean War, and it was around this time that the girls left the RHMS and attended the separate Drummond School in the Chapelizod area of Dublin. Students from the RHMS took part in the Great War; eighty of them were killed. One of the past pupils of the school to distinguish himself was Corporal Frederick J. Edwards. At twenty-one he won the VC on 26 September

1916 at Thiepval during the later stages of the Battle of the Somme while serving with the Middlesex Regiment. See *History of St Mary's Hospital Phoenix Park, Dublin* (St Mary's Hospital, Dublin) – booklet available from hospital administration. See also: O'Reilly, G. H., *History of Royal Hibernian Military School, Dublin* (The Genealogical Society of Ireland, Dún Laoghaire, 2004), p. 76.

7 Callan, P., 'Recruiting for the British Army in Ireland during the First World War', *The Irish Sword*, Vol. 17, Summer 1987, p. 42.

8 'Wall, 2nd Lieut Michael, 6th Royal Irish Regiment', RDFA Archive. Letter from Staff Captain R. B. Kelly, Ministry of Munitions, Dublin, 25 September 1915. Watt Ltd was a leading firm of engineers in Dublin.

9 *Ibid.* Letter from Captain Browne, Ministry of Munitions, Dublin to Michael, 16 November 1915.

10 *Ibid.* Letter from R. W. Smyth, RHMS, Dublin to Michael, 23 November 1915.

11 *Soldiers Died in the Great War, 1914–1919*, Part 73 (J. B. Hayward and Sons, Suffolk, 1989), p. 47.

12 Census of Ireland, 1911, http://www.census.nationalarchives.ie/pages/1911/Dublin/Malahide/Portmarnock/5285/.

13 Brockie (1988), pp. 24–38. Peadar Kearney – author of the Irish national anthem, 'The Soldier's Song' – was also a Joey's boy who was active in the Easter Rising. Kearney left St Joseph's in 1897 at the age of fourteen after spending a few months playing truant. Of the twenty-four Joey's boys who fought in the Rising, two were killed – Seán Connolly and James Fox.

14 'Wall, 2nd Lieut Michael, 6th Royal Irish Regiment', RDFA Archive. British Army Form W.3074 and British Army Form MT. 348. Medical report on Michael Wall, 26 November 1915.

15 *Ibid.* British Army Form B.210, 22 December 1915.

16 *Ibid.* Letter from Assistant Military Secretary, Irish Command, 32 Nassau Street, Dublin, 8 January 1916.

17 Denman, T., *Ireland's Unknown Soldiers: The 16th (Irish) Division in the Great War* (Irish Academic Press, Dublin, 1992), p. 44.

18 Cooper, B., *The Tenth (Irish) Division in Gallipoli* (Irish Academic Press, Dublin, 1993), p. 26.

19 Hanna, H., *The Pals at Suvla* (E. Ponsonby Ltd, Dublin, 1916), p. 202.

20 *Ibid.*, p. 18. William Boyd noted in a letter home after arriving at the Curragh: 'We picked two fellows for our officers out of our company two days after we came down but hardly any of us knew them well.' Also found in 'Boyd, Private William, 7th Royal Dublin Fusiliers', RDFA Archive, Dublin.

21 Hanna (1916), p. 196.

22 Beckett, I. and Simpson, K., *A Nation in Arms: A Social Study of the British Army in the First World War* (Manchester University Press, Manchester, 1985), p. 79.

23 Whitton, F. E., *The History of the Prince of Wales's Leinster Regiment (Royal Canadians) 1914–1922*, Vol. 2 (Schull Books, Cork, 1998), p. 100.

24 Denman (1992), p. 57.

25 'Parsons, Lieut General Sir L. W.', Liddell Hart Centre for Military Archives (LHCMA), King's College London, GB99 KCLMA, 29 November 1914.

26 Whitton (1998), p. 100.

27 'Parsons, Lieut General Sir L. W.', LHCMA.

28 'Wall, 2nd Lieut Michael, 6th Royal Irish Regiment', RDFA Archive. Letter from Assistant Military Secretary, Irish Command, 32 Nassau Street, Dublin, 8 January 1916.

29 *Ibid.* Letter from the War Office, 25 January 1916.

30 *Ibid.* Letter from Major and Commandant, Dublin University Officers' School of Instruction, 25 January 1916.

31 *Ibid.* Standing Orders of Dublin University OTC, 2 February 1916.

3 'Fancy the Royal Irish captured Moore Street'

1 'Wall, 2nd Lieut Michael, 6th Royal Irish Regiment', RDFA Archive. Letter from Michael to Bernard Wall, 18 April 1916.

2 *Ibid.* Letter from Michael to his mother, 25 April 1916. 'Sinn Feiners' was a generic term often incorrectly used to identify those who led the 1916 Rising.

3 *Ibid.* Letter from Michael to his mother from Ballykinlar Camp, County Down. Michael dated this letter 6 April 1916 in error. It is more than likely that he should have dated it 6 May 1916. Michael also misspelt Lieutenant Ramsay's surname as Ramsey. While serving with the 2nd

Royal Irish Regiment near St Julien near Mouse Trap Farm in early May 1915, 2nd Lieutenant A. L. Ramsay was wounded by gas shells and sent back to Dublin to recover. Subsequently promoted to captain, he was killed in the Easter Rising.

4   Denman (1992), p. 142.

5   'Monica Roberts Collection', RDFA Archive, Dublin. Letter from Private George Soper, 2nd RDF to Miss Roberts, 20 May 1916. Monica Roberts was a young lady who lived in Stillorgan, County Dublin. During the First World War she and a lady friend collected comforts for the troops, such as tobacco, blades and soap, which they sent in parcels to the Dublin Fusiliers at the Front. Many of the men to whom she sent the parcels wrote to her in Dublin. These letters were donated to the archive of the RDFA in April 2005 by Monica's daughter, Mrs Mary Shackleton.

6   Barry, Tom, *Guerilla Days in Ireland* (Mercier Press, Cork, 2013), p. 17.

7   Denman (1992), p. 142.

8   Ó Comhraí, Cormac, *Ireland and the First World War: A Photographic History* (Mercier Press, Cork, 2014), p. 172.

9   Denman (1992), p. 130. Roger Casement (1864–1916) was a distinguished British diplomat born in Dublin. In 1905 he was awarded a Companion of the Order of St Michael and St George for his work in the Congo, and in 1911 he was given a knighthood for his work on behalf of the Amazon Indians. He became involved in the fight for Irish independence and on 3 August 1916 was hanged in Pentonville Prison in London on a charge of treason, for attempting to import arms into Ireland.

10   Leonard, J., 'The Reactions of Irish Officers in the British Army to the Easter Rising of 1916', in H. Cecil and P. H. Liddle (eds), *Facing Armageddon: The First World War Experienced* (Leo Cooper, London, 1996), p. 260. On 26 July 1914 Irish Volunteers illegally landed German guns from a yacht named the *Asgard* at the fishing village of Howth. Some of the guns were used in the Easter Rising. The importation of these guns by the Irish Volunteers was a direct response to a similar illegal importation of German guns by a unionist paramilitary group named the Ulster Volunteer Force in Larne, County Antrim, in April 1914.

11   'Monica Roberts Collection'. Letter from Private George Soper, 2nd RDF, 20 May 1916.

12   For more details on this see Geoghegan, S., *The Campaigns and History*

of the Royal Irish Regiment 1900–1922, Vol. 2 (Schull Books, Cork, 1997), pp. 102–104. On Easter Monday 24 April 1916 the 3rd (Reserve) Battalion of the Royal Irish Regiment was stationed at Richmond Barracks in Inchicore, Dublin. The battalion was under the command of Lieutenant Colonel R. L. Owens. The participation of the 3rd Royal Irish in putting down the rebellion is recorded by the historian of the Royal Irish (18th Foot), Brigadier General Stannus Geoghegan CB. The main function of the 3rd Royal Irish was to train new recruits for the regiment at the front in Flanders and France. According to Geoghegan: 'On the morning of 28 April a party under Major Morrogh and Company Sergeant Major Banks succeeded in capturing the republican flag from the roof of the Post Office.' Geoghegan seems to have been wrong about the timing here, as the General Post Office (GPO) was not evacuated by its Volunteer garrison until the evening of 28 April; by that point the building was ablaze and it was unlikely it could have been entered that evening. For many years the captured flag was kept in the Imperial War Museum (IWM) in London as a kind of battle trophy. Soon after it was taken from the GPO it was photographed being held up by a group of officers, one of whom was a young man named Captain Richard (Dick) Burke, from Dingle in County Kerry. Dick won the Military Cross at the Battle of Messines Ridge in June 1917. In an act of reconciliation on the fiftieth anniversary of the Rising in 1966, the flag was returned by the IWM to the National Museum of Ireland at Collins Barracks, Dublin.

13   Leonard in Cecil and Liddle (1996), p. 262.

14   For further discussion on the reaction of Irish soldiers serving in the British Army during the Easter Rising of 1916 see Burke, T., 'Fancy the Royal Irish Captured Moore Street', *The Blue Cap: Journal of The Royal Dublin Fusiliers Association*, Vol. 13, December 2006, pp. 22–36.

15   'Wall, 2nd Lieut Michael, 6th Royal Irish Regiment', RDFA Archive. Letter from Michael to his mother, 14 April 1917.

16   'Monica Roberts Collection'. Letter from Private Christy Fox, 2nd RDF, 12 May 1916.

17   *Ibid.* Letter from Private Joseph Clarke, 2nd RDF, 11 May 1916. The Sherwood's refers to The Sherwood Foresters (Nottinghamshire and Derbyshire Regiment), who were involved in some of the heaviest fighting during the Rising.

18   'Lockhart, Private Andrew, 11th Royal Inniskilling Fusiliers', RDFA
     Archive, Dublin. Letter from Andrew Lockhart to his sister Mina, 18
     May 1916.

19   'Monica Roberts Collection'. Letter from Private Christy Fox, 2nd
     RDF, 12 May 1916.

20   Denman (1992), p. 151.

21   *Ibid.*, p. 144.

22   Leonard in Cecil and Liddle (1996), p. 264.

23   Denman, T., *A Lonely Grave: The Life and Death of William Redmond*
     (Irish Academic Press, Dublin, 1995), p. 97. Patrick Henry Pearse
     (1879–1916), born in Dublin, was a school teacher, barrister, poet, wri-
     ter, Irish nationalist, political activist and one of the leaders of the Easter
     Rising. At the start of the Rising he read out the Proclamation of the
     Irish Republic outside the GPO in Dublin. He was one of the seven
     signatories to the Proclamation, all of whom were tried and executed by
     a British Army firing squad. Pearse was executed on the morning of 3
     May 1916.

24   *Ibid.*, p. 123.

25   Lyons, J. B., *The Enigma of Tom Kettle* (The Glendale Press, Dublin,
     1983), p. 284.

26   Leonard in Cecil and Liddle (1996), p. 261. The quotation used by
     Leonard is taken from the service record in the Robert Barton Papers in
     the National Archives, Dublin, 1093/9. In December 1918 Barton was
     elected Sinn Féin MP for West Wicklow and was one of the signatories
     to the Anglo-Irish Treaty in December 1921.

27   Dungan, M., *They Shall Grow Not Old* (Four Courts Press, Dublin,
     1997), p. 31. On 20 September 1914 the leader of the Irish Parliamen-
     tary Party, John Redmond, MP, made a speech at Woodenbridge Golf
     Course in which he called upon members of the Irish Volunteers to en-
     list in the British Army following the outbreak of the First World War.
     His speech caused a split in the Irish Volunteer movement, resulting in
     the formation of the National Volunteers. The vast majority of men fol-
     lowed Redmond and joined the National Volunteers.

28   Leonard in Cecil and Liddle (1996), p. 261.

29   Lyons (1983), p. 285.

30   Leonard in Cecil and Liddle (1996), p. 266. Seán Heuston (1891–

1916) was born in Dublin and educated by the Christian Brothers. He worked as a railway clerk in Limerick. On 4 May 1916 he was tried in Richmond Barracks in Dublin for his part in the Rising. He was executed on 7 May 1916.

31 Denman (1992), p. 143.

32 Jeffrey, K., *Ireland and the Great War* (Cambridge University Press, Cambridge, 2000), p. 54. A Carsonite was a follower of Edward Henry Carson (1854–1935). Born in Harcourt Street in Dublin and educated at Portarlington School, Wesley College and Trinity College, Dublin, Carson became a prominent barrister. A devout believer in Irish unity with Britain, he became leader of the Irish Unionist Alliance and later the Ulster Unionist Party. He served in the British cabinet during the First World War as attorney general. When he died in 1935 he was given a state funeral in Belfast. Cathleen Ni Houlihan is a mythical symbol and emblem of Irish nationalism found in poetry, literature and art. The name is often used by Irish writers, notably W. B. Yeats, to represent Ireland as a personified woman. Thomas MacDonagh (1878–1916) was born in Cloughjordan, County Tipperary. Educated at Rockwell College in Tipperary, he was a political activist, poet and teacher. A friend of Patrick Pearse, MacDonagh took a prominent part in the Rising and was one of the seven signatories to the Proclamation. He was court-martialled for his role in the Rising and was executed by firing squad on 3 May 1916. Francis Ledwidge (1887–1917) was killed on 31 July 1917 while serving with the Royal Inniskilling Fusiliers at the opening of the Third Battle of Ypres.

33 Dungan, M., *Irish Voices from the Great War* (Irish Academic Press, Dublin, 1995), p. 53.

34 Satterthwaite D., 'How Did the Easter Rising affect the Nationalism of Irish Soldiers serving in the British Army during the Great War?', unpublished MA thesis, The Queen's College, Oxford, Spring 2006, p. 36.

35 Denman (1992), p. 143. The Irish Guards were – and continue to be – an Irish regiment in the British Army. Soldiers were recruited from all over Ireland, although the regiment was strongly rural and Catholic in its composition.

36 Leonard in Cecil and Liddle (1996), p. 259.

37 Denman (1992), p. 143.

38   Bowman, T., *Irish Regiments in the Great War: Discipline and Morale* (Manchester University Press, Manchester, 2003), p. 127.

39   Leonard in Cecil and Liddle (1996), p. 263.

40   Brennan-Whitmore, W. J., *Dublin Burning: The Easter Rising from Behind the Barricades* (Gill & Macmillan, Dublin, 1996), p. 122.

41   Leonard in Cecil and Liddle (1996), p. 260. Captain Sheehy was the son of a former Home Rule MP and the brother-in-law of Tom Kettle.

42   'Dickson, Major T. C. H., 4th Royal Dublin Fusiliers', RDFA Archive, Dublin. The 4th RDF trained both officers and men of other ranks before they were sent to the 1st and 2nd (Regular) RDF Battalions in France and/or Gallipoli. In April 1916 the 4th RDF had a battalion strength of 1,600 officers and men divided into five companies. Some 85 per cent of the new recruits were Roman Catholic and 15 per cent were Protestant. In contrast, about 70 per cent of the officers were Protestant and 30 per cent were Roman Catholic.

43   Leonard in Cecil and Liddle (1996), p. 260. Joseph Mary Plunkett (1887–1916) was born in Dublin and educated at the Catholic University School, Belvedere College SJ, and later at Stonyhurst College in Lancashire. In 1915 he joined the Irish republican movement and became a planner for the Easter Rising, in which he took part. He was a signatory to the Proclamation and, for his prominent role in the Rising, he was executed on 4 May 1916.

44   *Ibid.*, p. 261.

45   Brennan-Whitmore (1996), p. 121.

46   McCann, B. P., 'The Diary of 2nd Lieut. Arthur V. G. Killingley. 'A' Company. 4th Battalion Royal Dublin Fusiliers Easter Week, 1916', *The Irish Sword*, Vol. 20, No. 81, Summer 1997, p. 247. Killingley's doubts about his troops' loyalty were discussed amongst his fellow RDF officers. He noted in his diary on 24 April, during the Rising: 'We had a general discussion as to how men will behave if ordered to fire on their fellow countrymen.'

47   'Dickson, Major T. C. H., 4th Royal Dublin Fusiliers', RDFA Archive. Dickson took a Maxim gun, a sergeant and two other men with him to carry out the order. Facing where the cattle market used to be on the North Circular Road in Dublin is a line of beautiful red-brick, three-storey, terraced houses known as Altona Terrace. At this point on the North Circular the road rises. Standing on the roof of one of these

terraced houses, the men had a panoramic view of the Grangegorman area, a very poor part of Dublin's north-west inner city with a large number of narrow streets. The area was well-known for the mental hospital built in its midst – then known as the Richmond Asylum. From the rooftop of one of these houses on Altona Terrace, according to Dickson, the Dublins gave Grangegorman 'a good spraying of about 1,000 rounds which must have broken several hundred slates and windows and kept everyone indoors for a while'.

48 McCann, (1997), p. 247.

49 Denman (1995), p. 97.

50 Denman (1992), p. 142.

51 Satterthwaite (2006), p. 21.

52 Dungan (1997), p. 32.

53 *Ibid.*, p. 31.

54 'Diary of Fr Henry Gill SJ', Jesuit Archive, Dublin, CHP 1/27, p. 123. In fact Fr Gill accused a sergeant in an English regiment of treachery: 'Later on when the attack (on Wijtschate) was over, it was discovered that a sergeant of an English regiment had given information to the enemy.' For further information on Fr Gill and other Irish Jesuits who served in the First World War, see: Burke, D., *Irish Jesuit Chaplains in the First World War* (Messenger Publications, Dublin, 2014).

55 'Wall, 2nd Lieut Michael, 6th Royal Irish Regiment', RDFA Archive. Paper cutting from the *Irish Independent* in early May 1916.

56 Brennan-Whitmore (1996), p. 125.

57 Leonard in Cecil and Liddle (1996), p. 260.

58 *Ibid.*

59 Denman (1992), p. 62.

60 Wylly, H. C., *Neill's Blue Caps 1914–1922*, Vol. 3 (Schull Books, Cork, 2000), p. 39, and 'War Diary 2nd Royal Dublin Fusiliers, August 1914 to September 1916', NAK WO95/1481.

61 For further discussion on morale in the British Army see Englander, D., 'Discipline and Morale in the British Army, 1917–1918', in J. Horne (ed.), *State, Society and Mobilisation in Europe During the First World War* (Cambridge University Press, Cambridge, 1997), pp. 125–143.

62 'Monica Roberts Collection'. Letter from Sgt Edward Heafey, 8th RDF, August 1917. Cold weather and the loss of comrades could have added

to Sergeant Heafey's depression more than the Rising, although the insurrection no doubt added to his poor state of mind.

63 Bowman (2003), pp. 127 and 194.

64 Denman (1992), p. 144.

65 'Monica Roberts Collection.' Letter from Private George Soper, 2nd RDF, 20 May 1916.

66 Lemisko, L., 'Morale in the 16th (Irish) Division, 1916–1918', *The Irish Sword*, Vol. 20, No. 81, Summer 1997, p. 230. Colonel Rowland Fielding was a Roman Catholic and commanding officer of the 6th Connaught Rangers.

67 'Wall, 2nd Lieut Michael, 6th Royal Irish Regiment', RDFA Archive. Letter from Michael to his mother, 16 May 1916.

68 *Ibid.* Letter from F. G. Smith to Michael Wall, 3 September 1916. It is interesting to note that Smith addressed his letter to Michael as 'Lt M. Wall. 3rd Bat. R.I. Regt, Carrick Hill, Malahide, Co. Dublin.' In addressing his letter in this way, Smith didn't seem to be too concerned about the possibility of any republican sympathisers or informers who may have been around Portmarnock and Carrick Hill.

69 *Ibid.* Letter from Michael to his mother, not dated. The 'nonsense about travel in Dublin' was due to the travel restrictions imposed by martial law following the Easter Rising.

4 Dear Mother, You Are Not to Worry

1 'Wall, 2nd Lieut Michael, 6th Royal Irish Regiment', RDFA Archive. Letter from Michael to his mother, 5 September 1916.

2 *Ibid.* Letter from Michael to his brother Joseph, 8 September 1916.

3 *Ibid.* Letter from Michael's friend R. W. Smyth to Michael, 28 September 1916. 'Tommy Atkins' was the slang title given to common soldiers in the British Army during the First World War. 'Fritz' being the pet name of Friedrich, was one of a variety of nicknames British soldiers used to identify German soldiers. 'The Hun' was another.

4 *Ibid.* Letter from Michael to his mother, 21 October 1916.

5 The Road to Wijtschate

1 Stevenson, D., *1914–1918: The History of the First World War* (Penguin Books, London, 2004), p. 161.

2   *Ibid.*

3   Edmonds, Sir (Brigadier-General) J. E. , *History of the Great War. Military Operations, France and Belgium 1917.* Vol. 2 (His Majesty's Stationery Office, London, 1948), p. 2.

4   Keegan, J., *The First World War* (Vintage Books, New York, 2000), p. 190.

5   Terraine, J., *The Road to Passchendaele: The Flanders Offensive of 1917. A Study in Inevitability* (Lee Cooper, London, 1977), p. 12.

6   Taylor, A. J. P., *English History 1914–1945* (Book Club Associates, London, 1977), p. 84.

7   Edmonds, *History of the Great War. France and Belgium, 1917* (1948), p. 102.

8   Sheffield, G. and Bourne, J. (eds), *Douglas Haig: War Diaries and Letters, 1914–1918* (Phoenix, London, 2005), pp. 172–173.

9   Holmes, R., *The Western Front* (BBC Worldwide, London, 1999), p. 121.

10 Stevenson (2004), p. 168.

11 Edmonds, *History of the Great War. France and Belgium, 1917* (1948), p. 2.

12 *Ibid.*, p. 4.

13 Steel, N. and Hart, P., *Passchendaele: The Sacrificial Ground* (Cassell Military Paperbacks, London, 2000), p. 30.

14 Wolff, L., *In Flanders Fields* (Longmans, London, 1959), p. 87.

15 Edmonds, *History of the Great War. France and Belgium, 1917* (1948), pp. 2–3. See also p. 27.

16 Sheffield and Bourne (2005), p. 178.

17 Passingham, I., *Pillars of Fire: The Battle of Messines Ridge June 1917* (Sutton Publishing, Glouchestershire, 1998), p. 55.

18 Terraine, J., *Douglas Haig: The Educated Soldier* (Cassell Military Publisher, London, 1963), p. 315.

19 Edmonds, *History of the Great War. France and Belgium, 1917* (1948), pp. 3–4.

20 *Ibid.*, p. 6.

21 *Ibid.*

22 *Ibid.*

23 For a discussion of the mines placed along the Irish lines facing Wijtschate, see Burke, T., *The 16th (Irish) and 36th (Ulster) Divisions at the Battle of Wijtschate–Messines Ridge, 7 June 1917* (The Royal Dublin Fusiliers

Association, Ieper, 2007). Edmonds' *History of the Great War. France and Belgium, 1917* (1948), p. 53, records that the mine at Maedelstede Farm contained 34,000 pounds of explosive charge. However, Passingham (1998), p. 57, records that the same mine contained 94,000 pounds of explosive. This script uses the official figures provided by Edmonds.

24 Edmonds, *History of the Great War. France and Belgium, 1917* (1948), pp. 6–7.

25 *Ibid.*, p. 8.

26 Taylor (1977), p. 80.

27 Edmonds, *History of the Great War. France and Belgium, 1917* (1948), p. 13.

28 *Ibid.*, p. 14.

29 *Ibid.*

30 *Ibid.*, p. 15.

31 *Ibid.*

32 *Ibid.*, p. 17. The eventual gap between the attacks was approximately forty-seven days – that is between 14 June and 31 July 1917 – and this proved to have dire consequences for Haig's dream of routing the Germans out of Belgium.

33 *Ibid.*, p. 25. A reconnaissance report by a tank officer, Captain G. le Q. Martel, in April stated that the sector of attack was unsuited to the employment of tanks, owing to the narrow defiles between the three woods that guarded the approaches, and to the broken surface and woods on the high ground itself.

34 *Ibid.*

35 Passingham (1998), p. 20. Passingham has cited Plumer's quotation as being in Edmonds, *History of the Great War. France and Belgium, 1917* (1948), pp. 24–25. There is, however, no reference on those pages to Plumer making this statement.

6 Michael's New Home in Flanders

1 'War Diary 9th Corps. No. Gs 75/3. Appendix 8', 15 July 1916, NAK WO95/835.

2 Falls, C., *The History of the 36th (Ulster) Division* (McCaw, Stevenson & Orr, Belfast, 1922), p. 65.

3 *Ibid.*, p. 64.

4   'War Diary 16th (Irish) Division', 11 September 1916, NAK WO95/1955/3.

5   'War Diary 8th Royal Dublin Fusiliers', 15 September 1916, NAK WO95/1974. The 8th Dublins relieved the 73rd Canadian Battalion in the front line facing Wijtschate.

6   'War Diary 9th Corps. Operation Order No. 9', 19 September 1916, NAK WO95/835.

7   Scott, Major General H. L., *The Attack of the British Ninth Corps at Messines Ridge* (The War Department, Washington, 1917), pp. 11–12. See also Falls (1922), p. 79.

8   'Western Front: Maps. Supplement to 1:10000 (British) Series I. Trenches corrected to: 1.4.17. Sheet Name and No. 28SW 2. Edition No. 5A. Lines: A/G Production: OS GSGS No. 3062', NAK WO297/6580. That road still exists and is today called Wijtschatestraat.

9   'Diary of R. H. Newman, Royal Artillery. MD 1169', The Royal Artillery Museum, Woolwich.

10 'War Diary 36th (Ulster) Division. Defence Scheme, issued 20 November 1916', NAK WO95/2491.

11 'Western Front: Maps. Supplement to 1:10000 (British) Series I. Trenches corrected to: 1.4.17. Sheet Name and No. 28SW 2. Edition No. 5A. Lines: A/G Production: OS GSGS No. 3062', NAK WO297/6580.

12 Laird, F., *Personal Experiences of the Great War (an Unfinished Manuscript)* (Eason & Son, Dublin, 1925), p. 142.

13 'Western Front: Maps. Supplement to 1:10000 (British) Series I. Trenches corrected to: 1.4.17. Sheet Name and No. 28SW 2. Edition No. 5A. Lines: A/G Production: OS GSGS No. 3062', NAK WO297/6580.

14 Gilbert, M., *The First World War: A Complete History* (Weidenfeld and Nicolson, London, 1994), p. 311.

15 Mulligan, W., *The Great War for Peace* (Yale University Press, New Haven, 2014), p. 200.

16 Gilbert (1994), p. 220. Six are buried in the New Irish Farm Cemetery at Ypres. Other Commonwealth war cemeteries in which Chinese people are buried are Croonaert Chapel Cemetery north of Wijtschate and Lijssenthoek Cemetery in Poperinge.

17 'War Diary 8th Royal Dublin Fusiliers', 15 September 1916, NAK WO95/1974.

18 Laird (1925), p. 113.

19 Fielding, R., *War Letters to a Wife: France and Flanders, 1915–1919* (The Medici Society, London, 1929), p. 124.

20 'Beater, Captain O. L., 9th Royal Dublin Fusiliers. 3385 – 86/65/1', IWM, London.

21 'Western Front: Maps. Supplement to 1:10000 (British) Series I. Trenches corrected to: 1.4.17. Sheet Name and No. 28SW 2. Edition No. 5A. Lines: A/G Production: OS GSGS No. 3062', NAK WO297/6580.

22 Whitton (1998), p. 413.

23 'War Diary 9th Royal Dublin Fusiliers', 28 January 1917, NAK WO95/1974.

24 'Western Front: Maps. Supplement to 1:10000 (British) Series I. Trenches corrected to: 1.4.17. Sheet Name and No. 28SW 2. Edition No. 5A. Lines: A/G Production: OS GSGS No. 3062', NAK WO297/6580.

25 'Drury, Captain Noel, 6th Royal Dublin Fusiliers', RDFA Archive, Dublin, p. 129.

26 'Wall, 2nd Lieut Michael, 6th Royal Irish Regiment', RDFA Archive. Letter from Michael to his mother from France, 23 October 1916.

27 *Ibid.* Letter from Michael to his mother from France, 24 October 1916. The word I have transcribed here as nauseous is difficult to read, hence the [?] marking some uncertainty in the interpretation.

28 Denman (1992), pp. 65–75. Pereira was originally commissioned into the Grenadier Guards and had previously served as a military attaché in China. He was fluent in Chinese. He was known to his men as 'Hoppy' because of his lameness following a horse riding accident. He was a firm disciplinarian and concerned only for the welfare of his men. See 'Brett, C., 6th Connaught Rangers. 76/134/1', IWM, London, p. 13.

29 Pope, S. and Wheal, E., *The Macmillan Dictionary of the First World War* (Macmillan, London, 1997), p. 322.

30 'War Diary 8th Royal Dublin Fusiliers', 3 January 1917, NAK WO95/1974.

31 'War Diary 6th Royal Irish Regiment', 25 October 1916, NAK WO95/1970.

32 'Wall, 2nd Lieut Michael, 6th Royal Irish Regiment', RDFA Archive. Letter from Michael to his mother, 25 October 1916.

33   See The Commonwealth War Graves Commission, http://www.cwgc. org. Pat had formerly served with the Royal Inniskilling Fusiliers and was married. He lived with his wife, Elizabeth, at 21 Osborne Street in the Rosemount area of Londonderry. He was twenty-eight when he died.

34   'War Diary 6th Royal Irish Regiment', 26 October 1916, NAK WO95/1970.

35   'Wall, 2nd Lieut Michael, 6th Royal Irish Regiment', RDFA Archive. Letter from Michael to his mother, 28 October 1916.

36   'War Diary 6th Royal Irish Regiment', 29 October 1916, NAK WO95/1970.

37   'Wall, 2nd Lieut Michael, 6th Royal Irish Regiment', RDFA Archive. Letter from Michael to his mother, 30 October 1916. *Nash's Magazine* was a British literary magazine which in 1914 joined with the *Pall Mall Magazine* to form *Nash's and Pall Mall Magazine*.

38   Tommy Hughes survived the First World War and returned home to Hazlebrook. He was a keen golfer; in 1921 he became Hon. Secretary of The Island Golf Club, Donabate, County Dublin. See O'Doherty-Murphy, W. R. M., *A Century of Golf on the Island: A History of the Island Golf Club* (The Island Golf Club, Dublin, 1990), p. 98.

39   Laird (1925), pp. 113–117.

40   'War Diary 6th Royal Irish Regiment', 1 November 1916, NAK WO95/1970.

41   'Wall, 2nd Lieut Michael, 6th Royal Irish Regiment', RDFA Archive. Letter from Michael to his brother Joseph, 1 November 1916.

42   *Ibid.* Letter from Michael to his aunt, 2 November 1916.

43   Fielding (1929), p. 126.

44   'Wall, 2nd Lieut Michael, 6th Royal Irish Regiment', RDFA Archive. Letter from Michael to his mother, 2 November 1916.

45   'War Diary 6th Royal Irish Regiment', 4 November 1916, NAK WO95/1970.

46   'War Diary 9th Royal Dublin Fusiliers', 4 November 1916, NAK WO95/1974.

47   Romer, C. F. and Mainwaring, A. E., *The 2nd Battalion Royal Dublin Fusiliers in the South African War* (A. L. Humphreys, London, 1908), p. 255.

48   'War Diary 8th Royal Dublin Fusiliers', 3 November 1916, NAK WO95/1974.

49   'Simon, Lieut Frank, 1st Otago Regiment. 1st New Zealand Brigade. New Zealand Division II Anzac Corps', RDFA Archive, Dublin, p. 16.

50   'Wall, 2nd Lieut Michael, 6th Royal Irish Regiment', RDFA Archive. Letter from Michael to his mother, 5 November 1916.

51   'War Diary 6th Royal Irish Regiment', 7 November 1916, NAK WO95/1970.

52   'Wall, 2nd Lieut Michael, 6th Royal Irish Regiment', RDFA Archive. Letter from Michael to his mother, 13 November 1916.

53   'War Diary 6th Royal Irish Regiment', 13 November 1916, NAK WO95/1970.

54   For more details on these men, see The Commonwealth War Graves Commission (CWGC), http://www.cwgc.org. Although the CWGC lists Phillips' date of death as 14 November, the regimental diary was written at the time and is more likely to be accurate. Recruiting difficulties back in Ireland had resulted in 245 men from the Guernsey Militia being voluntarily drafted into the 6th Battalion of the Royal Irish as 'D' Company; roughly half of them could not speak English. A further 230 men from the Jersey Militia were also attached to the 6th Royal Irish Regiment. Both units joined the battalion on 5 March 1915. The Channel Islanders preferred to be with the Royal Irish, apparently due to the fact that the 2nd Battalion of the regiment was stationed on the island just before the outbreak of the war and the Irishmen seemed to have built up a good relationship with the islanders. See Editorial, 'Guernsey's Contribution to the 16th (Irish) Division', The Irish Sword, Vol. 18, No. 37, Summer 1992, pp. 305–306. See also Becke, A. F., History of the Great War Based on Official Documents. Order of Battle of Division, Part 3A: New Army Divisions (9–26) (His Majesty's Stationery Office, London, 1938), p. 65.

55   'War Diary 8th Royal Dublin Fusiliers', 21 November and 4 December 1916, NAK WO95/1974.

56   Ibid., 29 November 1916.

57   Wylly, Neill's Blue Caps (2000), pp. 205–206.

58   'Our Heroes', Irish Life, Vol. XXII, No. 2, 22 January 1915, p. 47. Mrs Loveband was the wife of the commanding officer of the 2nd RDF, Lieutenant Colonel Arthur Loveband. On 24 May 1915, four months

after this notice appeared in the January edition of 'Our Heroes', Colonel Loveband was killed during the German gas attack at Mouse Trap Farm, north-east of Ypres.

59   Wylly, *Neill's Blue Caps* (2000), pp. 205–206. The County Kildare Committee operated from The Courthouse, Naas, County Kildare, and their honorary president was the Countess of Mayo. Two further committees were established from this Central Advisory Committee: the Dublin County Association for the Administration of Voluntary Work, and the Regimental Care Committee for Prisoners of War. The establishment of both these committees was approved by the War Office. The Dublin Committee, Prisoners of War, whose honorary president was Lady Arnott, operated from 65 Merrion Square.

60   Hurley, M. J., *A View from the Grandstand* (Greencastle Press, Dublin, 1989), p. 60.

61   'Monica Roberts Collection'. Letter from Private J. Kirwin, 2nd RDF, 22 February 1917.

62   *Ibid.* Letter from Private P. Byrne, 2nd RDF, 5 April 1916.

63   'War Diary 2nd Royal Dublin Fusiliers, August 1914 to September 1916', 20 April 1916, NAK WO95/1481.

64   For more on these men see the Commonwealth War Graves Commission, http://www.cwgc.org.

7 Back to School

1   'War Diary 6th Royal Irish Regiment', 21 November 1916, NAK WO95/1970.

2   'Wall, 2nd Lieut Michael, 6th Royal Irish Regiment', RDFA Archive. Letter from Michael to his mother, 18 November 1916. See also letter to his aunt dated 19 November 1916.

3   'War Diary 6th Royal Irish Regiment', 26, 27, 29 and 30 November 1916, NAK WO95/1970.

4   'Wall, 2nd Lieut Michael, 6th Royal Irish Regiment', RDFA Archive. Field Service Card sent by Michael to his mother, 28 November 1916. If a man didn't want to write a letter but simply wanted to inform his family he was fine and all was well, there was Form A.2042, the standard Field Service Post Card (also known as the Quick Firer). He would cross out whatever was not appropriate.

5   *Ibid.* Letter from Michael to his mother, 1 December 1916.

6   'War Diary 8th Royal Dublin Fusiliers', end of December 1916 report written by the commanding officer of the 8th Dublins, Lieut. Col. Edward Bellingham, NAK WO95/1974.

7   *Ibid.*

8   *Ibid.*

9   *Ibid.*

10   For more on these men see The Commonwealth War Graves Commission, http://www.cwgc.org.

11   Passingham (1998), p. 1.

12   Denman (1992), p. 105. Also see Fielding (1929), p. 148.

13   'War Diary 8th Royal Dublin Fusiliers', end of December 1916 report written by the commanding officer of the 8th Dublins, Lieut. Col. Edward Bellingham, NAK WO95/1974.

14   'Wall, 2nd Lieut Michael, 6th Royal Irish Regiment', RDFA Archive. Letter from Michael to his mother, 2 December 1916.

15   Griffith, P., *Battle Tactics of the Western Front: The British Army's Art of Attack 1916–1918* (Yale University Press, New Haven, 1994), pp. 188–191.

16   Kingston, G. P., *History of the 4th (British) Infantry Division 1914–1919* (The London Press, London, 2006), p. 129.

17   Griffith (1994), p. 170.

18   Kingston (2006), p. 197.

19   'War Diary 8th Royal Dublin Fusiliers', 24 December 1916, NAK WO95/1974. The Central School of the 2nd Army was at Wisques, a town about forty-two kilometres directly west of Bailleul.

20   'Brett, C., 6th Connaught Rangers. 76/134/1', IWM.

21   Robbins, S., *British Generalship on the Western Front 1914–1918: Defeat into Victory* (Frank Cass and Co. Ltd, Abingdon, 2005), p. 91.

22   'War Diary 2nd Royal Dublin Fusiliers, August 1914 to September 1916', 16 September 1916, NAK WO95/1481.

23   'Ministry of Munitions, Trench Warfare and Chemical Warfare Departments, and War Office, Chemical Warfare Research Department and Chemical Defence Experimental Stations (Later Establishments), Porton: Reports and Papers. Director of Gas Services, France (Dgs) Series. General: Files Nos. Dgs/16–28', NAK WO142/91.

24   'War Diary 9th Royal Dublin Fusiliers', 14 January and 4 March 1917, NAK WO95/1974.

25 Laird (1925), pp. 129–130.

26 'Wall, 2nd Lieut Michael, 6th Royal Irish Regiment', RDFA Archive. Letter from Michael to his mother, 7 December 1916.

27 Laird (1925), pp. 129–130. When Michael visited Bailleul, he wasn't very impressed by it. This is apparent in the letter he wrote to his sister, Agatha, on 11 December 1916, when he told her that the town he was near (Bailleul) 'had nothing worth while [*sic*] sending. Most of the shops only stock military wants.' See 'Wall, 2nd Lieut Michael, 6th Royal Irish Regiment', RDFA Archive. Letter from Michael to his sister, 11 December 1916.

28 Gilbert (1994), p. 303.

29 'Wall, 2nd Lieut Michael, 6th Royal Irish Regiment', RDFA Archive. Letter from Michael to his mother, 7 December 1916.

30 *Ibid*. Letter from Michael to his mother, 12 December 1916.

31 'War Diary 6th Royal Irish Regiment', 16 December 1916, NAK WO95/1970.

32 See The Commonwealth War Graves Commission, http://www.cwgc.org. For example, Private Timothy Brett came from Thurles; Lance Corporal William Meehan came from Killenaule; Private James Fitzgerald came from Clonmel; and Private Henry Barago came from Cashel.

33 'Wall, 2nd Lieut Michael, 6th Royal Irish Regiment', RDFA Archive. Letter from Michael to his mother, 17 December 1916. On 12 December 1916 the German chancellor, Theobald von Bethmann Hollweg, in a speech in the Reichstag, offered to open negotiations with the British, French and Russians (the Entente Powers) in a neutral country. His terms, which asserted that Germany's possession of most of Belgium and much of France was a negotiable asset, were rejected by the new British cabinet. Following the Allied rejections of the German peace offer, the Germans began unrestricted submarine warfare on 1 February 1917. The aim of their decision was, according to the German submarine leader Commodore Bauer, 'to force England to make peace and thereby decide the whole war'. In January 1917, the last month in which the restrictions were in force, German submarines sank fifty-one British and sixty-three other Allied ships, which came to more than 300,000 tons, a third of which was British. See Gilbert (1994), p. 306.

34   'War Diary 8th Royal Dublin Fusiliers', 18 December 1916, NAK WO95/1974.

35   'Kingdon, Ernest William, Royal Field Artillery. Manuscript Memoirs of Service with 153rd and 56th Brigades Royal Field Artillery: "Through Mud, through Blood to the Green Fields Beyond, 1914–1918". MD 1327', The Royal Artillery Museum, Woolwich. Officers who wore a red band around their head caps were mainly generals.

36   'Wall, 2nd Lieut Michael, 6th Royal Irish Regiment', RDFA Archive. Letter from Michael to his mother, 20 December 1916.

37   'Diary of Fr P. Wrafter SJ', Jesuit Archive, Dublin, CHP 1/63. The Provincial was and is the title given to the head of the Jesuit Provincialate or Curia in Ireland.

38   'Wall, 2nd Lieut Michael, 6th Royal Irish Regiment', RDFA Archive. 1916 Christmas card Michael sent to his brother Joseph.

39   'War Diary 6th Royal Irish Regiment,' 20 December 1916, NAK WO95/1970.

40   'War Diary 8th Royal Dublin Fusiliers', 25–26 December 1916, NAK WO95/1974. See also 'War Diary 16th (Irish) Division', 25–26 December 1916, NAK WO95/1955. The 16th (Irish) Division's section of the front line was subdivided into three further sections: that on the left was the Vierstraat section; the centre was the Wijtschate section; and the right section was the Spanbroek section.

41   'War Diary 9th Royal Dublin Fusiliers', 25 December 1916, NAK WO95/1974. It wasn't until they came out of the line at the end of December 1916 that the 9th Dublins and 6th Connaught Rangers received their Christmas dinner. Before they did, Canon Ryan PP, VG, from Tipperary, gave them a morning sermon in the church at Loker. The dinner turned out to be a bit disappointing. According to Rowland Fielding it was 'a dismal affair'. Some of the food was dished out cold and, because there were no cups, the beer had to be drunk from the same mess tins from which the men ate their dinner. They even had to sit on the floor while eating their dinner; there were no tables available for them to sit at. See Fielding (1929), p. 141.

42   'Monica Roberts Collection'. Letter from Private Christy Fox, 2nd RDF, 28 December 1916.

43   'Brett, C., 6th Connaught Rangers. 76/134/1', IWM, p. 18.

44   *Ibid.*

45   'War Diary 8th Royal Dublin Fusiliers', 26 December 1916, NAK WO95/1974.

46   'War Diary 2nd Royal Dublin Fusiliers, 1 October 1916 to 30 April 1919', 13 January 1917, NAK WO95/1974. The battalion held its Christmas dinner of 1916 on Sunday evening 14 January 1917.

47   'Monica Roberts Collection'. Letter from Private Christy Fox, 2nd RDF, 19 January 1917.

48   'Wall, 2nd Lieut Michael, 6th Royal Irish Regiment', RDFA Archive. Letter from Michael to his mother, 25 December 1916.

49   'War Diary 2nd Royal Dublin Fusiliers, 1 October 1916 to 30 April 1919', 26 December 1916, NAK WO95/1974.

50   'Wall, 2nd Lieut Michael, 6th Royal Irish Regiment', RDFA Archive. Letter from Michael's friend Jamie, 29 December 1916. The Empire Theatre may well have been the Empire Palace Theatre, which later became the Olympia Theatre in Dame Street.

51   Advertisement, *The Irish Times*, 2 January 1917. On 20 November 1925 the Masterpiece cinema was bombed by the IRA because it had shown the film *The Battle of Ypres*. See *The Irish Times*, 21 November 1925. I would like to thank Dr Denis Condon of the School of English, Media and Theatre Studies, Maynooth University, for information on this film.

52   'War Diary 6th Royal Irish Regiment', 30 December 1916, NAK WO95/1970.

53   'Wall, 2nd Lieut Michael, 6th Royal Irish Regiment', RDFA Archive. Letter from Michael to his mother, 30 December 1916.

54   'War Diary 6th Royal Irish Regiment', 31 December 1916, NAK WO95/1970. Lieutenant Rennison's name is on the Menin Gate Memorial, Ypres.

55   'War Diary 8th Royal Dublin Fusiliers', 31 December 1916, NAK WO95/1974.

56   Fielding (1929), p. 142.

8 'Shamrock grows nowhere else but Ireland'

1   'War Diary 9th Royal Dublin Fusiliers', 28 January 1917, NAK WO95/1974.

2   'Monica Roberts Collection'. Letter from Private Christy Fox, 2nd RDF, 20 February 1917.

3   *Ibid.*

4   'War Diary 8th Royal Dublin Fusiliers', 1 January 1917, NAK WO95/1974.

5   'War Diary 6th Royal Irish Regiment', 1 January 1917, NAK WO95/1970.

6   'Wall, 2nd Lieut Michael, 6th Royal Irish Regiment', RDFA Archive. Letter from Michael to his brother Joseph, 2 January 1917. Michael erroneously dated this letter 2 January 1916.

7   *Ibid.* Letter from Michael to his mother, 6 January 1917.

8   'War Diary 2nd Royal Dublin Fusiliers, 1 October 1916 to 30 April 1919', 5 January 1917, NAK WO95/1974.

9   *Ibid.*

10   'War Diary 6th Royal Irish Regiment', 7 January 1917, NAK WO95/1970.

11   Passingham (1998), p. 14.

12   'Kingdon, Ernest William, Royal Field Artillery. Manuscript Memoirs of Service with 153rd and 56th Brigades Royal Field Artillery: "Through Mud, through Blood to the Green Fields Beyond, 1914–1918". MD 1327.'

13   'Diary of 2nd Lieut J. F. B. O'Sullivan, 6th Connaught Rangers. 77/167/1', IWM, London, p. 16.

14   'Lockhart, Private Andrew, 11th Royal Inniskilling Fusiliers', RDFA Archive.

15   'Wall, 2nd Lieut Michael, 6th Royal Irish Regiment', RDFA Archive. Letter from Michael to his mother, 16 January 1917. Michael served in the 6th Royal Irish Regiment in the 9th Corps. He presumably wrote 8th Corps by mistake.

16   For a broader discussion on trade union disputes and strikes throughout Europe during the First World War, see Mulligan (2014), pp. 147–160.

17   Fielding (1929), pp. 135–136.

18   Ferguson, N., *The Pity of War* (Penguin Books, London, 1998), pp. 270–271.

19   'Labour Unrest in Dublin', 3 November and 'Dublin Labour Unrest' 15 November 1917, *The Irish Times*. One of the arbitrators between the

management of Boland's and its workers' representative was Mr Henry Hanna KC, the author of the history of 'D' Company, 7th Royal Dublin Fusiliers, called *The Pals at Suvla* (1916).

20 'Wall, 2nd Lieut Michael, 6th Royal Irish Regiment', RDFA Archive. Letter from Michael to his mother, 22 January 1917. On 20 January 1917 *The Evening Herald*, on page 3, presented a notice entitled 'Another Strike Threatened'. Dublin dockers threatened to strike for an increase in their wages. Right beside this notice there was an advertisement from Dublin University Officers' Training Corps seeking new recruits.

21 See The Commonwealth War Graves Commission, http://www.cwgc. org. Toohey is buried in Pond Farm Cemetery near the village of Wulverghem; grave reference H.4.

22 'Wall, 2nd Lieut Michael, 6th Royal Irish Regiment', RDFA Archive. Letter from Michael to his mother, 22 January 1917.

23 'War Diary 6th Royal Irish Regiment', 28 January 1917, NAK WO95/1970.

24 'Wall, 2nd Lieut Michael, 6th Royal Irish Regiment', RDFA Archive. Letter from Michael to his mother, 28 January 1917.

25 'War Diary 8th Royal Dublin Fusiliers', 1–31 January 1917, NAK WO95/1974.

26 See The Commonwealth War Graves Commission, http://www.cwgc. org, for details.

27 Whitton (1998), p. 408.

28 'War Diary 8th Royal Dublin Fusiliers', 8 and 9 February 1917, NAK WO95/1974.

29 'Diary of 2nd Lieut J. F. B. O'Sullivan, 6th Connaught Rangers. 77/167/1', IWM, p. 12.

30 *Ibid.*, p. 34.

31 *Ibid.*, p. 26.

32 Fielding (1929), pp. 149–150. Fielding did not give the men's names.

33 'War Diary 8th Royal Dublin Fusiliers', 11 February 1917, NAK WO95/1974.

34 See The Commonwealth Graves Commission, http://www.cwgc.org, for details.

35 Good, W., 'Bandon's Youngest Soldier to Die', *The New Ranger: Journal of the Connaught Rangers Association*, Vol. 21, No. 2, January 2005, pp. 9–10.

36   See The Commonwealth Graves Commission, http://www.cwgc.org, for details.

37   'War Diary 6th Royal Irish Regiment,' 4 February 1917, NAK WO95/1970. Roche-Kelly had served with the South Irish Horse in 1915.

38   Pegler, M., *British Tommy* (Osprey Publishing, Oxford, 1996), pp. 27–28.

39   Fielding (1929), p. 157.

40   Ferguson (1998), p. 353.

41   'Beater, Captain O. L., 9th Royal Dublin Fusiliers. 3385 – 86/65/1', IWM.

42   'Monica Roberts Collection'. Letter from Private Christy Fox, 2nd RDF, 15 March 1917.

43   'Wall, 2nd Lieut Michael, 6th Royal Irish Regiment', RDFA Archive. Letter from Michael to his mother, 8 February 1917.

9 'I stick to my rosary'

1   'Wall, 2nd Lieut Michael, 6th Royal Irish Regiment', RDFA Archive. Letter from Michael to Joseph Wall, 13 February 1917. On 1 February 1917 Germany resumed its policy of unrestricted submarine warfare. Michael referred to this German move as being Germany's 'new mad dog policy'. For further discussion on Germany's resumption of unrestricted submarine warfare in February 1917, see Mulligan (2014), pp. 188–196.

2   'Wall, 2nd Lieut Michael, 6th Royal Irish Regiment', RDFA Archive. Letter from Michael to his mother, 11 February 1917.

3   'War Diary 6th Royal Irish Regiment', 13 February 1917, NAK WO95/1970.

4   Middlebrook, M., *The First Day on the Somme* (Penguin Books, London, 1971), pp. 94 and 279.

5   *Ibid.*, pp. 278–279. See also Samuels, M., *Doctrine and Dogma: German and British Infantry Tactics in the First World War* (Greenwood Press, London, 1992), p. 159.

6   'War Diary 86th Brigade, March 1916 to December 1917', account of 1 July battle, NAK WO95/2298.

7   Edmonds, Sir (Brigadier-General) J. E., *History of the Great War. Military Operations, France and Belgium 1916.* Vol. 2 (His Majesty's Stationery Office, London, 1948), p. 572. 'The best formation, as was proved later in the War, consisted of small groups each trained to use

ground and covering fire to the best advantage, and to work on its own initiative whilst affording support and assistance to other groups.'

8   Lee, J., 'Some Lessons of the Somme: The British Infantry in 1917', in The British Commission for Military History, *Look to Your Front: Studies in the First World War* (Spellmount, Kent, 1999), pp. 80–81. As part of a tactical team, Sergeant Robert Downie of the 2nd RDF won the VC on 23 October charging a German machine-gun position using such tactics. His citation appeared in *The London Gazette* on 25 November 1916. Also see Wylly, H. C., *Crown and Company: The Historical Records of the 2nd Battalion Royal Dublin Fusiliers 1911–1922*, Vol. 2 (Schull Books, Cork, 2000), p. 74.

9   McCarthy, C., 'Queen of the Battlefield: The Development of Command, Organisation and Tactics in the British Infantry Battalion during the Great War', in G. Sheffield and D. Todman (eds), *Command and Control on the Western Front: The British Army's Experience 1914–1918* (Spellmount, Gloucestershire, 2007), p. 182.

10   These comments were made by Peter Simkins as part of his address to the Haig Fellowship in January 2000. See http://www.scotsatwar.co.uk/AZ/HaigFellows%27Addresses00.html.

11   For further discussion on the learning-curve concept specifically as applied to battalion level, see Burke, T., 'The Learning Experiences of the Royal Dublin Fusiliers in Trench Warfare in the First World War, August 1914 to December 1916', unpublished MLitt thesis, University College Dublin, 2013.

12   'War Diary 6th Royal Irish Regiment', 16 February 1917, NAK WO95/1970.

13   'Wall, 2nd Lieut Michael, 6th Royal Irish Regiment', RDFA Archive. Letter from Michael to his mother, 16 February 1917. On occasion German biplanes would fly over the Irish lines. Michael's account of them 'bagging' a 'Bosche' plane may be a bit of an exaggeration. Although the battalion diarist noted that German biplanes flew over, he made no mention of them ever 'bagging' one.

14   'Wall, 2nd Lieut Michael 6th Royal Irish Regiment', RDFA Archive. Letter from Michael to his mother, 19 February 1917. Second Lieutenant Charlie Adams (RDF) survived the war and returned to live in Malahide, County Dublin. Before the war he had played rugby for Ireland and

cricket for Malahide Cricket Club, of which Tom Kettle was also a member. As a rugby international, Charlie was first capped for Ireland in 1908 when Ireland played England. He was a member of Old Wesley Rugby Football Club and continued to play for Ireland right up to the outbreak of the war. After the war Charlie became president of Malahide Cricket Club. His son, Norman Adams, was a member of the RDFA.

15   Denman (1992), p. 106.

16   'War Diary 6th Royal Irish Regiment', 19 February 1917, NAK WO95/1970.

17   For more details see The Commonwealth War Graves Commission, http://www.cwgc.org.

18   Jourdain, H. F. N., *The Connaught Rangers*, Vol. 3 (Schull Books, Cork, 1999), p. 236.

19   'War Diary 2nd Royal Dublin Fusiliers, 1 October 1916 to 30 April 1919', 13 February 1917, NAK WO95/1974.

20   'Monica Roberts Collection'. Letter from Private George Soper, 2nd RDF, 5 March 1917.

21   'War Diary 6th Royal Irish Regiment', 21 February 1917, NAK WO95/1970. Via Gellia was a communication trench in the 16th (Irish) Division's sector. Although the term was used widely by Allied (most often British and Commonwealth) servicemen to describe any form of German field-artillery shells, the 'whizz bang' was originally attributed to the noise made by shells from German 77mm field guns. See http://www.firstworldwar.com/atoz/whizzbang.htm.

22   'Wall, 2nd Lieut Michael, 6th Royal Irish Regiment', RDFA Archive. Letter from Michael to his mother, 21 February 1917.

23   'Beater, Captain O. L., 9th Royal Dublin Fusiliers. 3385 – 86/65/1', IWM.

24   'Wall, 2nd Lieut Michael, 6th Royal Irish Regiment', RDFA Archive. Letter from Michael to his mother, 26 February 1917.

25   *Ibid*. Letter from Michael to his mother, 28 February 1917.

26   *The Irish Times*, 6 and 8 February 1917.

27   On 19 January 1917 the recently appointed German foreign minister, Dr Alfred von Zimmerman, sent a coded telegram to the German ambassador in Mexico City. Zimmerman's telegram outlined a scheme whereby Germany would seek the alliance of Mexico by offering it generous financial support if America entered the war as a result of

unrestricted submarine warfare. Germany would also assist Mexico to reconquer the territories it had lost seventy years previously: Texas, New Mexico and Arizona. The message was intercepted and decoded by the British and handed to the Americans. Although President Woodrow Wilson did not declare war immediately on Germany, he did announce to Congress that he had brought two and a half years of war diplomacy to an end. This was the policy referred to in *The Irish Times* article 'Senate Approves Break With Germany'.

28 'War Diary 8th Royal Dublin Fusiliers', 22 February 1917, NAK WO95/1974.

29 The Commonwealth War Graves Commission, http://www.cwgc.org.

30 'Wall, 2nd Lieut Michael, 6th Royal Irish Regiment', RDFA Archive. Letter from Fr Francis Gleeson to Michael, 2 March 1917. The church was opened on Sunday 12 December 1915 and was a temporary building, mainly constructed from corrugated iron. A more permanent chapel now stands on the site of the old chapel in what is now Sean MacDermott Street. See 'New Church Opened in Dublin', *The Irish Independent*, 13 December 1915.

31 'Wall, 2nd Lieut Michael, 6th Royal Irish Regiment', RDFA Archive. Letter from Michael to his mother, 1 March 1917.

10 Life in the Reserve around Loker, Kemmel and Dranouter

1 Ferguson (1998), p. 351.

2 'McClure, Private Thomas, 15th Royal Irish Rifles', memoir, The Somme Heritage Centre, Newtownards, p. 65.

3 'War Diary 6th Royal Irish Regiment', 1 March 1917, NAK WO95/1970.

4 Denman (1992), p. 104.

5 'McClure, Private Thomas', The Somme Heritage Centre, p. 56. The Shankill Camp at Neuve Église was just under six-and-a-half kilometres to the east of Bailleul.

6 Ferguson (1998), p. 352.

7 Englander (1997), p. 130.

8 'Wall, 2nd Lieut Michael, 6th Royal Irish Regiment', RDFA Archive. Letter from Michael to his mother, 1 March 1917.

9 'Diary of R. H. Newman, Royal Artillery. MD 1169', The Royal Artillery Museum, Woolwich.

10 'Monica Roberts Collection'. Letter from Private Christy Fox, 2nd RDF. Although no date was given on the letter, the postmark on the envelope was 20 February 1917.

11 'War Diary 6th Royal Irish Regiment', 13 February 1917, NAK WO95/1970.

12 'Kitchener's Orders to Soldiers Attached to All Active Service Pay Books', RDFA Archive, Dublin, 10 August 1914.

13 Bourke, J., *The Misfit Soldier: Edward Casey's War Story 1914–1918* (Cork University Press, Cork, 1999), back cover and pp. 46–47.

14 *Ibid.*, p. 35.

15 'May, Lieut. A.G., 49th Machine Gun Company. 88/46/1', IWM, London.

16 Laird (1925), p. 102. 'First Hundred Thousand' was a term given to the first 100,000 men of Kitchener's new armies designated as Kitchener's Army or K1. The term is also the title of a book written by John Hay Beith published in 1915.

17 'Schweder, Captain Ronald Paul, 173rd Brigade Royal Field Artillery, 36th (Ulster) Division. MD 2472', The Royal Artillery Museum, Woolwich.

18 Orr, P., *The Road to the Somme* (Blackstaff Press, Belfast, 1987), p. 81.

19 'War Diary 2nd Royal Dublin Fusiliers, August 1914 to September 1916', 2 November 1914, NAK WO95/1481.

20 Ferguson (1998), p. 353.

21 Simpson, K., 'Dr James Dunn and Shell Shock', in Cecil and Liddle (1996), p. 508.

22 'McClure, Private Thomas', The Somme Heritage Centre, p. 57.

23 Ferguson (1998), p. 351.

24 *Ibid.*

25 *Ibid.*

26 Orr (1987), p. 164.

27 Bowman (2003), p. 14.

28 Pegler (1996), p. 30.

29 'Beater, Captain O. L., 9th Royal Dublin Fusiliers. 3385 – 86/65/1', IWM.

30 Fielding (1929), p. 175.

31 Lemisko (1997), p. 227.

32 Denman (1992), p. 151.

33 Bowman (2003), Table 2.1, p. 42; Table 3.1, p. 87; Table 5.1, p. 157.

34   Satterthwaite (2006), p. 48.

35   'War Diary 8th Royal Dublin Fusiliers', 3 October 1916, NAK WO95/1974.

36   *Ibid.*, 16 October 1916. See also The Commonwealth Graves Commission, http://www.cwgc.org.

37   'War Diary 8th Royal Dublin Fusiliers', 10 October 1916, NAK WO95/1974.

38   *Ibid.*, 22 November 1916.

39   The Commonwealth Graves Commission, http://www.cwgc.org. Sergeant Roache died in England on 25 August 1918. He was buried in Portsmouth.

40   'Monica Roberts Collection'. Letter from Private Christy Fox, 2nd RDF, 1 December 1916.

41   'Jeffreys, Lieut. Col. R. G. B., 2nd Royal Dublin Fusiliers', RDFA Archive, Dublin.

42   'Monica Roberts Collection'. Papers of Sgt Bob Downie VC donated by the Downie family. Sergeant Downie may have known Sergeant Stephen Ward of the 2nd RDF, who was burned to death in an accident at training. On the morning of Sunday 23 October 2016 a paving stone located at the Doulton Fountain outside the People's Palace on Glasgow Green, dedicated to Sergeant Downie, was unveiled by the Lord Provost of Glasgow, The Right Honourable Councillor Sadie Docherty. Attending the ceremony were Mr Mark Hanniffy, Consul General of Ireland to Scotland; members of the large Downie family; and members of the RDFA Committee. The unveiling was followed by a civic reception kindly hosted by the Lord Provost in the City Chambers. Bob was a life-long Glasgow Celtic supporter. His day was made with the dedicated stone, and to top it off, his beloved Celtic beat Rangers one goal to nil in the old firm match that took place in the afternoon.

43   'War Diary 2nd Royal Dublin Fusiliers, 1 October 1916 to 30 April 1919', 28 December 1916, NAK WO95/1974.

44   'Monica Roberts Collection'. Letter from Private Christy Fox, 2nd RDF, 28 December 1916.

11 'Curious times'

1   'War Diary 6th Royal Irish Regiment', 10 March 1917, NAK WO95/1970.

2 'War Diary 2nd Royal Dublin Fusiliers, 1 October 1916 to 30 April 1919', 8 March 1917, NAK WO95/1974.

3 'War Diary 16th (Irish) Division, 1 December 1915 to 30 April 1917', Report by General Hickie of German raid on 8 March 1917, NAK WO95/1955.

4 'War Diary 16th (Irish) Division', Report by Brigadier General Ramsay on German raid of 8 March 1917, NAK WO95/1955.

5 'Beater, Captain O. L., 9th Royal Dublin Fusiliers. 3385 – 86/65/1', IWM.

6 'War Diary 6th Royal Irish Regiment', 12–13 March 1917, NAK WO95/1970. As a result of his wounds, Second Lieutenant Laracy lost his leg. When he had joined the battalion on 17 October 1916, the battalion diarist had noted that he 'was six feet seven inches in his socks', an ideal target for German snipers.

7 'Wall, 2nd Lieut Michael, 6th Royal Irish Regiment', RDFA Archive. Letter from Michael to his mother, 11 March 1917.

8 The contentious meeting is reported in 'Alderman O'Neill Elected', *The Irish Times*, 24 February 1917.

9 *The Irish Times*, 8 March 1917.

10 For text of the full speech see The Dublin Committee, Patron Lord Wimborne, *In Memoriam Major Willie Redmond M.P., B.L., Souvenir Booklet* (1918). Available in the National Library of Ireland, Call Number P 2375.

11 *Ibid.*

12 Denman (1995), p. 111.

13 *Ibid.*, pp. 106 and 111.

14 'No Enforced Home Rule', *The Irish Times*, 8 March 1917.

15 Denman (1995), p. 112.

12 Paddy's Day at Loker

1 'War Diary 6th Royal Irish Regiment', 14 March 1917, NAK WO95/1970.

2 'Wall, 2nd Lieut Michael, 6th Royal Irish Regiment', RDFA Archive. Letter from Bernard Wall to Michael, 15 March 1917.

3 'Monica Roberts Collection'. Letter from Corporal Arthur Brennan, 2nd RDF, 17 March 1917.

4   'War Diary 2nd Royal Dublin Fusiliers, 1 October 1916 to 30 April 1919', 15 March 1917, NAK WO95/1974.

5   'War Diary 7th Royal Dublin Fusiliers', 17 March 1917, NAK WO95/4296.

6   Whitton (1998), p. 411.

7   'Glass, Corporal Joseph, 10th Royal Irish Rifles', The Somme Heritage Centre, Newtownards.

8   'Wall, 2nd Lieut Michael, 6th Royal Irish Regiment', RDFA Archive. Letter from Michael to his mother, 18 March 1917. The sensational news about Russia was that, on 15 March 1917, the Great War had claimed its first sovereign. The Tsar of Russia had abdicated and Russia was in turmoil.

9   'War Diary 6th Royal Irish Regiment', 22 March 1917, NAK WO95/1970.

10 'Wall, 2nd Lieut Michael, 6th Royal Irish Regiment', RDFA Archive. Letter from Michael to his mother, 22 March 1917.

11 'War Diary 8th Royal Dublin Fusiliers', 1–31 March 1917, NAK WO95/1974.

12 'War Diary 6th Royal Irish Regiment', 26 March 1917, NAK WO95/1970.

13 'Wall, 2nd Lieut Michael, 6th Royal Irish Regiment', RDFA Archive. Letter from Michael to his mother, 30 March 1917.

13 The Swallows Have Arrived

1   'War Diary 6th Royal Irish Regiment', 1 April 1917, NAK WO95/1970.

2   'Western Front: Maps. Supplement to 1:10000 (British) Series I. Trenches corrected to: 1.4.17. Sheet Name and No. 28SW 2. Edition No. 5A. Lines: A/G Production: OS GSGS No. 3062', NAK WO297/6580.

3   'War Diary 6th Royal Irish Regiment', 2 April 1917, NAK WO 95/1970.

4   The Commonwealth War Graves Commission, http://www.cwgc.org.

5   Dorrington, N., 'Live and Let Die: The British Army's Experience of Trench Raiding 1915–1918', *Journal of the Centre of First World War Studies*, Vol. 3, No. 1, September 2007, p. 3.

6   Edmonds, Sir (Brigadier-General) J. E., *History of the Great War. Military Operations, France and Belgium 1916*. Vol. 1 (His Majesty's Stationery

Office, London, 1948), Appendix 6, 'Organisation and Execution of a Raid', p. 42.

7   Griffith (1994), p. 62.

8   Haynes, A. D., 'The Development of Infantry Doctrine in the Canadian Expeditionary Force: 1914–1918', *Canadian Military Journal*, Vol. 8, No. 3, 2007, p. 66. For further reading on infantry–artillery co-operation see Farndale, M., *History of the Royal Regiment of Artillery Western Front 1914–1918* (Dorset Press, Dorchester, 1986).

9   Passingham (1998), p. 85.

10   'War Diary 6th Royal Irish Regiment', 5 April 1917, NAK WO95/1970.

11   Passingham (1998), p. 199.

12   The Commonwealth War Graves Commission, http://www.cwgc.org. Second Lieutenant M. C. Day was buried in Tanga Memorial Cemetery in Tanzania. See also *Irish Independent*, 12 April 1917.

13   The Commonwealth War Graves Commission, http://www.cwgc.org, 199065 Captain Edward Day. Grave reference III.B.60.

14   'Burke, Capt Dick, 6th Royal Irish Regiment', RDFA Archive, Dublin. Dick Burke survived the war and returned to his job in the National Bank at Camden Street in Dublin. After the war he lived with his wife and two daughters in one of the ex-servicemen's cottages in Killester on the north side of Dublin city, where he died in January 1977.

15   'War Diary 6th Royal Irish Regiment', 7 April 1917, NAK WO95/1970.

16   The Commonwealth War Graves Commission, http://www.cwgc.org.

17   'Wall, 2nd Lieut Michael, 6th Royal Irish Regiment', RDFA Archive. Letter from Michael to his mother, 7 April 1917. Michael stated that the raid took place at night. It actually took place just as dawn broke.

18   'War Diary 6th Royal Irish Regiment', 8 April 1917, NAK WO95/1970.

19   'Wall, 2nd Lieut Michael, 6th Royal Irish Regiment', RDFA Archive. Letter from Michael's mother to Michael, 3 April 1917.

20   *Ibid.* Letter from Bernard Wall to Michael, 11 April 1917. Brooks Thomas was a well-known Dublin timber merchant that had timber yards where the Irish Life complex is now situated in Abbey Street, Dublin.

21   *Ibid.* Letter from Michael to his mother, 14 April 1917.

22   *Ibid.* Letter from Michael to his mother, 20 April 1917.

23   Callan (1987), p. 42

24 'British Great Offensive, Gigantic Battle', *The Cork Examiner*, 10 April 1917; 'Brilliant Drive by the British', *Irish Independent*, 10 April 1917.

25 *Irish Independent*, 11 April 1917.

26 'War Diary 6th Royal Irish Regiment', 28 April 1917, NAK WO95/1970.

27 'Wall, 2nd Lieut Michael, 6th Royal Irish Regiment', RDFA Archive. Letter from Michael to his aunt, 27 April 1917.

14 Training and Away from the Guns for a While

1 Passingham (1998), p. 33. See also Neillands, R., *The Great War Generals on the Western Front 1914–19* (Robinson, London, 1999), pp. 364–365.

2 'War Diary 8th Royal Dublin Fusiliers', 19 March 1917, NAK WO95/1974.

3 'War Diary 9th Royal Dublin Fusiliers', 25 March 1917, NAK WO95/1974. It's a pity Charlie Adams had been reported missing; he would have made a fine addition to the Dubs rugby team. See also O'Rahilly, A., *Father William Doyle S. J.* (Longmans Green and Co., London, 1920), p. 481.

4 'War Diary 6th Royal Irish Regiment', 28 April 1917, NAK WO95/1970.

5 'War Diary 8th Royal Dublin Fusiliers', 31 March 1917, NAK WO95/1974.

6 *Ibid.* St Omer is approximately forty-five kilometres west of Loker.

7 'Monica Roberts Collection'. Letter from Private George Soper, 2nd RDF, 31 March 1917.

8 Laird (1925), p. 133.

9 O'Rahilly (1920), p. 276. In August 2015, with a broken right hand, I cycled from Loker to St Omer on the same journey. It was a difficult cycle; marching it with full pack would have been very tough indeed.

10 *Ibid.*, p. 277. The church in Nordausques is still there today. On Sunday 15 July 1917 Fr Willie Doyle SJ offered a sermon in the Cathedral of Notre Dame in St Omer. Hundreds of men from the 2nd RDF were in attendance. A little over one month later, in August 1917, Fr Doyle was killed at Frezenberg Ridge, north-east of Ypres. See *Ibid.*, pp. 520–525.

11 *Ibid.*, p. 277. See also 'War Diary 8th Royal Dublin Fusiliers', 31 March 1917, NAK WO95/1974.

12   Passingham (1998), p. 33.

13   O'Rahilly (1920), p. 277.

14   Such manuals included *SS 135: Instructions for the Training of Infantry Divisions for Offensive Action* (December 1916) and *SS 143: Instructions for the Training of Platoons for Offensive Action* issued by GHQ in February 1917.

15   Jourdain (1999), p. 241. Alquines is some seventy-four kilometres east of Loker, and roughly eighteen kilometres east of St Omer.

16   'War Diary 8th Royal Dublin Fusiliers', 10 April 1917, NAK WO95/1974.

17   'War Diary 6th Royal Irish Regiment', 31 May 1917, NAK WO95/1970.

18   *Ibid.*, 1–4 May 1917.

19   Falls (1922), p. 83.

20   'War Diary 6th Royal Irish Regiment', 5 May 1917, NAK WO95/1970.

21   'War Diary 8th Royal Dublin Fusiliers', 15 April 1917, NAK WO95/1974. Also, the 56th Squadron had a training centre at Bailleul.

22   Passingham (1998), pp. 43–44. At dusk on 31 May one of these kite balloons was shot down over Clare Camp by a German aeroplane. See 'War Diary 6th Royal Irish Regiment', 31 May 1917, NAK WO95/1970.

23   'Brett, C., 6th Connaught Rangers. 76/134/1', IWM, p. 11.

24   Passingham (1998), p. 33. This is a fine example of the learning curve debate among military historians.

25   The Commonwealth War Graves Commission, http://www.cwgc.org.

26   'War Diary 6th Royal Irish Regiment', 25–27 May 1917, NAK WO95/1970.

27   I would like to thank Dr Tim Bowman, School of History at the University of Kent, for checking field general courts martial records and verifying Private Kenny's trial.

28   Laird (1925), pp. 139–140.

29   'Brierley, Private Ned, MM, 8th Royal Dublin Fusiliers', RDFA Archive, Dublin. The 8th Dublins had Ned Brierley playing with them. Ned won the Military Medal (MM) for bravery later in 1917. After the war he played League of Ireland Association Football for Shelbourne Football Club and St Mary's of Ballsbridge, Dublin.

30   The Commonwealth War Graves Commission, http://www.cwgc.org, 437823 Private James Hughes. James was born in Blanchardstown,

County Dublin. His parents, James and Mary, came from Porterstown, Clonsilla, County Dublin. He was twenty-four when he died and is buried in Mendinghem Military Cemetery. Grave reference IVB11.

31 Denman (1992), p. 110. For example, in mid-May, the 6th Connaught Rangers worked at burying telephone cables for the 16th Divisional Signal Company. Their work delayed their heading for 49th Brigade training at Alquines. See Jourdain (1999), pp. 240–241.

32 'Wall, 2nd Lieut Michael, 6th Royal Irish Regiment', RDFA Archive. Letter from Michael to his mother, 2 May 1917.

33 *Ibid.* Letter from Michael to his mother, 4 May 1917. A 'Blighty' was the name given to a wound that merited treatment at home in Ireland or Britain.

34 'War Diary 6th Royal Irish Regiment', 26 April 1917, NAK WO95/1970.

35 For most men, a wound had been looked upon as a ticket home.

36 'War Diary 6th Royal Irish Regiment', 7 May 1917, NAK WO95/1970.

37 Laird (1925), p. 146.

38 Johnstone, T., *Orange, Green and Khaki* (Gill & Macmillan, Dublin, 1992), p. 270.

39 Terraine (1977), p. 89.

40 Passingham (1998), p. 366.

41 'War Diary 6th Royal Irish Regiment', 10 May 1917, NAK WO95/1970.

42 The Commonwealth War Graves Commission, http://www.cwgc.org.

43 Geoghegan (1997), p. 115.

44 'War Diary 6th Royal Irish Regiment', 19 May 1917, NAK WO95/1970.

45 Alquines is right beside the village of Journy, where the 7th Leinsters were billeted.

46 'War Diary 6th Royal Irish Regiment', 17 May 1917, NAK WO95/1970. In order to protect its African colonies of Angola and Mozambique from German ambitions in Africa, Portugal entered the war on the Allies' side in March 1916. See Strachan, H., *The First World War, to Arms!* (Oxford University Press, Oxford, 2001), p. 623.

47 Fielding (1929), p. 179.

48 'Wall, 2nd Lieut Michael, 6th Royal Irish Regiment', RDFA Archive. Letter from Michael to his mother, 12 May 1917.

49 Fielding (1929), p. 181.

15 'We'll hold Derry's Walls' – Relations between the Irish Divisions in Flanders

1   Denman (1992), p. 180.

2   Denman (1995), p. 114. The article appeared in *Irish Life* on 11 May 1917.

3   *Ibid.*, p. 116. Despite the rhetoric used by Redmond, and agreeing sentiments expressed by others on Irish unity in Flanders and Ireland, they were rejected by some people back in Ireland. A couple of days before that article appeared in *Irish Life*, Ennis Rural District Council passed a resolution that called for Willie Redmond to resign his seat 'and give the people of East Clare an opportunity of selecting a person who would represent their views and wishes'. See *Ibid.*, p. 113.

4   'The Irish Troops', *The Irish Times*, 8 June 1917.

5   Liddle Hart, B. H., *The Real War 1914–1918* (Faber and Faber, London, 1930), p. 358.

6   On the road leading into Wijtschate from Kemmel, just near Maedelstede Farm, there are two stone markers that mark the actual location of the divisional interface where these two battalions met on 7 June 1917.

7   Bowman (2003), p. 140.

8   Callan (1987).

9   Denman (1992), p. 140.

10   Burke, T., 'Whence Came the Royal Dublin Fusiliers?', *The Irish Sword*, Vol. 24, No. 98, Winter 2005, p. 449. Note: the balances to bring percentages up to 100% came mainly from Welsh and Scottish drafts.

11   'War Diary 8th Royal Dublin Fusiliers', 21 December 1916, NAK WO95/1974.

12   Perry, N., 'Politics and Command: General Nugent, the Ulster Division and Relations with Ulster Unionism, 1915–1917', in The British Commission for Military History, *Look to Your Front: Studies in the First World War* (Spellmount, Kent, 1999), p. 116.

13   *Ibid.*, p. 118.

14   Bowman (2003), pp. 140–142.

15   'War Diary 9th Corps. Proceedings of Corps Commander's Conference 3 October 1916', NAK WO95/835.

16   Geoghegan (1997), p. 44. See also Wylly, *Crown and Company* (2000), p. 73.

17   McCance, S., *History of the Royal Munster Fusiliers 1861 to 1922*, Vol. 2 (Schull Books, Cork, 1995), p. 67.

18   'Monica Roberts Collection'. Letter from Private Christy Fox, 2nd RDF, 1 December 1916. Note: the 10th Royal Dublin Fusiliers were not part of the 16th (Irish) Division's order of battle at Wijtschate on 7 June 1917. They joined the division on 23 June 1917.

19   Denman (1992), p. 140.

20   Burke, T., 'Some Further Debate on Recruitment in Ireland into the British Army during the First World War', *The Blue Cap: Journal of The Royal Dublin Fusiliers Association*, Vol. 19, 2014. See also 'Commission to Enquire into Conditions of British Ex-Servicemen in Irish Free State', NAK PIN 15/757.

21   'War Diary 14th Royal Irish Rifles', 26 May 1917, NAK WO95/251.

22   'War Diary 9th Royal Irish Fusiliers', 30 April 1917, NAK WO95/2505.

23   Fielding (1929), p. 169.

24   'War Diary 9th Royal Irish Fusiliers', 30 April 1917, NAK WO95/2505.

25   Fielding (1929), p. 170.

26   'War Diary 6th Connaught Rangers', 30 April 1917, NAK WO95/1970.

27   Bowman (2003), p. 154.

28   Jourdain (1999), pp. 230–238.

29   Gwynn, S., *Ireland in Ten Days* (George G. Harrap & Co., London, 1935), p. 83. See also Macrory, Lieut Col F. S. N., 'Contribution to the "History of the 36th (Ulster) Division"', NAK WO95/2491, p. 45. A report of this event was also written in *The Galway Observer*, 21 September 1918.

30   Macrory, 'Contribution to the "History of the 36th (Ulster) Division"', NAK WO95/2491, p. 46.

31   Bowman (2003), p. 154.

32   'Papers of Sir Percy McElwaine, 14th Royal Irish Rifles. Box Reference 92/35/1', IWM, London.

33   'Collins, Rifleman Walter, 9th Royal Irish Rifles', The Somme Heritage Centre, Newtownards.

34   'Monica Roberts Collection'. Letter from Private Joseph Elley, 2nd RDF, 20 November 1915.

35   *Ibid.*, 5 December 1915. John Redmond visited France in November 1915 where he 'met the Dublin Fusiliers and the men of a battalion of the Ulster Division (the Royal Irish Rifles) side by side in the trenches'.

See Kerr, S. P., *What the Irish Regiments Have Done* (Fisher Unwin Ltd, London, 1916), p. 17.

36 Bowman (2003), p. 182.

37 Carswell, S., 'The First World War Diary of Henry Gill SJ', unpublished thesis, Trinity College, Dublin, 3 April 1998.

38 Burke (2014), p. 64.

39 The 36th (Ulster) and 16th (Irish) Divisions included men from the Ulster Volunteers and Irish National Volunteers respectively. It is quite possible they would have faced each other in a civil war had it not been for the outbreak of war abroad. Whatever camaraderie developed among the Irishmen from north and south in Flanders, sadly, with time, became polarised and lost in the opposing political and religious cultures when the men of Belfast and Derry returned home. By and large, post-war commemorations in Ulster parted along sectarian lines. On 29 July 1919 a fete was held in Celtic Park, Belfast, in honour of the Belfast men of the 16th (Irish) Division. General Hickie addressed the gathering of men, who were exclusively ex-servicemen from his old division. See *The Freeman's Journal*, 30 July 1919. There were some exceptions, however. In Tyrone, the Castlederg Comrades of the Great War were allowed to use the Killen Orange Hall for a concert on condition that Catholic members would not attend. Afterwards fighting broke out between some of the Orangemen and some of the war veterans upset at their comrades' exclusion. See Leonard, J., *The Culture of War Commemoration* (Cultures of Ireland, Dublin, 1996), p. 20.

16 'God grant that I come through ... we have let Hell loose'

1 Laird (1925), p. 149. See also 'War Diary 6th Royal Irish Regiment', 31 May and 1 June 1917, NAK WO95/1970.

2 'Wall, 2nd Lieut Michael, 6th Royal Irish Regiment', RDFA Archive. Letter from Michael to his mother, 1 June 1917.

3 'War Diary 2nd Royal Dublin Fusiliers, 1 October 1916 to 30 April 1919', 1 June 1917, NAK WO95/1974.

4 Liddle Hart (1930), p. 357.

5 Passingham (1998), p. 47. See also Wolff (1959), p. 94 and Edmonds *History of the Great War. Military Operations, France and Belgium 1917* (1948), pp. 33 and 41.

6   Liddle, P. H., *The 1916 Battle of the Somme: A Reappraisal* (Leo Cooper, London, 1992), p. 23.

7   Passingham (1998), p. 89. German artillery retaliation took its toll too. On 1 June Private Richard Lester, 2nd RDF, was killed by German artillery fire concentrated on the Dublins' sector of the line near the part of the Chinese Wall named Hong Kong Trench. The battalion had finished its term of front-line duty and was preparing to go into reserve. The 6th Connaught Rangers were lined up to take their place. Richard came from Bermondsey in Surrey. He had previously served with the 6th London Rifles and was either conscripted or 'called back'. When he died, he left a wife and three young daughters behind: Catherine, aged seven; Hannah, aged three; and Norah, aged two. His wife, also Catherine, never remarried and reared the three girls as best she could. She had lost her brother in the same war. Catherine and Norah are now dead, but in November 2000, for the first time in her life, Richard's daughter Hannah laid a wreath at the grave of her father, whom she never got to know. He is buried in Kemmel Chateau Military Cemetery near Ypres. (Source: Correspondence between author and Mrs H. E. Cowley (née Lester), Surrey, England.) On 2 June German artillery hit the headquarters of the 8th RDF at Rossignol *estaminet*, situated just outside Kemmel. It hit the kitchen and killed Company Sergeant Major Daniel Doyle, who was running for cover to the basement. Private James Downes was also killed. The same shell blast accounted for three more men who had run into the house looking for cover, two from the Royal Engineers and one from the Royal Irish Rifles. Daniel Doyle came from a poor tenement area of Dublin's north inner city, 110 Summerhill. James Downes came from Tallaght (Ballinascorney) in south County Dublin. Both men are buried in La Laiterie Military Cemetery. See 'War Diary 8th Royal Dublin Fusiliers', 1 June 1917, NAK WO95/1974 and The Commonwealth War Graves Commission, http://www.cwgc.org.

8   Prior, R. and Wilson, T., *Passchendaele: The Untold Story* (Yale University Press, London, 1996), p. 60.

9   'War Diary 8th Royal Dublin Fusiliers', 2 June 1917, NAK WO 95/1974. Private Ryland had been sent to France from the 5th RDF.

10 *Ibid.*, 3 June 1917. The 1911 Census notes that George Ryland from

Kingstown (sometimes called Kingston), Finglas (St Margaret's was a parish in Finglas), son of Edward, a Land Steward, and Caroline Ryland, was eleven years of age. He was born in St Margaret's and was his parents' only child. See http://www.census.nationalarchives.ie/pages/1911/Dublin/Finglas/Kingstown/7033/.

11   Geoghegan (1997), p. 124. It's anybody's guess why George returned to France. For what it's worth, mine is that it may have been out of loyalty to his friends and comrades. George Ryland's remains lie in the Roncq Communal Cemetery, Nord, France. See The Commonwealth War Graves Commission, http://www.cwgc.org.

12   'War Diary 109th Brigade Instructions For The Offensive', Instruction No. 20, dated 20 April 1917, NAK WO95/2508.

13   'War Diary 6th Royal Irish Regiment', 3 June 1917, NAK WO95/1970. During the German March offensive of 1918 Lieutenant Jones was taken prisoner. He later died of wounds received during the offensive. He is buried in Caudry British Cemetery, east of Cambrai, France.

14   Fielding (1929), p. 185. See also Passingham (1998), p. 90. These oil-drum bombs may well be similar to the barrel bombs dropped from helicopters into civilian areas by the Syrian Air Force in 2014/2015.

15   'Wall, 2nd Lieut Michael, 6th Royal Irish Regiment', RDFA Archive. Letter from Michael to his mother, 3 June 1917.

16   See Fielding (1929), p. 187 and 'War Diary 6th Connaught Rangers', report on raid 4/5 June 1917, NAK WO95/1970.

17   'War Diary 7th Leinster Regiment', 4 June 1917, NAK WO95/1970.

18   Denman (1995), p. 116.

19   Jourdain (1999), p. 242.

20   Johnstone (1992), p. 273. General Hickie was being a little over-enthusiastic when he claimed the capture of Wijtschate was assigned to his division. In fact only the northern half of the village was assigned to the 16th Division; the southern half was assigned to his comrades from Ulster.

21   'War Diary 6th Royal Irish Regiment', 5 June 1917, NAK WO95/1970. 'C' and 'D' companies remained at Renmore Lines.

22   'Wall, 2nd Lieut Michael, 6th Royal Irish Regiment', RDFA Archive. Letter from Michael to his mother, 5 June 1917.

23   'War Diary 6th Royal Irish Regiment', 6 June 1917, NAK WO95/1970.

24 Terraine (1977), p. 118.

25 Passingham (1998), p. 60.

26 Geoghegan (1997), p. 115.

27 Denman (1995), p. 119.

28 *In Memoriam Major Willie Redmond M.P., B.L.* (1918).

29 Wylly, *Crown and Company* (2000), p. 83.

30 O'Rahilly (1920), p. 298.

17 'Come on the Royal Irish'

1   Whitton (1998), p. 416.

2   Conversation between author and Mrs Marjorie Quarton from Nenagh, County Tipperary, whose father was a serving officer with the 2nd Dublins at Wijtschate in June 1917. Also see *The Irish Times*, 7 November 1998.

3   'War Diary 8th Royal Dublin Fusiliers, Operation Instructions', 5 June 1917, NAK WO95/1974.

4   Falls (1922), p. 91.

5   Fielding (1929), p. 187. See also Oldham, P., *Messines Ridge: Battleground Europe* (Pen and Sword, South Yorkshire, 1998), p. 74.

6   Passingham (1998), p. 98.

7   *Ibid.*, p. 102.

8   *Ibid.*, p. 101.

9   'War Dairy 36th (Ulster) Division, 109th Infantry Brigade', 8 April 1917, and Daily Intelligence Summary, 17 April and 13 May 1917, NAK WO95/2508.

10 'War Diary 8th Royal Dublin Fusiliers', 1 June 1917, NAK WO95/1974.

11 Passingham (1998), p. 98.

12 Oldham (1998), p. 80.

13 Denman (1992), p. 112.

14 Whitton (1998), p. 417.

15 Oldham (1998), p. 88.

16 *Ibid.*, p. 80.

17 O'Rahilly (1920), pp. 298–301.

18 Dungan (1995), p. 157.

19 'Glanville, 2nd Lieut Arthur, 2nd Royal Dublin Fusiliers', RDFA Archive. Letter to his mother, 15 June 1917.

20 *Ibid.*

21 'War Diary 36th (Ulster) Division. Instructions for the Offensive 36th Division Artillery. Extracts from 9th Corps Royal Artillery Orders for the Preliminary Bombardment'. See Section 33 entitled 'Action on Z Day', 1 June 1917, NAK WO95/2491.

22 Whitton (1998), p. 417.

23 *In Memoriam Major Willie Redmond M.P., B.L.* (1918).

24 Whitton (1998), p. 418. See also Denman (1992), p. 112.

25 Fielding (1929), p. 191.

26 Myers, K., 'An Irishman's Diary', *The Irish Times*, 14 March 2001. See also 'Irishwoman who became the mother of British ballet' in the same edition of *The Irish Times*. Colonel Tom Stannus and his wife, Lilith Graydon-Smith, a distinguished glassmaker and collector of Waterford glass, had two young daughters in their home at Blessington, County Wicklow. One of Stannus's daughters, Edris, became a ballet dancer of international fame. It's nice to know, however, that her journey to ballet fame began when, as a little girl of seven, she entertained the gathering at a party with a display of an Irish jig taught to her by Kate, the family's cook. Edris Stannus, or Dame Ninette de Valois as she was later known, died on 8 March 2001 at the great age of 102.

27 Dungan (1995), p. 162.

28 Denman (1995), pp. 118–120.

29 Whitton (1998), p. 418.

30 Fielding (1929), p. 192.

31 Whitton (1998), p. 418.

32 McCance (1995), p. 70. Second Lieutenant Edmund Thornber Hussey came from No. 24 Vanbrugh Hill, Blackheath, London. He is buried in Irish House Cemetery near Wijtschate. See The Commonwealth War Graves Commission, http://www.cwgc.org.

33 *Ibid.*, p. 70.

34 'War Diary 8th Royal Dublin Fusiliers', 7 June 1917, NAK WO95/1974.

35 'War Diary 16th (Irish) Division', 7 June 1917, NAK WO95/1955.

36 Fielding (1929), pp. 190–194.

37 *Ibid.*, p. 194.

38 Passingham (1998), p. 152.

39 Denman (1992), p. 114.

40   Falls (1922), p. 100.

41   'War Diary 6th Royal Irish Regiment', 7 June 1917, NAK WO95/1970.

42   'Glanville, 2nd Lieut Arthur, 2nd Royal Dublin Fusiliers', RDFA Archive. Letter to his mother, 9 June 1917.

43   *Ibid.* Letter to his mother, 15 June 1917.

44   'War Diary 16th (Irish) Division', 11 September 1916, NAK WO95/1955.

45   Denman (1992), p. 114. The 'Soldiers Died Series' lists 136 other ranks who were killed in action or died of wounds between 6 and 8 June 1917 inclusive.

46   Walsh, O., *An Englishwoman in Belfast: Rosamond Stephen's Record of the Great War* (Cork University Press, Cork, 2000), p. 59. The Wijtschate sports hall and grounds now stand on the site where L'Hospice once stood.

47   Falls (1922), p. 100. See also 'War Diary 36th (Ulster) Division, Narrative of part taken by 36th (Ulster) Division in the operations against the Messines-Wytschaete [*sic*] Ridge', 7 June 1917, NAK WO95/2491. Report not dated in war diary.

48   *Soldiers Died in the Great War* (CD), Version 1.1 issued in 1998 by The Naval and Military Press. See also '"109th Infantry Brigade's Report on the Operations culminating in the capture of the Wytschaete [*sic*]–Messines Ridge on 7th June, 1917", War Diary 109th Brigade, 36th (Ulster) Division', 17 June 1917, NAK WO95/2508.

49   Orr (1987), p. 243. Orr uses data estimated by Martin Middlebrook. See Middlebrook (1971), pp. 224, 243 and 226.

50   Prior and Wilson (1996), pp. 63–64.

51   'War Diary 6th Royal Irish Regiment', 7 June 1917, NAK WO95/1970.

52   Geoghegan (1997), p. 115. The number quoted by Geoghegan is twenty-seven men plus four officers. Out of the nine officers killed with the 16th (Irish) Division, four were from the 6th Royal Irish Regiment. See 'War Diary 6th Royal Irish Regiment', 7 June 1917, NAK WO95/1970.

53   'War Diary 150th Field Company, Royal Engineers', 7 June 1917, NAK WO95/2497.

54   'Diary of Rev. John Redmond CF', The Somme Heritage Centre, Newtownards.

55   Wylly, *Crown and Company* (2000), p. 83.

56   Fielding (1929), pp. 191–192.

57   Denman (1995), p. 122.

58   The Commonwealth War Graves Commission, http://www.cwgc.org, Captain Capel Desmond O'Brien Butler. 197795 Captain Charles Paget O'Brien Butler, brother of Desmond, was killed on 31 October 1914 while serving with The Royal Army Medical Corps.

59   'War Diary 6th Royal Irish Regiment,', 9 June 1917, NAK WO95/1970.

18 One Haversack and Six Religious Medallions

1   'Wall, 2nd Lieut Michael, 6th Royal Irish Regiment', RDFA Archive. Letter from Michael to his mother, 28 February 1917.

2   Kettle, T., *The Day's Burden and Other Essays* (Gill & Macmillan, Dublin, 1968), p. 47.

3   'War Diary 9th Royal Dublin Fusiliers', 4 June 1917, NAK WO95/1974.

4   Laird (1925), p. 149.

5   'Ireland's Roll of Honor', *The Irish Times*, 16 June 1917.

6   The Commonwealth War Graves Commission, http://www.cwgc.org.

7   'Wall, 2nd Lieut Michael, 6th Royal Irish Regiment', RDFA Archive. Telegram from the War Office to Mrs Wall informing her of Michael's death.

8   *Ibid.* Letter from Lieutenant Colonel E. Roche-Kelly to Michael's mother, 11 June 1917.

9   *Ibid.* Letter from Company Quartermaster Sergeant, 'B' Co. 6th Royal Irish Regiment, Henry Kellard to Michael's mother, 12 June 1917.

10   *Ibid.* Telegram from Buckingham Palace to Mrs Wall, 17 June 1917.

11   'Sunday List of Casualties', *The Irish Times*, 18 June 1917.

12   'Wall, 2nd Lieut Michael, 6th Royal Irish Regiment', RDFA Archive. Letter from The War Office, Graves Registration and Enquiries section to Michael's mother. In June 1917 Kemmel Chateau Military Cemetery was located near a communication trench known as Sackville Street, after the main street (now O'Connell Street) that ran through the centre of Dublin city.

13   *Ibid.* Card from Imperial (later Commonwealth) War Graves Commission.

14   File on Michael Wall at NAK WO339/53192. A copy of this file is also available in Michael Wall's papers in the RDFA Archive.

15   *Ibid.* Army Form 126A.

16 *Ibid.*

17 *Ibid.* Letter from Michael's mother to the War Office, 30 July 1917.

18 *Ibid.* Letter from the War Office to Michael's mother, 7 August 1917.

19 *Ibid.* Letter from Miss L. G. Willan to the War Office, 17 September 1917. Note the wrong date of death is given for Michael, 9 July.

20 *Ibid.* Form 107. This form essentially asked if the dead soldier had left any money to his relatives. Theresa's friend Fr Carrick died in 1932 at the great age of 99 years and 364 days, just one day off his 100th birthday. He died on the eve of the Eucharistic Congress, and since he was the oldest working priest in Ireland at the time, a special VIP chair had been set aside for him at the open air mass in the Phoenix Park, Dublin. Sadly, the chair remained vacant for the ceremony. See Hurley (1989), p. 45.

19 Remembrance

1 'Poppy Snatching in Dublin: An Anti-Imperialist Meeting', *The Irish Times*, 11 November 1927.

2 *Ibid.*

3 Conversation between author and Miss Jane O'Reilly (RIP), Dublin.

4 'Report by Supt. David Neligan on Outrages carried out in November 1928', National Archives, Dublin, File JUS 8/64.

5 'Poppies Worn by Deputies. Translations, Some Smiles but a Dull Debate', *The Irish Times*, 12 November 1927. No member of the opposition parties, namely Fianna Fáil or the Labour Party, was reported wearing a poppy, and only five out of sixty-two members of Cumann na nGaedheal, which was the party in government, wore a poppy in the Dáil on Friday 11 November 1927.

6 *Ibid.*

7 *Ibid.*

8 *Irish Independent*, 12 November 1927.

9 *Ibid.*

10 'Dept. of Justice. Armistice Celebrations "Poppy Day" 1928–1936', National Archives, Dublin, File JUS B/684.

11 That ceremony, which now takes place in the Four Courts, was carried out for several years in the late 1990s by Mr Anthony Quinn and Mr Pat Hogarty, both members of the RDFA and now, sadly, deceased.

12 'Remembrance Day Services in Dublin', *The Irish Times*, 12 November 1927.

13 *Ibid.*

14 *Ibid.*

15 *Ibid.*

16 'Remembrance Day in Dublin', *Irish Independent*, 12 November 1927.

17 *History of St Mary's Hospital Phoenix Park, Dublin*. By 1929 all the pupils at the RHMS had transferred to a similar school in England. During the Second World War, the school was used by the Irish Army as a military depot/hospital. The 22nd Infantry Battalion was stationed there. In 1947 Dublin Corporation took over the management of infectious diseases and, under the supervision of Dr Noel Browne, the building was converted into a hospital known as St Mary's Chest Hospital. It became one of the foremost hospitals in the treatment of tuberculosis by medication. With the demise of the disease, from 1958 onwards the chest patients decreased in number and in 1960 the hospital was used for geriatric patients, as it still is. In the grounds at the back of the hospital is a cemetery that contains the remains of young boys – pupils of the school – who died during a typhoid epidemic. The memorial to the ex-pupils of the RHMS who died in the Great War still stands in the front lawn of St Mary's Hospital.

18 'Remembrance Day in Dublin', *The Irish Independent*, 12 November 1927.

19 'Wreath on the Cross', *The Irish Times*, 12 November 1927.

20 Michael's Belated Funeral – a Personal Reflection

1 Brockie (1988), p. 73.

2 Burke (2007), p. 145.

3 Since then, I have visited Michael's grave many times. My wife, Michele, and I have two sons and one daughter, named Carl, Jamie and Rachel. But now I feel like I have three sons; the third is named Michael Wall.

4 Part of a speech made by Ms Trees Vannesste in September 2000. Note held by author.

Bibliography

PRIMARY SOURCES
Christian Brothers School, Fairview, County Dublin
School records of Michael Wall, Glentora, Howth, County Dublin

Imperial War Museum (IWM), London
Captain O. L. Beater, 9th Royal Dublin Fusiliers. 3385 – 86/65/1
C. Brett, 6th Connaught Rangers. 76/134/1
Lieut A.G. May, 49th Machine Gun Company. 88/46/1
Diary of 2nd Lieut J. F. B. O'Sullivan, 6th Connaught Rangers. 77/167/1
Papers of Sir Percy McElwaine, 14th Royal Irish Rifles. 92/35/1

Jesuit Archive, Dublin
Diary of Fr Henry Gill SJ, CHP 1/27
Diary of Fr P. Wrafter SJ, CHP 1/63

Liddell Hart Centre for Military Archives, King's College London
Lieut General Sir L. W. Parsons, File Reference GB99 KCLMA, 29
    November 1914

National Archives, Dublin
Department of Justice. Armistice Celebrations 'Poppy Day' 1928–1936. File
    JUS B/684
Report by Supt. David Neligan on Outrages carried out in November 1928.
    File JUS 8/64
Census of Ireland 1901 and 1911, http://www.census.nationalarchives.ie/
Dublin County Council Minutes of Meeting, 17 June 1915

National Archives, Kew (NAK), London
Ministry of Munitions, Trench Warfare and Chemical Warfare Departments,
    and War Office, Chemical Warfare Research Department and Chemical
    Defence Experimental Stations (Later Establishments), Porton: Reports
    and Papers. Director of Gas Services, France (Dgs) Series. General: Files
    Nos. Dgs/16–28. WO142/91
Commission to Enquire into Conditions of British Ex-Servicemen in Irish
    Free State 1930. PIN 15/757

File on Michael Wall. WO 339/53192 (a copy of this file is also available in Michael Wall's papers in the RDFA Archive)

Lieut Col F. S. N. Macrory, Contribution to the 'History of the 36th (Ulster) Division'. WO95/2491

'Western Front: Maps. Supplement to 1:10000 (British) Series I. Trenches corrected to: 1.4.17. Sheet name and no. 28SW 2. Edition No. 5A. Lines: A/G Production: OS GSGS No. 3062'. WO297/6580

War Diaries

2nd Royal Dublin Fusiliers, August 1914 to September 1916. WO95/1481
2nd Royal Dublin Fusiliers, 1 October 1916 to 30 April 1919. WO95/1974
7th Royal Dublin Fusiliers. WO95/4296
8th Royal Dublin Fusiliers. WO95/1974
9th Royal Dublin Fusiliers. WO95/1974
6th Connaught Rangers. WO95/1970
6th Royal Irish Regiment. WO95/1970
7th Leinster Regiment. WO95/1970
9th Royal Irish Fusiliers. WO95/2505
14th Royal Irish Rifles. WO95/251
86th Brigade, March 1916 to December 1917. WO95/2298
109th Brigade, 1 April 1917 to 29 June 1917. WO95/2508
150th Field Company, Royal Engineers. WO95/2497
16th (Irish) Division, 1 December 1915 to 30 April 1917. WO95/1955
36th (Ulster) Division. WO95/2491
9th Corps. No. Gs 75/3. Appendix 8, dated 15 July 1916. WO95/835
9th Corps. Operation Order No. 9, 19 September 1916. WO95/835
9th Corps. Proceedings of Corps Commander's Conference 3 October 1916. WO95/835

The National Library of Ireland
In Memoriam Willie Redmond M.P., B.L. Souvenir Booklet. Call Number P 2375

The Royal Artillery Museum, Woolwich
Diary of R. H. Newman, Royal Artillery. MD 1169
Ernest William Kingdon, Royal Field Artillery. Manuscript Memoirs of Service with 153rd and 56th Brigades Royal Field Artillery: 'Through Mud, through Blood to the Green Fields Beyond, 1914–1918'. MD 1327
Captain Ronald Paul Schweder, 173rd Brigade Royal Field Artillery, 36th (Ulster) Division. MD 2472

The Royal Dublin Fusiliers Association (RDFA) Archive
Second Lieutenant Arthur Glanville, 2nd Royal Dublin Fusiliers
Lieutenant Colonel R. G. B. Jeffreys, 2nd Royal Dublin Fusiliers
Major T. C. H. Dickson, 4th Royal Dublin Fusiliers
Captain Noel Drury, 6th Royal Dublin Fusiliers
Private William Boyd, 7th Royal Dublin Fusiliers
Private Ned Brierley, MM, 8th Royal Dublin Fusiliers
Private Andrew Lockhart, 11th Royal Inniskilling Fusiliers
Captain Dick Burke, 6th Royal Irish Regiment
Second Lieutenant Michael Wall, 6th Royal Irish Regiment
Lieutenant Frank Simon, 1st Otago Regiment, 1st New Zealand Brigade, New Zealand Division II Anzac Corps
Monica Roberts Collection
Kitchener's Orders to Soldiers Attached to All Active Service Pay Books, 10 August 1914

The Somme Heritage Centre, Newtownards
Rifleman Walter Collins, 9th Royal Irish Rifles
Diary of Rev. John Redmond, CF
Corporal Joseph Glass, 10th Royal Irish Rifles
Private Thomas McClure, 15th Royal Irish Rifles

BOOKS

Barry, Tom, *Guerilla Days in Ireland* (Mercier Press, Cork, 2013)
Becke, A. F., *History of the Great War Based on Official Documents. Order of Battle of Division, Part 3A: New Army Divisions (9–26)* (His Majesty's Stationery Office, London, 1938)
Beckett, I. and Simpson, K., *A Nation in Arms: A Social Study of the British Army in the First World War* (Manchester University Press, Manchester, 1985)
Bourke, J., *The Misfit Soldier: Edward Casey's War Story 1914–1918* (Cork University Press, Cork, 1999)
Bowman, T., *Irish Regiments in the Great War: Discipline and Morale* (Manchester University Press, Manchester, 2003)
Brennan-Whitmore, W. J., *Dublin Burning: The Easter Rising from Behind the Barricades* (Gill & Macmillan, Dublin, 1996)
Brockie, G., *St. Joseph's C.B.S. Fairview 1888–1988* (St Joseph's CBS, Dublin, 1988)

Burke, D., *Irish Jesuit Chaplains in the First World War* (Messenger Publications, Dublin, 2014)

Burke, T., *The 16th (Irish) and 36th (Ulster) Divisions at the Battle of Wijtschate–Messines Ridge, 7 June 1917* (The Royal Dublin Fusiliers Association, Ieper, 2007)

Cooper, B., *The Tenth (Irish) Division in Gallipoli* (Irish Academic Press, Dublin, 1993)

Corcoran, M., *Through Streets Broad and Narrow: A History of Dublin Trams* (Midland Publishing, Leicester, 2000)

Denman, T., *Ireland's Unknown Soldiers: The 16th (Irish) Division in the Great War* (Irish Academic Press, Dublin, 1992)

Denman, T., *A Lonely Grave: The Life and Death of William Redmond* (Irish Academic Press, Dublin, 1995)

Dungan, M., *Irish Voices from the Great War* (Irish Academic Press, Dublin, 1995)

Dungan, M., *They Shall Grow Not Old* (Four Courts Press, Dublin, 1997)

Edmonds, Sir (Brigadier-General) J. E., *History of the Great War. Military Operations, France and Belgium, 1916.* Vol. 1 (His Majesty's Stationery Office, London, 1948)

Edmonds, Sir (Brigadier-General) J. E., *History of the Great War. Military Operations, France and Belgium, 1916.* Vol. 2 (His Majesty's Stationery Office, London, 1948)

Edmonds, Sir (Brigadier-General) J. E., *History of the Great War. Military Operations, France and Belgium 1917.* Vol. 2 (His Majesty's Stationery Office, London, 1948)

Falls, C., *The History of the 36th (Ulster) Division* (McCaw, Stevenson & Orr, Belfast, 1922)

Farndale, M., *History of the Royal Regiment of Artillery Western Front 1914–1918* (Dorset Press, Dorchester, 1986)

Ferguson, N., *The Pity of War* (Penguin Books, London, 1998)

Fielding, R., *War Letters to a Wife: France and Flanders, 1915–1919* (The Medici Society, London, 1929)

Geoghegan, S., *The Campaigns and History of the Royal Irish Regiment 1900–1922.* Vol. 2 (Schull Books, Cork, 1997)

Gilbert, M., *The First World War: A Complete History* (Weidenfeld and Nicolson, London, 1994)

Griffith, P., *Battle Tactics of the Western Front: The British Army's Art of Attack 1916–1918* (Yale University Press, New Haven and London, 1994)

Gwynn, S., *Ireland in Ten Days* (George G. Harrap & Co., London, 1935)

Hanna, H., *The Pals at Suvla* (E. Ponsonby Ltd, Dublin, 1916)

History of St Mary's Hospital Phoenix Park, Dublin (St Mary's Hospital, Dublin: booklet available from hospital administration)

Holmes, R., *The Western Front* (BBC Worldwide Ltd, London, 1999)

Hurley, M. J., *A View from the Grandstand* (Greencastle Press, Dublin, 1989)

Jeffrey, K., *Ireland and the Great War* (Cambridge University Press, Cambridge, 2000)

Johnstone, T., *Orange, Green and Khaki* (Gill & Macmillan, Dublin, 1992)

Jourdain, H. F. N., *The Connaught Rangers*. Vol. 3 (Schull Books, Cork, 1999)

Keegan, J., *The First World War* (Vintage Books, New York, 2000)

Kennedy, T., *The Velvet Strand: A History of Portmarnock* (Confidential Report Printing, Dublin, 1984)

Kerr, S. P., *What the Irish Regiments Have Done* (Fisher Unwin Ltd, London, 1916)

Kettle, T., *The Day's Burden and Other Essays* (Gill & Macmillan, Dublin, 1968)

Kingston, G. P., *History of the 4th (British) Infantry Division 1914–1919* (The London Press, London, 2006)

Laird, F., *Personal Experiences of the Great War (an Unfinished Manuscript)* (Eason & Son, Dublin, 1925)

Leonard, J., *The Culture of War Commemoration* (Cultures of Ireland, Dublin, 1996)

Liddle, P. H., *The 1916 Battle of the Somme: A Reappraisal* (Leo Cooper, London, 1992)

Liddle Hart, B. H., *The Real War 1914–1918* (Faber and Faber, London, 1930)

Lyons, J. B., *The Enigma of Tom Kettle* (The Glendale Press, Dublin, 1983)

McBrierty, V. J., *The Howth Peninsula: Its History, Lore and Legend* (North Dublin Round Table, Dublin, 1981)

McCance, S., *History of the Royal Munster Fusiliers 1861 to 1922*. Vol. 2 (Schull Books, Cork, 1995)

Middlebrook, M., *The First Day on the Somme* (Penguin Books, London, 1971)

Mulligan, W., *The Great War for Peace* (Yale University Press, New Haven, 2014)

Neillands, R., *The Great War Generals on the Western Front 1914–19* (Robinson, London, 1999)

Ó Comhraí, Cormac, *Ireland and the First World War: A Photographic History* (Mercier Press, Cork, 2014)

O'Doherty-Murphy, W. R. M., *A Century of Golf on the Island: A History of the Island Golf Club* (The Island Golf Club, Dublin, 1990)

O'Rahilly, A., *Father William Doyle S.J.* (Longmans Green and Company, London, 1920)

O'Reilly, G. H., *History of Royal Hibernian Military School, Dublin* (The Genealogical Society of Ireland, Dún Laoghaire, 2004)

Oldham, P., *Messines Ridge: Battleground Europe* (Pen and Sword, South Yorkshire, 1998)

Orr, P., *The Road to the Somme* (Blackstaff Press, Belfast, 1987)

Paris, M., *Over the Top: The Great War and Juvenile Literature in Britain* (Praeger Publishers, Westport, CT, 2004)

Passingham, I., *Pillars of Fire. The Battle of Messines Ridge June 1917* (Sutton Publishing, Gloucestershire, 1998)

Pegler, M., *British Tommy* (Osprey Publishing, Oxford, 1996)

Pope, S. and Wheal, E., *The Macmillan Dictionary of the First World War* (Macmillan, London, 1997)

Portmarnock Youth Project Team, *Portmarnock: A Closer Look* (Wolfhound Press, Dublin, 1985)

Prior, R. and Wilson, T., *Passchendaele: The Untold Story* (Yale University Press, London, 1996)

Robbins, S., *British Generalship on the Western Front 1914–1918: Defeat into Victory* (Frank Cass and Co. Ltd, Abingdon, 2005)

Romer, C. F. and Mainwaring, A. E., *The 2nd Battalion Royal Dublin Fusiliers in the South African War* (A. L. Humphreys, London, 1908)

Samuels, M., *Doctrine and Dogma: German and British Infantry Tactics in the First World War* (Greenwood Press, London, 1992)

Scott, Major General H. L., *The Attack of the British Ninth Corps at Messines Ridge* (The War Department, Washington, 1917)

Sheffield, G. and Bourne, J. (eds), *Douglas Haig: War Diaries and Letters, 1914–1918* (Phoenix, London, 2005)

Soldiers Died in the Great War, Parts 71, 72 and 73 (J. B. Hayward and Sons, Suffolk, 1989)

Steel, N. and Hart, P., *Passchendaele: The Sacrificial Ground* (Cassell Military Paperbacks, London, 2000)

Stevenson, D., *1914–1918: The History of the First World War* (Penguin Books, London, 2004)

Strachan, H., *The First World War, to Arms!* (Oxford University Press, Oxford, 2001)

Taylor, A. J. P., *English History 1914–1945* (Book Club Associates, London, 1977)

Terraine, J., *Douglas Haig: The Educated Soldier* (Cassell Military Publisher, London, 1963)

Terraine, J., *The Road to Passchendaele: The Flanders Offensive of 1917. A Study in Inevitability* (Lee Cooper, London, 1977)

Walsh, O., *An Englishwoman in Belfast: Rosamond Stephen's Record of the Great War* (Cork University Press, Cork, 2000)

Whitton, F. E., *The History of the Prince of Wales's Leinster Regiment (Royal Canadians) 1914–1922*. Vol. 2 (Schull Books, Cork, 1998)

Wolff, L., *In Flanders Fields* (Longmans, London, 1959)

Wylly, H. C., *Crown and Company: The Historical Records of the 2nd Battalion Royal Dublin Fusiliers 1911–1922*. Vol. 2 (Schull Books, Cork, 2000)

Wylly, H. C., *Neill's Blue Caps 1914–1922*. Vol. 3 (Schull Books, Cork, 2000)

Articles in Books

Englander, D., 'Discipline and Morale in the British Army, 1917–1918', in J. Horne (ed.), *State, Society and Mobilisation in Europe during the First World War* (Cambridge University Press, Cambridge, 1997)

Lee, J., 'Some Lessons of the Somme: The British Infantry in 1917', in The British Commission for Military History, *Look to Your Front: Studies in the First World War* (Spellmount, Kent, 1999)

Leonard, J., 'The Reactions of Irish Officers in the British Army to the Easter Rising of 1916', in H. Cecil and P. H. Liddle (eds), *Facing Armageddon: The First World War Experienced* (Leo Cooper, London, 1996)

McCarthy, C., 'Queen of the Battlefield: The Development of Command, Organisation and Tactics in the British Infantry Battalion during the Great War', in G. Sheffield and D. Todman (eds), *Command and Control on the Western Front: The British Army's Experience 1914–1918* (Spellmount, Gloucestershire, 2007)

Perry, N., 'Politics and Command: General Nugent, the Ulster Division and Relations with Ulster Unionism, 1915–1917', in The British Commission for Military History, *Look to Your Front: Studies in the First World War* (Spellmount, Kent, 1999)

Simpson, K., 'Dr James Dunn and Shell Shock', in H. Cecil and P. H. Liddle (eds), *Facing Armageddon: The First World War Experienced* (Leo Cooper, London, 1996)

CD

Soldiers Died in the Great War, Version 1.1 issued in 1998 by The Naval and Military Press

CONFERENCE PAPERS

Muller, S., 'Toys, Games, and Juvenile Literature during the First World War in Germany and England: A Comparison', paper presented at 'Uncovering the First World War' conference, Trinity College, Dublin, 23–25 September 2005

JOURNALS

Irish Life, Vol. XXII, No. 2, 22 January 1915

The Catholic Bulletin, No. 7, April 1917

Burke, T., 'Whence Came the Royal Dublin Fusiliers?', *The Irish Sword*, Vol. 24, No. 98, Winter 2005, pp. 445–458

Burke, T., 'Fancy the Royal Irish Captured Moore Street', *The Blue Cap: Journal of The Royal Dublin Fusiliers Association*, Vol. 13, December 2006, pp. 22–36

Burke, T., 'Some Further Debate on Recruitment in Ireland into the British Army during the First World War', *The Blue Cap: Journal of The Royal Dublin Fusiliers Association*, Vol. 19, 2014, pp. 19–26

Callan, P., 'Recruiting for the British Army in Ireland during the First World War', *The Irish Sword*, Vol. 17, Summer 1987, pp. 42–56

Dorrington, N., 'Live and Let Die. The British Army's Experience of Trench Raiding 1915–1918', *Journal of the Centre of First World War Studies*, Vol. 3, No. 1, September 2007, pp. 1–31

Editorial, 'Guernsey's Contribution to the 16th (Irish) Division', *The Irish Sword*, Vol. 18, No. 37, Summer 1992, pp. 305–306

Good, W., 'Bandon's Youngest Soldier to Die', *The New Ranger: Journal of the Connaught Rangers Association*, Vol. 21, No. 2, January 2005, pp. 9–10

Haynes, A. D., 'The Development of Infantry Doctrine in the Canadian Expeditionary Force: 1914–1918', *Canadian Military Journal*, Vol. 8, No. 3, 2007, pp. 63–72

Lemisko, L., 'Morale in the 16th (Irish) Division, 1916–1918', *The Irish Sword*, Vol. 20, No. 81, Summer 1997, pp. 217–233

McCann, B. P., 'The Diary of 2nd Lieut. Arthur V. G. Killingley. 'A' Company. 4th Battalion Royal Dublin Fusiliers Easter Week, 1916', *The Irish Sword*, Vol. 20, No. 81, Summer 1997, pp. 246–252

'Our Heroes', *Irish Life*, Vol. XXII, No. 2, 22 January 1915

Paris, M., 'Boy's Books and the Great War', *History Today*, Vol. 50, No. 11, November 2000, pp. 44–49

NEWSPAPERS
The Cork Examiner
The Freeman's Journal
The Galway Observer
Irish Independent
The Irish Times

WEBSITES
http://www.census.nationalarchives.ie/
http://www.cwgc.org (The Commonwealth War Graves Commission)
http://www.firstworldwar.com/atoz/whizzbang.htm
http://www.scotsatwar.co.uk/AZ/HaigFellows%27Addresses00.html

UNPUBLISHED THESES AND ESSAYS
Burke, T., 'The Learning Experiences of the Royal Dublin Fusiliers in Trench Warfare in the First World War, August 1914 to December 1916', unpublished MLitt thesis, University College Dublin, 2013

Carswell, S., 'The First World War Diary of Henry Gill SJ', unpublished thesis, Trinity College, Dublin, 3 April 1998

Satterthwaite, D., 'How Did the Easter Rising affect the Nationalism of Irish Soldiers serving in the British Army during the Great War?', unpublished MA thesis, The Queen's College, Oxford, Spring 2006

Index